Henry Van Boynton

Sherman's Historical Raid

The Memoirs in the Light of the Record

Henry Van Boynton

Sherman's Historical Raid
The Memoirs in the Light of the Record

ISBN/EAN: 9783337116194

Printed in Europe, USA, Canada, Australia, Japan

Cover: Foto ©ninafisch / pixelio.de

More available books at **www.hansebooks.com**

SHERMAN'S HISTORICAL RAID.

THE MEMOIRS

IN THE LIGHT OF THE RECORD.

A REVIEW BASED UPON COMPILATIONS FROM
THE FILES OF THE WAR OFFICE.

H. V. BOYNTON,
WASHINGTON CORRESPONDENT OF THE CINCINNATI GAZETTE.

CINCINNATI:
WILSTACH, BALDWIN & CO.,
1875.

PREFACE.

GENERAL SHERMAN in the introduction to his Memoirs, says:

"What is now offered is not designed as a history of the war, or even as a complete account of all the incidents in which the writer bore a part; but merely as his recollection of events, corrected by a reference to his own memoranda, which may assist the future historian when he comes to describe the whole, and account for the motives and reasons which influenced some of the actors in the grand drama of the war."

The object of the present compilation, chiefly from the official records, is to show wherein the Memoirs of General Sherman fall far short of presenting the correct history of many great events of which they treat; how much they lack of giving a complete account of incidents which they relate; how far the author's recollection, even when corrected by his own memoranda, is at fault; and to furnish the future historian with facts which will guard him against perpetuating the error and the injustice which pervade both volumes of the work.

This book is a criticism upon Sherman as a general, only so far as the official records presented furnish such criticism. There is no attempt to contradict his statements, except as the records contradict them. Wherever these show that he has done grave injustice both to the living and to the dead, they are produced with as little comment as is needed to set them in connected order, and point out the refutations which they contain. While by this method of review, his mistakes only are presented, there has been no intention to underrate the great and brilliant services which he performed.

If these pages serve in any degree to correct error and do justice, where error uncorrected, and injustice done, affect the reputations of men or officers, who, either in humble position or exalted station, freely periled their lives, or laid them down for the country, the object for which they have been written will be accomplished.

CONTENTS.

CHAP.	PAGE
I.—INTRODUCTORY	7
II.—FORTS HENRY AND DONELSON—THE CREDIT WHICH SHERMAN DENIES GRANT	10
III.—SHILOH—THE QUESTION OF SURPRISE—UNFAIR TREATMENT OF BUELL AND HIS ARMY	25
IV.—IUKA AND SECOND CORINTH—GENERAL ROSECRANS MISREPRESENTED	44
V.—CHICKASAW BAYOU—PLUNGING AN ARMY THROUGH SWAMPS AND AGAINST IMPREGNABLE BLUFFS	54
VI.—CHATTANOOGA AND CHICKAMAUGA—INJUSTICE TO ROSECRANS, THOMAS, AND THE ARMY OF THE CUMBERLAND . .	65
VII.—THE MERIDIAN CAMPAIGN—UNJUST ARRAIGNMENT OF GENERAL W. SOOY SMITH	89
VIII.—RESACA—THE FAILURE THERE ATTRIBUTED TO MCPHERSON	96
IX.—KENESAW—UNGENEROUS TREATMENT OF THOMAS; INACCURATE STATEMENTS	107
X.—THE BATTLE OF ATLANTA AND ITS POLITICAL GENERALS .	119
XI.—THE MARCH TO THE SEA—DID GRANT OR SHERMAN PLAN IT?	128
XII.—HARDEE'S ESCAPE FROM SAVANNAH	162
XIII.—AFFAIRS AT NASHVILLE CRITICISED FROM SAVANNAH	173

CONTENTS.

CHAP. PAGE
XIV.—Thomas' Troubles at Nashville—The History of his Contemplated Removal 183

XV.—The Captured Cotton at Savannah—Character of the Attack on Secretary Stanton; The Jeff. Davis Gold 198

XVI.—Battle of Bentonville—The Careless Advance of an Army 208

XVII.—The Terms with Johnston—First Draft Made by a Confederate Cabinet Officer—Fac-Simile of the Original 219

XVIII.—Opinions of Jeff. Davis' Cabinet Officers on Sherman's Terms 244

XIX.—Sneers at the Staff—The Controversy with the War Department Over the Control of the Staff Corps 259

XX.—Conclusion—The Case Against the Memoirs Summed Up 272

CHAPTER I.

INTRODUCTORY.

GENERAL SHERMAN is one of the most popular heroes of the late war. He has published his book after ten years of reflection upon events in which he bore most conspicuous and honorable part. During these years he has had uninterrupted access to the official records, including their most confidential papers; and in view of his high position, his opportunities for intimate knowledge and his popularity, what he has now written will, in spite of himself, be accepted as history by most readers who have not the means of testing his story by the records. It is believed that the extracts from these, presented in this volume, will prove sufficient to thoroughly fortify General Sherman in the claim that his book is not history, and so in part prevent the injustice which will be done to many distinguished officers and brave armies, if what he has written be received as accurate. No criticisms of the strategy or the tactics of General Sherman will be found in these pages, except such as are plainly called forth by the records produced.

High as is the position which he occupies, great as is the authority with which he speaks, there is nothing in either which should afford him the least protection in the eyes of his countrymen, if he be found detracting from the merit or the fame which belongs to his associates.

It might be pardoned in one who accomplished so much if he had contented himself with moderately magnifying his own achievements, but when he goes beyond this, and claims the merit which belongs to others, and steps still beyond and attempts to belittle the deeds of men in no respect his inferiors as generals or soldiers, and does cruel injustice to whole armies, the harmless vanity of the successful general becomes the gigantic wrong of the false historian.

In a broad and high sense, the merit of every man who bore a musket faithfully, and slept finally in the grave of the "unknown," is as great as his. His Memoirs arraign the dead as well as the living. The files of the War Department afford an answer for both. These orders, letters, telegrams, and reports, written either before, at the time, or immediately after the occurrence of the events ordered, in progress, or accomplished, photographed the truth, and in these the living and the dead find just defense. Here Thomas, McPherson, Stanton, and their companions, speak for themselves, and vindicate themselves from unjust aspersions. Here, in short, truth is made manifest, and exact justice done.

The position which General Sherman occupies now, and that which he held during the war, will naturally, and of necessity, give the force of history to what he has written, in spite of any disclaimer he may make, and this historical character will attach to these Memoirs so long as they remain uncorrected by the official record.

For the benefit of comrades living, who can not conveniently consult these records, and especially in vindication of such as are dead, it should be esteemed a duty by all who can reach the files, to search them carefully, with a view to overthrow error and establish truth. So far as General Sherman's book conforms to official papers, their production can only strengthen him; so far as it fails to agree with these, it not only deserves to be condemned, but its condemnation should be measured by the prominence of the author and his abundant facilities for obtaining accurate information.

Judged by the official record, the verdict must be that the work is intensely egotistical, unreliable, and cruelly unjust to nearly all his distinguished associates. Our erratic General thrusts his pen recklessly through reputations which are as dear to the country as his own. He detracts from what rightfully belongs to Grant; misrepresents and belittles Thomas; withholds justice from Buell, repeatedly loads failures for which he was responsible, now upon Thomas, now upon Schofield, now upon McPherson, and again upon the three jointly; is unjust in the extreme to Rosecrans; sneers at Logan and Blair; insults Hooker, and slanders Stanton.

The salient points of the long story are readily found by those who either followed, or made themselves familiar by study with his campaigns. The reader turns naturally for explanations of the surprise and attending disgrace at Shiloh; the ill-judged and fatal assault at Chickasaw Bayou; the protest against the move by which Vicksburg was captured; his failure to carry the point assigned him at the battle of Chattanooga; the escape of Johnston from Dalton and Resaca; the terrible mistake of the assault on Kenesaw; the plunging of his army, marching by the flank, into Hood's line of battle under the supposition that Atlanta was evacuated; the escape of the rebel army from Savannah; the careless and inexcusable periling and narrow escape of his own army at Bentonville; and lastly, the political surrender to Johnston at Raleigh: these are points upon which every reader desires light. But instead of gaining it, he finds that for most, the chief aim of the author seems to be to make the darkness more impenetrable.

The succeeding chapters will treat, in their order, of the prominent movements and battles which General Sherman passes in review in his Memoirs, and in each of these the version of his book will be compared with the facts as disclosed by the records now on file in the War Department.

CHAPTER II.

FORTS HENRY AND DONELSON—THE CREDIT WHICH SHERMAN DENIES TO GRANT.

OF the many remarkable things in General Sherman's book few will excite more comment than the deliberate attempt to take from General Grant the credit which belongs to him for several very important movements, and either assign it to others, as in the case of the move against Forts Henry and Donelson, or appropriate it for himself, as is done in claiming that he planned the "March to the Sea." No one general officer of his rank was under greater obligations to another throughout the war than Sherman to Grant, and on this account any unjust treatment of the latter deserves severer condemnation.

General Sherman wrote his book while in Washington. A staff officer at his headquarters copied the rough manuscript daily. All the records of the War Department, including reports, field telegrams, and all other species of official correspondence pertaining to every movement of which he wrote, and arranged for ready reference, were at his disposal. He had only to ask for them, or to send an orderly after them. And yet, incredible as it may seem, he scarcely availed himself of this collection of records, but wrote from memory and from some portions of these which happened to be in his own possession.

In reviewing the campaign up the Cumberland and Tennessee Rivers, Sherman thus gives the credit to Halleck—or to "Cullum or I"—on page 219 of Vol. I:

"Though it was midwinter, General Halleck was pushing his preparations most vigorously, and surely he brought order out of chaos in St. Louis with commendable energy. I remember one night sitting in his room, on the second floor of the Planters' House, with him and General Cullum, his chief of staff, talking of things generally, and the subject then was of the much-talked-of 'advance,' as soon as the season would permit. Most people urged the movement down the Mississippi River; but Generals Polk and Pillow had a large rebel force with heavy guns in a very strong position at Columbus, Ky., about eighteen miles below Cairo; Commodore Foote had his gun-boat fleet at Cairo; and General U. S. Grant, who commanded the district, was collecting a large force at Paducah, Cairo, and Bird's Point. General Halleck had a map on his table, with a large pencil in his hand, and asked, 'Where is the rebel line?' Cullum drew the pencil through Bowling Green, Forts Donelson and Henry, and Columbus, Ky. 'That is their line,' said Halleck; 'now where is the proper place to break it?' And either Cullum or I said, '*Naturally* the center.' Halleck drew a line perpendicular to the other, near its middle, and it coincided nearly with the general course of the Tennessee River, and he said, 'That's the true line of operations.'

"This occurred more than a month before General Grant began the movement, and as he was subject to General Halleck's orders, I have always given General Halleck the full credit for that movement, which was skillful, successful, and extremely rich in military results; indeed it was the first real success on our side in the civil war. The movement up the Tennessee began about the 1st of February, and Fort Henry was captured by the joint action of the navy under Commodore Foote, and the land forces under General Grant, on the 6th of February, 1862. About the same time General S. R. Curtis had moved forward from Rolla, and on the 8th of March, defeated the rebels under McCulloch, Van Dorn and Price at Pea Ridge.

"As soon as Fort Henry fell, General Grant marched straight across to Fort Donelson, on the Cumberland River, invested the place, and, as soon as the gun-boats had come round from the Tennessee, and had bombarded the water front, he assaulted; whereupon Buckner surrendered the garrison of twelve thousand men, Pillow and ex-Secretary of War General Floyd having personally escaped across the river at night, occasioning a good deal of fun and criticism at their expense."

If General Sherman had taken the trouble to send for General Halleck's letter-book for the time he mentions above, he would have found a letter to General McClellan, then General-in-Chief of the army, showing that he (Halleck) had no settled plans for a movement up the Cumberland and the Tennessee, and only general ideas of it at most, and that he did not expect such a movement could take place till long after the time General Grant actually captured both Forts Henry and Donelson, and effectually opened these rivers.

This letter, lying at General Sherman's very elbow, is dated at Headquarters Department of the Missouri, St. Louis, January 20, 1862. The following extracts are sufficient to settle the question at issue:

I have received no information in respect to the general plan of campaign, and therefore feel much hesitation in recommending any line of operations for these and other troops which I may be able to withdraw from Missouri. Of course this line must be subordinate to some general plan. I take it for granted General, that what has heretofore been done has been the result of political policy rather than military strategy, and that the want of success on our part is attributable to the politicians rather than to the generals. * *

I am aware General, that you are in no way responsible for this; these movements have been governed by political expediency, and in many cases directed by politicians in order to subserve party interest. * * * But is it not possible, with the new Secretary of War, to introduce a different policy, and make our future movements in accordance with *military principles*. On this supposition I venture to make a few suggestions in regard to operations in the West.

The idea of moving down the Mississippi by steam, is in my opinion impracticable, or at least premature. It is not the proper line of operations, at least now. A much more feasible plan is to move up the Cumberland and Tennessee, making Nashville the present objective point. This would threaten Columbus, and force the abandonment of Bowling Green. * * * *

This line of the Cumberland and the Tennessee is the great central line of the Western theater of war, with the Ohio below the mouth of Green River as the base, and two great navigable rivers extending far into the theater of operations. But the plan should not be attempted without a large force—not less than sixty thousand effective men. * * * The main central line will also require the withdrawal of all available troops from this State, also those in Illinois, Indiana, Iowa, Wisconsin, and Ohio, which are armed, or still to be armed, and also the transfer to that route, or near it, of all the Kentucky troops not required to secure the line of Green River.

The force at Cairo and on the Ohio River below the mouth of Green River is now about fifteen thousand. Seven regiments have just been ordered there from Missouri.

By the middle or last of February I hope to send fifteen thousand more. If thirty thousand or forty thousand can be added from the sources indicated, these will be sufficient for holding Cairo, Fort Holt, and Paducah, and form the column proposed. * * * *

These suggestions are hastily written out, but they are the result of much anxious inquiry and mature deliberation. I am confident that the plan, if properly carried out, will produce important results. I also believe it to be feasible.

I have not designated any particular line or lines of movement; that must be a matter for further study, if the general idea should be approved. Perhaps the main column should move from Smithland, between the rivers, by Dover, etc. Perhaps the line east of the Cumberland, or that west of the Tennessee, would be preferable. These questions, however, are matters easily determined. * * *

H. W. HALLECK, *Major-General.*

As General Grant formally proposed, on January 28th, to General Halleck to take Fort Henry, captured it on the 6th of February, moved on Fort Donelson the next day, and took it on the 16th of February, it will be seen from the above letter, that General Halleck, at the time Grant had accomplished this work and opened both rivers, did not expect to have men enough by thirty or forty thousand to begin the vague movement he had in his mind.

But if General Sherman had searched the records with the least care he would have found that even these identical ideas of Halleck, about a move on a line perpendicular to one joining Bowling Green and Columbus were suggested by General Buell.

For the records show that as early as November of the preceding year, Buell had proposed to General McClellan to move around the right flank of the rebels at Bowling Green, and advance on Nashville, while supplies and troops from Halleck should move up the Cumberland, guarded by the fleet. General McClellan urged coöperation on Halleck, who delayed answering dispatches for some time. Finally, on January 3d, at the request of President Lincoln, General Buell wrote General Halleck, setting forth most of the ideas that Halleck afterward submitted as his own to McClellan, and which are given above in the letter dated January 20th.

The records give a connected history of the discussion at this time between the authorities at Washington, and Generals Buell and Halleck.

WASHINGTON, D. C., *December* 31, 1861.

General BUELL, *Louisville, Ky.*

General McClellan is sick. Are General Halleck and yourself in concert? When you move on Bowling Green, what hinders it being reënforced from Columbus? Answer.

A. LINCOLN.

LOUISVILLE, KY., *January* 1, 1862.

To A. LINCOLN, *President.*

There is no arrangement between General Halleck and myself. I have been informed by General McClellan that he would make suitable disposition for concerted action.

There is nothing to prevent Bowling Green being reënforced from Columbus, if a military force is not brought to bear on the latter place.

D. C. BUELL, *Brigadier-General*

LOUISVILLE, 11 P. M., *January* 1, 1862.

To *President* LINCOLN.

I have already telegraphed General Halleck with a view to arranging a concert of action between us, and am momentarily expecting his answer.

D. C. BUELL, *Brigadier General.*

WASHINGTON, D. C., *December* 31, 1861.

General HALLECK, *St. Louis.*

General McClellan is sick. Are General Buell and yourself in concert? When he moves on Bowling Green, what hinders it being reënforced from Columbus? A simultaneous move by you on Columbus might prevent it. Answer. A. LINCOLN.

HEADQUARTERS DEPARTMENT OF THE MISSOURI,
ST. LOUIS, *January* 1, 1862.

A. LINCOLN, *President U. S. A., Washington.*

I have never received a word from General Buell. I am not ready to coöperate with him; hope to do so in a few weeks. Have written fully on this subject to General McClellan. Too much haste will ruin everything here.

H. W. HALLECK, *Major-General.*

LOUISVILLE, KY., *January* 1, 1862.

Major-General HALLECK, *St. Louis.*

I understand General McClellan is sick. Has any concerted action been arranged for us? If not, can any be arranged between us? If possible, it is desirable it should be done speedily.

D. C. BUELL, *Brigadier-General commanding.*

HEADQUARTERS DEPARTMENT OF THE MISSOURI,
ST. LOUIS, *January* 2, 1862.

Brigadier-General BUELL, *Louisville.*

I have had no instructions respecting coöperation. All my available troops are in the field, except those at Cairo and Paducah, which are barely sufficient to threaten Columbus, etc. A few weeks hence I hope to be able to render you very material assistance, but now a withdrawal of my troops from this State is almost impossible. Write me fully.

H. W. HALLECK, *Major-General.*

HEADQUARTERS DEPARTMENT OF THE OHIO,
LOUISVILLE, *January* 3, 1862.

General W. H. HALLECK, *Commanding Department of the Missouri.*

GENERAL: I received your dispatch, and, with more delay than I meant, proceed to the subject of it, in compliance with your request, and I may add also, at the wish of the President.

I do not underrate the difficulties in Missouri, but I think it is not extravagant to say that the great power of the rebellion in the West is arranged on a front, the flanks of which are Columbus and Bowling Green, and the center about where the railroad between those points crosses the Tennessee and Cumberland Rivers, including Nashville and the fortified points below. It is, I have no doubt, within bounds to estimate their force on that line at eighty thousand men, including a column about Somerset, Ky. In rear of their right flank it is more.

Of their force, forty thousand may be set down as at Bowling Green, twenty thousand at Columbus—though you, doubtless, have more information on that point than I have—and twenty thousand at the center. Considering the railroad facilities, which enable the enemy to concentrate in a few hours on any single point of this front, you will at once see the importance of a combined attack on its center and flanks, or at least of demonstrations which may be converted into real attacks, and fully occupy the enemy on the whole front. It is probable that you may have given the subject, as far as Columbus and the center are concerned, more attention than I have. With reference to the former, at least, I can make no more than the general suggestion already expressed, that it should be fully occupied.

The attack upon the center should be made by two gun-boat expeditions, with, I should say, twenty thousand men on the two rivers. They should, of course, be organized with reference to the depth of water in the rivers; and whether they should be of equal or unequal strength, would depend upon that and other considerations, and can hardly be determined until the moment of departure. The mode of attack must depend on the strength of the enemy at the several points and the features of the localities. It will be of the first importance to break the railroad communication, and, if possible, that should be done by columns moving rapidly to the bridges over the Cumberland and Tennessee. The former probably would not be reached at first, being some thirty-one miles above the first principal battery that I know of at Dover. The other is eighteen miles above Fort Henry—the first I know of on the Tennessee. If the expeditions should not be strong enough to do the work alone, they should establish themselves firmly at the nearest possible point, and remain at least until they ascertained that reënforcements from my columns, or some other source, would not reach them. By uniting, they could establish themselves permanently under the protection of the gun-boats.

I say this much rather to lay the subject before you than to propose any definite plan for your side. Whatever is done should be done speedily, within a few days. The work will become more difficult every day. Please let me hear from you at once. Very truly yours,

D. C. BUELL, *Brigadier-General commanding.*

Four days later General Buell telegraphed as follows:

LOUISVILLE, *January* 7, 1862.

General HALLECK, *St. Louis.*

I am telegraphed by the President. Can you fix a day for concerted action?

D. C. BUELL, *Brigadier-General.*

To which Halleck replied:

ST. LOUIS, January 7, 1862.

General BUELL, *Louisville.*

Designate a day for a demonstration. I can do nothing more. See my letter of yesterday.
H. W. HALLECK, *Major-General.*

The letter thus referred to was as follows:

HEADQUARTERS DEPARTMENT OF THE MISSOURI, }
ST. LOUIS, *January* 6, 1862.

Brigadier-General D. C. BUELL, *Louisville, Ky.*

GENERAL: I have delayed writing to you for several days in hopes of getting some favorable news from the South-west. The news received to-day, however, is unfavorable, it being stated that Price is making a stand near Springfield, and that all our available forces will be required to dislodge and drive him out.

My last advices from Columbus represent that the enemy has about twenty-two thousand men there. I have only about fifteen thousand at Cairo, Fort Holt, and Paducah, and after leaving guards at these places I could not send into the field over ten or eleven thousand. Moreover, many of these are very imperfectly armed.

Under these circumstances, it would be madness for me to attempt any serious operation against Camp Beauregard or Columbus. Propably, in the course of a few weeks, I will be able to send additional troops to Cairo and Paducah to coöperate with you, but at present it is impossible; and it seems to me that, if you deem such coöperation necessary to your success, your movement on Bowling Green should be delayed. I know nothing of the plan of campaign, never having received any information on the subject; but it strikes me that to operate from Louisville and Paducah, or Cairo, against an enemy at Bowling Green, is a plain case of exterior lines, like that of McDowell and Patterson, which, unless *each* of the exterior columns is superior to the enemy, leads to disaster ninety-nine times in a hundred.

Very respectfully, your obedient servant,

H. W. HALLECK, *Major-General.*

On the 6th of January McClellan wrote to Buell as follows: "Halleck, from his own accounts, will not soon be in condition to support properly a movement up the Cumberland." And again on the 13th: "Halleck is not yet in condition to afford you the support you need when you undertake the movement on Bowling Green."

On the 10th of January Halleck telegraphed Buell:

HEADQUARTERS DEPARTMENT OF THE MISSOURI,
ST. LOUIS, *January* 10, 1862.

General BUELL, *Louisville.*

Troops at Cairo and Paducah are ready for a demonstration on Mayfield, Murray, and Dover. Six additional regiments will be there next week. Fix the day when you wish a demonstration; but put it off as long as *possible*, in order that I may increase the strength of the force.

H. W. HALLECK, *Major-General.*

On the same day Halleck telegraphed Grant: "Reënforcements are receiving arms. Delay your movements until I telegraph. Let me know when the channel is clear."

And on the next day: "I can hear nothing from Buell, so fix your own time for the advance. Three regiments will come down Monday."

Subsequently the following passed between Halleck and Buell:

ST. LOUIS, *February* 2, 1862.

Brigadier-General BUELL, *Louisville, Ky.*

GENERAL: Yours of the 30th ultimo is received. At present it is only proposed to take and occupy Fort Henry and Dover, and, if possible, cut the railroad from Columbus to Bowling Green. * * * But it will take some time to get troops ready to advance far south of Fort Henry.

Very respectfully, your obedient servant,

H. W. HALLECK, *Major General.*

ST. LOUIS, *February* 7, 1862.

To General BUELL, *Louisville.*

You say you regret that we could not have consulted on this matter earlier. So do I most sincerely. I had no idea of commencing the movement before the 15th or 20th inst., until I received General McClellan's telegram about the reënforcements sent to Tennessee and Kentucky by Beauregard. Although not ready, I deemed it important to move instantly. I believe I was right. Fort Henry must be held at all hazards.

H. W. HALLECK, *Major-General.*

From all of which it will appear that General Halleck had not originated, up to the time General Grant was ready to execute it, any such move as the latter was anxious and waiting to make, and General McClellan did not even consider Halleck as prepared to afford a support.

As a matter of fact, General Grant began preparations for the move he had in contemplation the latter part of December, and consequently before the date of the correspondence between President Lincoln and Generals Buell and Halleck. Nor is there any thing in the records to indicate that General McClellan, the President, or General Buell communicated with General Grant upon the subject of a move up the Tennessee or Cumberland. In fact, as he was subordinate to General Halleck, they would not have written him directly.

On the 6th of January, 1862, General Grant, then in command at Cairo, telegraphed to General Halleck for permission to visit St. Louis, for the purpose of obtaining authority from General Halleck to move against Forts Henry and Donelson. At first, leave to visit headquarters was refused; but on the 22d of January it was granted, and on the 23d Grant started for St. Louis, called on Halleck, and suggested a move on Fort Henry. According to Badeau, who wrote by authority, when Grant "attempted to broach the subject, Halleck silenced him so quickly and sharply that Grant said no more on the matter, and went back to Cairo with the idea that his commander thought him guilty of proposing a great military blunder."

Grant, however, had been quietly engaged for three weeks in preparing for this move, had studied it carefully, and quite set his heart upon it. He was the more convinced of its feasibility, from a report of a partial reconnoissance of Fort Henry, made by General C. F. Smith, and forwarded to General Halleck on January 24th.

Upon reaching Cairo he telegraphed Halleck :

CAIRO, *January* 28, 1862.

Major-General H. W. HALLECK, *St. Louis, Mo.*

With permission I will take Fort Henry on the Tennessee, and establish and hold a large camp there. U. S. GRANT, *Brigadier-General.*

On the same day Commodore Foote, then in command of the gun-boats in that section, and in full accord with General Grant, also telegraphed Halleck as follows :

CAIRO, *January* 28, 1862.

Major-General H. W. HALLECK, *St. Louis, Mo.*

Commanding General Grant and myself are of opinion that Fort Henry, on the Tennessee River, can be carried with four iron-clad gun-boats and troops to permanently occupy. Have we your authority to move for that purpose when ready? A. H. FOOTE, *Flag Officer*

On the 29th General Grant wrote Halleck as follows :

HEADQUARTERS DISTRICT OF CAIRO, }
CAIRO, *January* 29, 1862. }

Major-General H. W. HALLECK, *St. Louis Mo.*

In view of the large force now concentrating in this district, and the present feasibility of the plan, I would respectfully suggest the propriety of subduing Fort Henry, near the Kentucky and Tennessee line, and holding the position. If this is not done soon, there is but little doubt but that the defenses on both the Tennessee and Cumberland Rivers will be materially strengthened. From Fort Henry it will be easy to operate, either on the Cumberland, only twelve miles distant, Memphis, or Columbus. It will, besides, have a moral effect upon our troops to advance them toward the rebel States. The advantages of this move are as perceptible to the General commanding as to myself, therefore, further statements are unnecessary.

U. S. GRANT, *Brigadier-General.*

To these dispatches of Grant and Commodore Foote, Halleck replied:

HEADQUARTERS DEPARTMENT OF THE MISSOURI, }
ST. LOUIS, *January* 29, 1862. }

Brigadier-General GRANT, *Cairo.*

Make your preparations to take and hold Fort Henry. I will send you written instructions by mail. H. W. HALLECK, *Major-General.*

HEADQUARTERS DEPARTMENT OF THE MISSOURI,
ST. LOUIS, *January* 29, 1862.

Commodore FOOTE, *Cairo*

I am waiting for General Smith's report on the road from Smithland to Fort Henry. As soon as that is received will give orders. In the meantime have every thing ready.   H. W. HALLECK, *Major-General*

On the 1st of February permission to make the movement arrived from Halleck, and on the 2d Grant began the campaign with seventeen thousand men, less than one-third the force Halleck had in mind for the operations he thought might be carried on along this general line. On the 6th of February Fort Henry was taken, and on the 8th Grant telegraphed Halleck that he should immediately take Fort Donelson and return to Fort Henry.

On the 16th he had accomplished the work, and the campaign for which Halleck wanted "not less than sixty thousand effective men," thirty thousand of which he hoped to have "by the middle or last of February," had been made a success by Grant with a force of seventeen thousand men and four gun-boats.

General Sherman closes the chapter in which he treats of the movements on Forts Henry and Donelson as follows:

"From the time I had left Kentucky General Buell had really made no substantial progress; though strongly reënforced, beyond even what I had asked for, General Albert Sidney Johnston had remained at Bowling Green until his line was broken at Henry and Donelson, when he let go Bowling Green and fell back hastily to Nashville, and on Buell's approach he did not even tarry there, but continued his retreat southward."

Three chapters previous to the one containing this unkind allusion to General Buell, General Sherman, writing of his selection as Superintendent of the Louisiana Military College, says: "For this honorable position I was indebted to Major D. C. Buell and General G. Mason Graham, to whom I have made full and due acknowledgment."

While the General of the army should have felt himself, by virtue of his position and opportunities for obtaining exact information, under strong obligations to correctly present all matters of which he wrote, he was thus peculiarly bound to treat General Buell with common fairness. But in the above extract he wholly ignores the fact that after he left Kentucky, General Buell had organized and made efficient the Army of the Ohio, which, from that time forward, under Buell, Rosecrans, and Thomas, held high rank among the armies of the Union. A portion of it under General Buell's directions and the immediate command of General Thomas, had broken the Confederate right at Mill Springs, killed the commander of its army, captured its fortified camp, with all its artillery, several thousand stand of small arms, transportation, and stores, and there achieved a victory which at the time was regarded by the nation as a most important one. It was the Western Bull Run for the Confederacy. General Thomas, in his report upon the battle, thus speaks of the captures:

"On reaching the intrenchments we found that the enemy had abandoned every thing and retired during the night. Twelve pieces of artillery, with their caissons packed with ammunition, one battery wagon and two forges, a large amount of small arms, mostly the old flint-lock muskets, and ammunition for the same, one hundred and fifty or sixty wagons, and upward of one thousand of horses and mules, a large amount of commissary stores, intrenching tools, and camp and garrison equipage, fell into our hands. A correct list of all the captured property will be forwarded as soon as it can be made up and the property secured.

"The steam and ferry-boats having been burned by the enemy on their retreat, it was found impossible to cross the river and pursue them; besides, their command was completely demoralized, and retreated with great haste and in all directions, making their capture in any numbers quite doubtful if pursued."

Besides this, General Buell had contributed a considerable force to aid General Grant in the movement on Fort Donelson, and Bowling Green was evacuated in the face of an advance upon it by General Buell, and before Fort Donelson had fallen.

But whether any "substantial progress" had been made by

General Buell after General Sherman left Kentucky, will best appear from portions of three letters written by General Sherman while in Kentucky, the first two bearing date about ten days before he relieved General Robert Anderson in command, and the third about a week before he was in turn relieved by General Buell. Muldraugh's Hill is about forty miles south of Louisville, on the railroad to Nashville, and was one of the first points of consequence occupied on that line by the Union forces. General Sherman gives the following account of the movement upon it, and the condition of affairs after his troops were established there:

> HEADQUARTERS MULDRAUGH'S HILL, }
> *September* 27, 1861. }

Captain OLIVER D. GREEN, *Adjutant-General.*

SIR: When I left Louisville on the cars in charge of the Home Guards, followed by Rosseau's brigade, I understood my orders to be to station parties along the road at all the bridges, secure the road and occupy Muldraugh's Hill. * * * *

This is not an isolated hill, but a range separating the waters of the Rolling Fork of Salt Creek and Green River, the ascent from the north being very abrupt, and the descent to the south being very gradual.

Our position is far from being a strong one when held against a superior force. Roads will enable the enemy with cavalry to pass round us and cut off our communications and starve us out. I have no safe line of retreat, but must stand our ground let what will happen.

Our opponents, led by General Buckner, who is familiar with the ground, are now supposed to be along the railroad from Green River to Bowling Green. Their forces are variously estimated from seven thousand to twenty thousand men; and, I doubt not, they have fifteen thousand, some well and some poorly armed, but all actuated by the one purpose to destroy us. I am fully alive to the danger of our position and to all its disadvantages, especially that of supplies. Our provisions have been hauled up the rugged valley of Clear Creek by hired wagons, and by some which were brought along by the Thirty-ninth Indiana. We can barely supply our wants, and are liable at any moment to have these wagons seized. The reason I came to Muldraugh's Hill was for effect. Had it fallen into the hands of our enemy the cause would have been lost, and even with it in our possession for a week nobody has rallied to our support. I expected, as we had reason to, that the people of Kentucky would rally to our support, but, on the contrary, none have joined us, while hundreds, we are told, are going to Bowling Green. The railroad from Bowling Green toward us is broken at Nolin, ten miles off, and and at another trestle beyond some seven miles. I doubt if this was done by

Buckner's orders, but rather by the small parties of guards left to protect them and who are scared at our approach. I have from time to time given you telegraphic notice of these events, and must now await the developments.

We should have here at least twenty thousand men, but that has been an impossibility.   Truly yours,

W. T. SHERMAN, *Brigadier-General*.

From this first letter it appears how "the cause would have been lost" if the enemy had gained Muldraugh's Hill. The second one shows how the conduct of the Union troops after securing the Hill, was about to "ruin our cause."

HEADQUARTERS MULDRAUGH'S HILL,
September 29, 1861.

General ROBERT ANDERSON, *Louisville, Ky.*

DEAR GENERAL: I am sorry to report that in spite of my orders and entreaties, our troops are committing depredations that will ruin our cause. Horses and wagons have been seized, cattle, sheep, hogs, chickens, taken by our men, some of whom wander for miles around. I am doing and have done all in my power to stop this, but the men are badly disciplined and give little heed to my orders or those of their own regimental officers. We have received no accessions from the country, and I have only a few weak, scattered camps, such as Curran Pope's at New Haven, and General Ward's at Greenburg. Of course, the chief design of our occupying Muldraugh's Hill was to afford an opportunity for the people to organize and arm, but I can not learn that such is the case.

A great many people come into our camps, take the oath of allegiance and go away. I have no doubt spies could enter our camp and we can not conceal the strength of our command. Although Buckner is not at Green River he has many locomotives and cars there, and can march from there in a day or a day and a half, and I feel uneasy about our communications. The Home Guards have all returned, leaving us whom they deem outsiders alone, and the whole country would raise round about us, leaving us with an ambush all the way. To be effective, a force here should be very large, too large to be attacked in position. As to us we could make a good fight, but would soon be starved out. I know how you are situated and will do my best, and only want you not to draw too strong inferences from the destruction of the Green River bridges. This was, no doubt, intended as an obstruction to our advance, until other designs of theirs were completed, but as soon as Buckner is ready, he will surely advance on Elizabethtown where he lives. I hear nothing of Thomas' moves or those at Paducah. Our lines are broken and I have sent down to examine.   W. T. SHERMAN.

The third letter was written a few days before he was relieved by General Buell:

> HEADQUARTERS DEPARTMENT OF THE CUMBERLAND,
> LOUISVILLE, *November* 6, 1861.
>
> General L. THOMAS, *Adjutant-General.*
>
> SIR: General McClellan telegraphs me to report to him daily the situation of affairs here. * * * * We should have here a very large force, sufficient to give confidence to the Union men of the ability to do what should be done—possess ourselves of all the State. But all see and feel we are brought to a stand still, and this produces doubt and alarm. With our present force it would be simple madness to cross Green River, and yet hesitation may be as fatal. In like manner the other columns are in peril, not so much in front as rear; the railroads over which our stores must pass being much exposed. I have the Nashville Railroad guarded by three regiments, yet it is far from being safe, and the moment actual hostilities commence these roads will be interrupted and we will be in a dilemma. To meet this in part, I have put a cargo of provisions at the mouth of Salt River guarded by two regiments. All these detachments weaken the main force and endanger the whole. Do not conclude, as before, that I exaggerate the facts. They are as stated, and the future looks as dark as possible. It would be better if some man of sanguine mind were here, for I am forced to order according to my convictions. Yours truly,
>
> W. T. SHERMAN, *Brigadier-General commanding.*

In the light of these letters it would seem as if there had really been most "substantial progress" under General Buell after General Sherman left Kentucky.

CHAPTER III.

SHILOH—THE QUESTION OF SURPRISE; UNFAIR TREATMENT OF BUELL AND HIS ARMY.

AFTER the extended discussions over the events preceding and attending the battle of Shiloh, in some of which controversies General Sherman himself participated, and all of which have called out extracts from the official records, that, taken together, effectually settle some of the earlier questions in dispute, it must surprise all readers of the Memoirs to find their author ignoring these records, and at this late day presenting many inaccurate statements in regard to the operations about Pittsburgh Landing.

The main questions at issue have always been whether the Union army was surprised at Shiloh; if it was, who was mainly responsible, and how far Buell's army can lay claim to having made the victory possible?

General Sherman labors ingeniously, but inaccurately, as the official records show, to relieve himself from responsibility for it, and even attempts to create the impression that there was no general surprise. Ever since this battle, most who believed that the Union army was unexpectedly attacked on that occasion, have laid the chief load of responsibility upon General Grant, and he through all these years has made no effort to shift the burden. But now it will appear through the records which these Memoirs have called out, that General Sherman was mainly responsible, since he was encamped in advance; his division, as he wrote to the *United States Service Magazine* in 1865, "forming as it were the outlying picket," so that he was in charge of the picket front looking toward the roads over which an enemy must approach; and while not technically in command of the entire camp, in the absence of General Grant, whose headquarters were at Savannah, some twelve miles distant, he was constantly treated, trusted, and consulted by General Grant, as if he were the senior officer at the front. General Sherman, holding steadily till the last, and against all evidence, to the belief that no immediate attack was probable, by impressing his convictions upon General Grant, misled the latter as to the real condition of affairs along the front, and thus did the author of the Memoirs become primarily responsible for the surprise.

The records disclose both the blindness which prevailed as to the real situation, and where the responsibility for it mainly rested, and some comparison of these, with the statements of the Memoirs, will set the case in a clear light.

On the 14th of March General C. F. Smith, then in command at Savannah previous to the arrival of General Grant, "instructed me"—writes General Sherman—"to disembark my own division and that of General Hurlbut at Pittsburgh Landing; to take positions well back, and to leave room for his whole army; telling me that he would soon come up in person, and move out in force to make the lodgment on the railroad contemplated by General Halleck's orders."

"On the 16th we disembarked and marched out about ten miles toward Corinth to a place called Monterey or Pea Ridge, where the rebels had a cavalry regiment, which, of course, decamped on our approach, but from the people we learned that trains were bringing large masses of men from every direction into Corinth."–Page 228, Vol. I.

It might be supposed that such knowledge would have made General Sherman very watchful when he afterward encamped at Shiloh. And yet with this important fact ascertained, when he took position there, instead of camping in line of battle, he stationed three of his brigades a mile and a half from Hurlbut's division, and the fourth over two miles from the rest. Other divisions, as they arrived, selected camps to suit themselves. There was no line of battle determined, no rifle pits dug, none of the simplest forms of obstructions provided, and no sufficient picketing, as the result proved. And Sherman was the senior officer on the main front.

"On the 18th Hurlbut disembarked his division and took post about a mile and a half out, near where the roads branched—one leading to Corinth, the other toward Hamburgh. On the 19th I disembarked my division and took post about three miles back; three of the brigades covering the roads to Purdy and Corinth, and the other brigade, Stuart's, temporarily at a place on the Hamburgh road. * * * Within a few days Prentiss' division arrived and camped on my left, and afterward McClernand's and W. H. L. Wallace's divisions were formed in a line to our rear. * * * General C. F. Smith remained back at Savannah in chief command, and I was only responsible for my own division. I kept pickets well out on the roads, and made myself familiar with all the ground inside and outside my lines."

Of the events immediately preceding the battle, General Sherman writes as follows:

"I always acted on the supposition that we were an invading army; that our purpose was to move forward in force, make a lodgment on the Memphis & Charleston Road, and thus repeat the grand tactics of Fort Donelson, by separating the rebels in the interior from those at Memphis and on the Mississippi River. We did not fortify our camps against an attack, because we had no orders to do so, and because such a course would have made our raw men timid. The position was naturally strong, with Snake Creek on our right, a deep, bold stream, with a confluent (Owl Creek) to our right front, and Lick Creek, with a similar confluent on our left, thus narrowing the space over which we could be attacked to about a mile and a half or two miles.

"At a later period of the war we could have rendered this position impregnable in one night, but at this time we did not do it, and it may be it is well we did not. From about the 1st of April we were conscious that the rebel cavalry in our front were getting bolder and more saucy; and on Friday, the 4th of April, it dashed down and carried off one of our picket guards, composed of an officer and seven men, posted a couple of miles out on the Corinth road. Colonel Buckland sent a company to its relief, then followed himself with a regiment, and, fearing lest he might be worsted. I called out his whole brigade, and followed some four or five miles, when the cavalry in advance encountered artillery. I then, after dark, drew back to our lines and reported the fact by letter to General Grant at Savannah; but thus far (night of the 4th) we had not positively detected the presence of infantry, for cavalry regiments generally had a couple of guns along, and I supposed the guns that opened on us on the evening of Friday, April 4th, belonged to the cavalry that was hovering along our whole front.

"Saturday passed in our camps without any unusual event, the weather being wet and mild, and the roads back to the steamboat landing being heavy with mud; but, on Sunday morning, the 6th, early, there was a good deal of picket-firing, and I got breakfast, rode out along my lines, and, about four hundred yards to the front of Appler's regiment, received from some bushes in a ravine to the left front, a volley, which killed my orderly, Holliday. About the same time I saw the rebel lines of battle in front coming down on us as far as the eye could reach. All my troops were in line of battle ready, and the ground was favorable to us. I gave the necessary orders to the battery (Waterhouse's) attached to Hildebrand's brigade, and cautioned the men to reserve their fire till the rebels had crossed the ravine of Owl Creek, and had begun the ascent; also sent staff officers to notify Generals McClernand and Prentiss of the coming blow. Indeed, McClernand had already sent three regiments to the support of my left flank, and they were in position when the onset came.

"In a few minutes the battle of 'Shiloh' began with extreme fury and lasted two days."—Pages 229–230, Vol. I.

In August following the battle of Shiloh, when its events were fresh in his mind, General Sherman was sworn as a witness in the trial of Colonel Thos. Worthington, Forty-sixth Ohio Volunteers, who had severely criticized the management of the former previous to the battle. The following extracts from the official report of that testimony bear upon the questions under consideration; and some of them flatly contradict the statements of the book. This is notably the case upon the very important point whether Sherman had reason to know as early as Friday before the fight, that the enemy was in force in his immediate front.

General W. T. Sherman, sworn and examined:

"He (Colonel Worthington) says 'a slight abattis might have prevented an attack.' What business was it of his whether his superior officer invited an attack or not? The Army Regulations will show him that no fortification can be made except under order of the commanding general. To have erected fortifications would have been an evidence of weakness, and would have invited an attack. * * * And here I mention, for future history, that our right flank was well guarded by Owl and Snake Creeks, our left by Lick Creek, leaving us simply to guard our front. No stronger position was ever held by an army. Therefore, on Friday, two days before the battle, when Colonel Worthington was so apprehensive, I knew there was no hostile party within six miles, though there was reason to expect an attack. I suppose Colonel McDowell, like myself, had become tired of his constant prognostications, and paid no attention to him, especially when we were positively informed by men like Buckland, Kilby Smith, and Major Ricker, who went to the front to look for enemies, instead of going to the landing; and here I will state that Pittsburgh Landing was not chosen by General Grant, but by Major-General Smith. I received orders from General Smith, and took post accordingly; so did General Hurlbut; so did his own division. The lines of McClernand and Prentiss were selected by Colonel McPherson. I will not insult General Smith's memory by criticizing his selection of a field. It was not looked to so much for defense as for ground on which our army could be organized for offense. We did not occupy too much ground. General Buell's forces had been expected rightfully for two weeks, and a place was left for his forces, although General Grant afterward had determined to send Buell to Hamburgh as a separate command.

"But even as we were on the 6th of April, you might search the world over and not find a more advantageous field of battle—flanks well protected, and never threatened, troops in easy support; timber and broken ground giving good points to rally, and the proof is that forty-three thousand men, of whom at least ten thousand ran away, held their ground against sixty thousand chosen troops of the South with their best leaders. On Friday, the 4th, nor officer, nor soldier, not even Colonel Worthington looked for an attack, as I can prove.

"On Friday, April 4th, our pickets were disposed as follows: McDowell's brigade, embracing Worthington's regiment, looked to Owl Creek Bridge, and had nothing to do with any other road. Buckland and Hildebrand covered our line to the main Corinth road. Pickets, one company to a regiment, were thrown forward a mile and a half to the front, videttes a mile further, making a chain of sentinels. About noon of that day, Buckland's adjutant came to my tent and reported that a lieutenant and seven men of his guard had left their posts and were missing—probably picked up by a small cavalry force which had hovered around for some days, and which I had failed to bag. I immediately dispatched Major Ricker with all my cavalry in a tremendous rain to the front. Soon after I heard distant musketry, and finally three cannon shots, which I knew must be the enemy, as we had none there. This was the first positive information any intelligent mind on that field had of any approaching force. Before that, no scout, no officer, no responsible man, had seen an infantry or artillery soldier nearer than Monterey, five miles out. For weeks and months we had heard all sorts of reports, just as we do now. For weeks old women had reported that Beauregard was coming, sometimes with one hundred thousand; sometimes with three hundred thousand; when, in fact, he did not leave Corinth until after even Colonel Worthington had been alarmed for safety. As soon as I heard the cannon, I and my staff were in the saddle and off to the front. We overtook a party of Buckland's and Hildebrand's brigades going forward to the relief of the pickets. On reaching a position in advance of the guard-house, a mile and a half from Shiloh, they deployed into line of battle and I awaited the return of my cavalry and infantry, still to our front.

"Colonel Buckland and Major Ricker soon returned and reported encountering infantry, artillery, and cavalry near the fallen timbers six miles in front of our camp. We then knew that we had the elements of an army in our front, but did not know its strength or destination. The guard was strengthened, and, as night came on we returned to camp, and not a man in camp but knew we had an enemy to the front before we slept that night. But even I had to guess its purpose. No general could have detected or reported the approach of an enemy more promptly than was done."

The positive contradiction between these statements, and those of the book which deny that infantry and artillery had been discovered as early as Friday afternoon, will be observed.

On that very afternoon, however, General Sherman had written to General Grant, giving the result of the cavalry reconnoissance. That this did not agree with the present statement, that up to the night of the 4th, "we had not positively detected the presence of infantry," the following report by General Grant will show:

HEADQUARTERS DEPARTMENT WEST TENNESSEE,
SAVANNAH, *April* 5, 1862.

General H. W. HALLECK, *Commanding Department of Missouri, St. Louis, Mo.*

GENERAL: Just as my letter of yesterday to Captain McLean, Assistant-Adjutant-General, was finished, notices from Generals McClernand's and Sherman's Assistant-Adjutant-Generals were received, stating that our outposts had been attacked by the enemy apparently in strong force. I immediately went up, but found all quiet The enemy took two officers and four or five of our men prisoners, and killed four. We took eight prisoners, and killed several; number of the enemy wounded not known. They had with them three pieces of artillery, and cavalry and infantry. How much can not, of course, be estimated.

I have scarcely the faintest idea of an attack being made upon us (general one), but will be prepared should such a thing take place. General Nelson's division has arrived. The other two of General Buell's column will arrive to-morrow or next day. It is my present intention to send them to Hamburg, some four or five miles above Pittsburgh, when they all get here. From that point to Corinth the road is good, and a junction can be formed with the troops from Pittsburgh at almost any point. * * * *

I am, General, very respectfully your obedient servant.

U. S. GRANT, *Major-General.*

Immediately after the battle, General Sherman appears to have been won over to the idea that an abattis might be valuable as a protection to his camp, for in a compilation of his orders, made under his own direction, the very first of them which appears after the engagement, contains the following paragraph:

"Each brigade commander will examine carefully his immediate front; fell trees to afford his men a barricade, and clear away all underbrush for two hundred yards in front, so as to uncover an approaching enemy; with these precautions, we can hold our camp against any amount of force that can be brought against us."

There is no indication that General Sherman considered this order either an evidence of weakness, or an invitation to attack, or as calculated to make his "raw men timid."

That General Halleck supposed the officers in charge of the camp had taken means to strengthen their position, is shown by the following telegram:

HEADQUARTERS DEPARTMENT OF THE MISSOURI, }
ST. LOUIS, *April 8,* 1862. }

Hon. E. M. STANTON, *Secretary of War.*

The enemy attacked our works at Pittsburgh, Tennessee, yesterday, but was repulsed with heavy loss. No details given.

H. W HALLECK, *Major-General.*

General Buckland and Major Ricker have both written an account of the reconnoissance on the 4th. Starting at 2 P. M., General Buckland had come up with the enemy's cavalry about two miles in front of the camp. Of what happened, what was seen, and what reported to General Sherman, General Buckland thus writes:

"We pursued about a mile, when the enemy commenced firing artillery at us. We discovered that he had a large force of infantry and artillery. We therefore concluded to march back to camp with as little delay as possible.

"When we reached the picket lines, General Sherman was there with several regiments in line of battle. As I rode up to General Sherman at the head of my column, with about fifteen prisoners close behind me, the General asked me what I had been doing. His manner indicated that he was not pleased. I replied that I had accidentally got into a little fight, and there were some of the fruits of it, pointing to the prisoners. He answered that I might have drawn the whole army into a fight before they were ready, and ordered me to take my men to camp. Soon after reaching camp, one of General Sherman's aids came and said the General desired me to send him a written statement of what I had done and seen that day, which I did the same evening. General Sherman afterward informed me that he sent the statement to General Grant the same night.

"The next day, Saturday April 5th, I visited the picket line several times, and found that the woods were swarming with rebel cavalry along the entire front of my line, and the pickets claimed to have discovered infantry and artillery. Several times during the day I reported these facts to General Sherman. Colonel Hilderbrand, of the Third Brigade, and other officers, visited the picket line with me during the day. It was well understood all that day and night throughout Sherman's division, that there was a large rebel force immediately in our front. I consulted with Colonels Cockrell and Sullivan as to the proper measures to prevent a surprise. The pickets were strengthened, and Colonel Cockrell sent two companies of the Seventieth Ohio to take a position where they could best support the pickets in case of an attack. I also established a line of sentinels from my camp to the reserve of the pickets. Every officer in my brigade was fully aware of the danger, and such precautions were taken that a surprise was impossible." * * *

Concerning the same reconnoissance, Major Ricker wrote as follows:

* * * "When we got back to the picket lines we found General Sherman there with infantry and artillery in line of battle, caused by the heavy firing of the enemy on us. General Sherman asked me what was up. I told him I had met and fought the advance of Beauregard's army, that he was advancing on us. General Sherman said it could not be possible, Beauregard was not such a fool as to leave his base of operations and attack us in ours— mere reconnoissance in force."

General Bragg's official report shows that this reconnoitering party was really pushed up to the immediate vicinity of three corps of the Confederate army. Of the movement from Monterey to the battle-field, Bragg says:

"Moving from there, the command bivouacked for the night near the Meckey House, immediately in rear of Major-General Hardee's corps, Major-General Polk's being just in our rear * * * A reconnoissance in some force from the enemy made its appearance during the evening in front of General Hardee's corps, and was promptly driven back."

The following extracts from various official reports of the battle, bear pointedly upon the question of a surprise. General John McArthur, commanding Second Division, says:

"We had been in line but a few moments when the enemy made their appearance and attacked my left wing."

Colonel R. P. Buckland, Fourth Brigade, Sherman's division, says:

"Between six and seven o'clock on Sunday morning, I was informed that our pickets were fired upon. I immediately gave orders for forming the brigade on the color line, which was promptly done. About this time I was informed that the pickets were being driven in. I ordered the Forty-eighth Regiment, Colonel Sullivan, to advance in support of the pickets, which he did, but discovered that the enemy had advanced in force to the creek, about eighty to one hundred rods in front. I immediately ordered the brigade to advance in line of battle. We had marched about thirty to forty rods, when we discovered the enemy and opened fire upon him along the whole line, which checked his advance and caused him to fall back."

Colonel J. R. Cockerell, commanding Seventieth Ohio, says:

"On Sunday morning, April 6, 1862, an alarm was made in the front of this brigade, and I called my regiment from breakfast and formed it in line of battle on the color line. I then heard heavy firing on the left and in front of our line, and advanced my regiment about two hundred paces in the woods, and formed line of battle in pursuance of your order. I ordered my regiment to open fire, with the left thrown back, and did great execution among the enemy, who retired into the hollow."

Colonel Hilderbrand, commanding Third Brigade, Sherman's division, says:

"Early on the morning of Sunday, 6th inst., our pickets were fired on, and shortly after seven o'clock the enemy appeared in force, presenting himself in columns of regiments at least four deep. He opened upon our camp a heavy fire from infantry, which was immediately followed by shell. Having formed my brigade in line of battle, I ordered an advance. The Seventy-seventh and Fifty-seventh Regiments were thrown forward to occupy a certain position, but encountered the enemy in force within three hundred yards of our camp."

Captain Samuel E. Barrett, commanding First Regiment Illinois Artillery, says:

"We were stationed near the outposts, and on the alarm being given, at about half past seven o'clock on Sunday morning, the battery was promptly got in readiness, and in ten minutes thereafter commenced firing on the right of the log church, some one hundred yards in front of General Sherman's headquarters, where the attack was made by the enemy in great force."

Lieutenant-Colonel Parlin, commanding Forty-eighth Ohio Infantry, says:

"On the morning of the 6th our regiment met the enemy about two hundred yards in front of our color line; they came upon us so suddenly that for a short time our men wavered, but soon rallied again, when we kept him back for two hours and until General Sherman ordered us to fall back to the Purdy road."

As to the distances of the picket from his front, and the limits reached by his reconnoissance, it is notable that General Sherman fixes them much further from camp than all the other officers who have given testimony or made statements upon these points.

An officer of General Beauregard's staff, who was helping direct the rebel advance, wrote thus of the matter:

"The total absence of cavalry pickets from General Grant's army was a matter of perfect amazement. There were absolutely none on Grant's left, where Breckinridge's division was meeting him, so that we were able to come up within hearing of their drums entirely unperceived. The Southern generals always kept cavalry pickets out for miles, even when no enemy was supposed to be within a day's march of them. The infantry pickets of Grant's forces were not above three-fourths of a mile from his advance camps, and they were too few to make any resistance."

The officers of General Thomas' army, who had charge of

the pickets a few days after the battle, rode over the line from which the rebels moved to the attack. Every where were signs of the deliberation with which the enemy formed his forces. The routes by which each corps and division of the first line was to march to its position in the woods, were blazed upon the trees, and the entire force of the enemy went into line for the attack wholly undisturbed, and with as much order and precision, as if forming upon markers for a grand review. And the time that the enemy was thus forming his lines, scarcely out of rifled cannon range, "passed in our camps," says General Sherman, "without any unusual event."

Enough has been presented to show upon how slight a foundation that position of the book is built, by which General Sherman seeks to controvert the idea that "our army was taken completely by surprise" at Shiloh.

Two brief extracts from his own official report of the battle, dated on the field, April 10th, will show on what day and at what hour he, the trusted officer on the field, became satisfied that the rebels intended to attack:

"On Saturday the enemy's cavalry was again very bold, coming well down to our front, yet I did not believe they designed anything but a strong demonstration. * * * *

"About 8 A. M. (Sunday) I saw the glistening bayonets of heavy masses of infantry to our left front in the woods beyond the small stream alluded to, and became satisfied for the first time that the enemy designed a determined attack on our whole camp."

It is unnecessary to do more than call attention to some most absurd points made by General Sherman.

No rifle pits were dug or abattis laid down, because the army regulations stood in the way.

The line did not occupy too much ground, although space enough had been left for Buell's forces.

Although all the elements of an army were known to be in the front on Friday, yet no one knew its destination, and even General Sherman had to guess its purpose.

And for all this bungling, blundering, and criminal carelessness, General Sherman some years later had this excuse, in a letter to the *United States Service Magazine:*

"It was necessary that a combat, fierce and bitter, to test the manhood of the two armies, should come off, and that was as good a place as any. It was not then a question of military skill and strategy, but of courage and pluck, and I am convinced that every life lost that day to us was necessary, for otherwise, at Corinth, at Memphis, at Vicksburg, we would have found harder resistance, had we not shown our enemies, that rude and untutored as we then were, we could fight as well as they."

A well ordered line of battle, some rifle pits, and a vigilant watch for an approaching enemy, followed by such fighting as these precautions would have insured, might have made even a better impression upon the rebels with a great saving of life.

At Shiloh, for the first time since General Buell had obtained an "honorable position" for General Sherman in Louisiana, these two officers met on the battle-field. This time General Buell came when sorely needed, to aid Sherman and his associates in securing honorable victory. All would suppose that when the author of the Memoirs sat down to write his version of Shiloh he would at least have done bare justice to General Buell and his army, but the reader will look for it in vain. Whatever his impressions at the time may have been, the public discussions which have since taken place, and the whole official history of the movements, which was at his disposal, afforded every means of correcting previous errors. Although, toward the close of that first disastrous day, Grant's whole army was praying for "night or Buell," and Grant about noon was urging Buell on as follows:—"If you will get upon the field, leaving all your baggage over the river, it will be a move to our advantage, and *possibly* save the day to us,"— General Sherman finds little to recognize or praise in the gallantry and efficient aid rendered in time of need by his former friend, and has cold words of disparagement instead.

The closing portion of his chapter on Shiloh, is chiefly devoted to matters connected with General Buell and his forces, and is as follows:

* * * "General Grant did not make an official report of the battle of Shiloh, but all its incidents and events were covered by the reports of division commanders and subordinates. Probably no single battle of the war gave rise to such wild and damaging reports. It was publicly asserted at the North that our army was taken completely by surprise; that the rebels caught us in our tents; bayoneted the men in their beds; that General Grant was drunk; that Buell's opportune arrival saved the Army of the Tennessee from utter annihilation, etc. These reports were in a measure sustained by the published opinions of Generals Buell, Nelson, and others, who had reached the steamboat landing from the east just before night-fall of the 6th, when there was a large crowd of frightened, stampeded men, who clamored and declared that our army was all destroyed and beaten. Personally I saw General Grant, who with his staff visited me about 10 A. M. of the 6th, when we were desperately engaged. But we had checked the headlong assault of our enemy, and then held our ground. This gave him great satisfaction, and he told me that things did not look as well over on the left. He also told me that on his way up from Savannah that morning, he had stopped at Crump's Landing, and had ordered Lew. Wallace's division to cross over Lick Creek, so as to come up on my right, telling me to look out for him. He again came to me just before dark, and described the last assault made by the rebels at the ravine, near the steamboat landing, which he had repelled by a heavy battery collected under Colonel J. D. Webster and other officers, and he was convinced that the battle was over for that day. He ordered me to be ready to assume the offensive in the morning, saying that, as he had observed at Fort Donelson at the crisis of the battle, both sides seemed defeated and whoever assumed the offensive was sure to win. General Grant also explained to me that General Buell had reached the bank of the Tennessee River opposite Pittsburgh Landing, and was in the act of ferrying his troops across at the time he was speaking to me.

"About half an hour afterward General Buell himself rode up to where I was, accompanied by Colonels Fry, Michler, and others of his staff. I was dismounted at the time, and General Buell made of me a good many significant inquiries about matters and things generally. By the aid of a manuscript map made by myself, I pointed out to him our positions as they had been in the morning, and our then positions; I also explained to him that my right then covered the bridge over Lick Creek, by which we had all day been expecting Lew. Wallace; that McClernand was on my left, Hurlbut on his left, and so on. But Buell said he had come up from the landing, and had not seen our men—of whose existence, in fact, he seemed to doubt. I insisted that I had five thousand good men still left in line, and thought that McClernand had as many more, and that with what was left of Hurlbut's, W. H. L. Wallace's, and Prentiss' divisions, we ought to have eighteen thousand men fit for battle. I reckoned that ten thousand of our men were dead, wounded, or prisoners, and that the enemy's loss could not be much less. Buell said that Nelson's, McCook's, and Crittenden's divisions of his army, containing eighteen thousand men, had arrived, and could cross over in the night and be ready for the next day's battle. I argued that, with these reënforcements, we could sweep the field. Buell seemed to mistrust us, and repeatedly said that he did not like the looks of things, especially about the boat landing, and I really feared he would not cross over his army that night, lest he should become involved in our general disaster. He did not, of course, understand the shape of the ground, and asked me for the use of my map, which I lent him on the promise that he would return it. He handed it to Major Michler to have it copied, and the original returned to me, which Michler did two or three days after the battle. Buell did cross over that night, and the next day we assumed the offensive and swept the field, thus gaining the battle decisively. Nevertheless, the controversy was started and kept up, mostly to the personal prejudice of General Grant, who, as usual, maintained an imperturbable silence.

"After the battle, a constant stream of civilian surgeons, and sanitary commission agents, men and women, came up the Tennessee to bring relief to the thousands of maimed and wounded soldiers for whom we had imperfect means of shelter and care. These people caught up the camp stories, which, on their return home, they retailed through their local papers, usually elevating their own neighbors into heroes, but decrying all others. Among them was Lieutenant-Governor Stanton, of Ohio, who published in Bellefontaine, Ohio, a most abusive article about General Grant and his subordinate generals. As General Grant did not, and would not, take up the cudgels, I did so. My letter in reply to Stanton, dated June 10, 1862, was published in the *Cincinnati Commercial* soon after its date. To this Lieutenant-Governor Stanton replied, and I further rejoined in a letter dated July 12, 1862. These letters are too personal to be revived. By this time the good people of the North had begun to have their eyes opened, and to give us in the field more faith and support. Stanton was never again elected to any public office, and was commonly spoken of as 'the late Mr. Stanton.' He is now dead, and I doubt not in life he often regretted his mistake in attempting to gain popular fame by abusing the army leaders, then, as now, an easy and favorite mode of gaining notoriety, if not popularity. Of course, subsequent events gave General Grant and most of the other actors in that battle their appropriate place in history, but the danger of sudden popular clamor is well illustrated by this case.

"The battle of Shiloh, or Pittsburgh Landing, was one of the most fiercely contested of the war. On the morning of April 6, 1862, the five divisions of McClernand, Prentiss, Hurlbut, W. H. L. Wallace, and Sherman aggregated about thirty-two thousand men. We had no intrenchments of any sort, on the theory that, as soon as Buell arrived, we would march to Corinth to attack the enemy. The rebel army, commanded by General Albert Sidney Johnston, was, according to their own reports and admissions, forty-five thousand strong, had the momentum of attack, and beyond all question fought skillfully from early morning till about 2 P. M., when their commander-in-chief was killed by a Minié-ball in the calf of his leg, which penetrated the boot and severed the main artery. There was then a perceptible lull for a couple of hours, when the attack was renewed, but with much less vehemence, and continued up to dark. Early at night the division of Lew. Wallace arrived from the other side of Snake Creek, not having fired a shot. A very small part of General Buell's army was on our side of the Tennessee River that evening, and their loss was trivial.

"During that night the three divisions of McCook, Nelson, and Crittenden were ferried across the Tennessee, and fought with us the next day (7th.) During that night, also, the two wooden gun-boats, Tyler, commanded by Lieutenant Gwin, and Lexington, Lieutenant Shirk, both of the regular navy, caused shells to be thrown toward that part of the field of battle known to be occupied by the enemy. Beauregard afterward reported his entire loss as ten thousand six hundred and ninety-nine. Our aggregate loss, made up from official statements, shows seventeen hundred killed, seven thousand four hundred and ninety-five wounded, and three thousand and twenty-two prisoners; aggregate, twelve thousand two hundred and seventeen, of which twenty-one hundred and sixty-seven were in Buell's army, leaving for that of Grant ten thousand and fifty. This result is a fair measure of the amount of fighting done by each army."

And this of an army that occupied three-fourths of the line of battle on the second day, and carried it steadily forward till victory was attained! Instead of this last unworthy sentence, General Sherman might have had the fairness to say that, as Grant's force for the first day's fight consisted of five divisions, aggregating about thirty-two thousand men, and as Lew. Wallace's division, about six thousand strong, came up for the second day's fight—while Buell had only one brigade in action after 5 o'clock the first day, and only three divisions of eighteen thousand men the second day—the losses of each army were about in proportion to their respective numbers, and the time each was engaged. But it has never heretofore answered General Sherman's purpose to state the facts about Buell's army at Shiloh, and now he is attempting to perpetuate exploded errors.

The statement that General Grant made no official report of the battle of Shiloh is a good illustration of the careless manner in which General Sherman has prepared his book. Not only did Grant make such a report, but it was written before the reports of any of the division commanders had been handed in, as is shown by their respective dates, so that it is valuable as containing General Grant's own understanding of the events of the battle. It has long been in the regular files, with the reports of one hundred and sixteen other officers, upon the part taken by their commands in this battle. It was printed in the *Rebellion Record* for 1862.

And, as General Sherman, since the publication of his Memoirs, still maintains that General Grant made no official report of Shiloh, it is proper to present its formal official marks. It opens and closes as follows:

HEADQUARTERS DISTRICT OF WEST TENNESSEE,
PITTSBURGH, April 9th, 1862.

Captain N. H. MCLEAN, *A. A. Gen. Dept. of the Mississippi, St. Louis, Mo*

CAPTAIN: It becomes my duty again to report another battle fought between two great armies—one contending for the maintenance of the best government ever devised, the other for its destruction. It is pleasant to record the success of the army contending for the former principle.

(Then follows the body of the report.)

I am, very respectfully, your obedient servant,

U. S. GRANT, *Major-General commanding.*

The document was forwarded to the War Department from General Halleck's headquarters at St. Louis, thus officially certified:

HEADQUARTERS DEPARTMENT OF THE MISSISSIPPI,
ST. LOUIS, April 14th, 1862.

Official copy.

J. C. KELTON, *Assistant Adjutant-General.*

On account of some delay, it was not transmitted to the Senate when that body called for all the reports of the battle. Those forwarded in obedience to the call, were not described by Mr. Stanton in his letter accompanying them, as *all* the reports, but as "all the reports (one hundred and sixteen in number) which have yet been received by this Department."

It now occupies its proper place in the files with the other reports of that battle.

A paragraph from this report sets forth the part taken by General Buell's forces in repelling the assault near the steamboat landing, about the close of the first day's action, which is wholly ignored in General Sherman's account of Shiloh. Says General Grant:

"At a late hour in the afternoon a desperate effort was made by the enemy to turn our left and get possession of the landing, transports, etc. This point was guarded by the gun-boats Tyler and Lexington, Captains Gwinn and Shirk, U. S. N., commanding, four 20-pounder Parrott guns and a battery of rifled guns. As there is a deep and impassable ravine for artillery or cavalry, and very difficult for infantry at this point, no troops were stationed here except the necessary artillerists and a small infantry force for their support. Just at this moment the advance of Major-General Buell's column (a part of the division under General Nelson) arrived, the two Generals named both being present. An advance was immediately made upon the point of attack, and the enemy soon driven back."

It is, to say the least, quite improbable that when General Grant was detailing to Sherman the desperate attack at the ravine spoken of in his report, and had seen Buell's troops, with Buell and Nelson both present, advance and push back the enemy with the assistance of the gun-boats and the heavy artillery, he not only forgot to mention to Sherman the fact that Buell and part of his troops were across and had been engaged at the ravine, but should tell him that Buell was actually on the other side of the river.

General Buell's official report agrees exactly with that of General Grant, in regard to the attack at the landing. In speaking of his arrival, which was at 1 o'clock in the afternoon of the 6th, General Buell says:

"Finding General Grant at the landing, I requested him to send steamers to Savannah to bring up General Crittenden's division, which had arrived during the morning, and then went ashore with him. * * * In the meantime the enemy had made such progress against our troops that his artillery and musketry began to play into the vital spot of the position, and some persons were killed on the bank at the very landing. General Nelson arrived with Colonel Ammen's brigade at this opportune moment. It was immediately posted to meet the attack at that point, and with a battery of artillery, which happened to be on the ground, and was brought into action, opened fire on the enemy and repulsed him. The action of the gun-boats also contributed very much to that result. The attack at that point was not renewed, night having come on, and the firing ceased on both sides."

Concerning the actors in the battle, General Grant says:

"Of the part taken by each separate command I can not take special notice in this report, but will do so more fully when reports of division commanders are handed in.

"General Buell coming on the field with a distinct army long under his command, and which did such efficient service, commanded by himself in person on the field, will be much better able to notice those of his command, who particularly distinguished themselves, than I possibly can."

In this report General Grant says nothing of himself, and all that he could of good about others. There was no attempt here, nor has he ever attempted since to evade his full responsibility for Shiloh, but has trusted to time for a proper distribution of both honor and blame.

General Halleck's congratulatory order issued a week after the battle thus recognized the presence and the action of Buell's troops on the first day:

"1. The Major-General commanding this department thanks Major-General Grant and Major-General Buell, and the officers and men of their respective commands, for the bravery and endurance with which they sustained the general attacks of the enemy on the 6th, and for the heroic manner in which on the 7th instant they defeated and routed the entire rebel army. The soldiers of the Great West have added new laurels to those which they had already won on numerous fields."

The report made to General Halleck by General Grant on the evening of the 5th, that one of Buell's divisions had then arrived, and two others would arrive the next day, renders unnecessary the further discussion of a question indirectly presented by General Sherman. In previous controversies, it has been strenuously maintained by him, that General Grant ordered an advance for the second day without regard to the arrival of Buell's troops. The report to Halleck shows that this was impossible.

The connection sought to be established between the letters of Lieutenant-Governor Stanton upon the battle of Shiloh, and his non-election to public office after writing them, is certainly a curious conceit to indulge over the grave of such a man.

This treatment of the battle of Shiloh is a fair sample of the entire work. The two volumes, as will be shown by the records, teem with inaccuracies and instances of great injustice done to associate generals and coöperating armies.

CHAPTER IV.

IUKA AND SECOND CORINTH—GENERAL ROSECRANS MISREPRESENTED.

HOSTILE criticism of Generals Buell, Rosecrans, and Thomas, the successive commanders of the Army of the Ohio, forms one of the salient features of the Memoirs. General Rosecrans particularly distinguished himself in the battles of Iuka and Corinth, in the autumn following the first occupation of the latter place. From General Sherman's account, however, the reader would suppose that General Rosecrans had behaved badly in both these actions. Of the battle at Iuka, he says:

"In the early part of September the enemy in our front manifested great activity, feeling with cavalry at all points, and on the 13th General Van Dorn threatened Corinth, while General Price seized the town of Iuka, which was promptly abandoned by a small garrison under Colonel Murphy. Price's force was about eight thousand men, and the general impression was that he was *en route* for Eastport, with the purpose to cross the Tennessee River in the direction of Nashville, in aid of General Bragg, then in full career for Kentucky.

"General Grant determined to attack him in force, prepared to regain Corinth before Van Dorn could reach it. He had drawn Ord to Corinth, and moved him by Burnsville on Iuka, by the main road twenty-six miles. General Grant accompanied this column as far as Burnsville. At the same time he had dispatched Rosecrans by roads to the south, *via* Jacinto, with orders to approach Iuka by the two main roads coming into Iuka from the south, viz., the Jacinto and Fulton roads.

"On the 18th General Ord encountered the enemy about four miles out of Iuka. His orders contemplated that he should not make a serious attack until Rosecrans had gained his position on the south; but, as usual, Rosecrans had encountered difficulties in the confusion of roads. His head of column did not reach the vicinity of Iuka till 4 P. M. of the 19th, and then his troops were long drawn out on the single Jacinto road, leaving the Fulton road clear for Price's use. Price perceived his advantage, and attacked with vehemence the head of Rosecrans' column, Hamilton's division, beating it back, capturing a battery, and killing and disabling seven hundred and thirty-six men, so that when night closed in Rosecrans was driven to the defensive, and Price, perceiving his danger, deliberately withdrew by the Fulton road, and the next morning was gone. Although General Ord must have been within four or six miles of this battle, he did not hear a sound, and he or General Grant did not know of it till advised the next morning by a courier who had made a wide circuit to reach them. General Grant was much offended with General Rosecrans because of this affair; but in my experience these concerted movements generally fail, unless with the very best kind of troops, and then in a country on whose roads some reliance can be placed, which is not the case in northern Mississippi. If Price was aiming for Tennessee he failed, and was therefore beaten. He made a wide circuit by the south and again joined Van Dorn." * * * *

To what extent this action was a reverse for General Rosecrans, and in what degree General Grant was offended, the reports of the last-named officer will show:

IUKA, MISS., *September 20, 1862.*

To *Major-General* HALLECK, *General-in-Chief.*

General Rosecrans, with Stanley and Hamilton's divisions of Missouri cavalry, attacked General Price south of this village about two hours before dark yesterday, and had a sharp fight until night closed in.

General Ord was to the north with an armed force of about five thousand men, and had some skirmishing with rebel pickets. This morning the fight was resumed by General Rosecrans, who was nearest to the town, but it was found that the enemy had been evacuating during the night, going south. Hamilton and Stanley, with the cavalry, are in full pursuit.

This will, no doubt, break up the enemy, and possibly force them to abandon much of their artillery. The loss on either side in killed and wounded is from four to five hundred.

The enemy's loss in arms, tents, etc., will be large. We have about two hundred and fifty prisoners. I have reliable information that it was Price's intention to move over east of Tennessee. In this he has been thwarted. Among the enemy's loss are General Little, killed, and General Whitfield, wounded. I can not speak too highly of the energy and skill displayed by General Rosecrans in the attack, and of the endurance of the troops under him. General Ord's command showed untiring zeal, but the direction taken by the enemy prevented them taking the active part they desired. Price's force was about fifteen thousand.   U. S. GRANT, *Major-General.*

Subsequently, General Grant made an extended report of this battle, which bears date October 22d. The chief expression in it which can be construed into dissatisfaction with General Rosecrans' movements, is where he says, speaking of the delay of his column through the fault of a guide, "this caused some disappointment and made a change of plans necessary," and before closing his report he calls attention to the fact that this delay was "the fault of a guide."

This report sums up the movement and its results as follows:

> On the 16th of September we commenced to collect our strength to move upon Price at Iuka, in two columns; the one to the right of the railroad, commanded by Brigadier-General (now Major-General) W. S. Rosecrans; the one to the left, commanded by Major-General O. E. C. Ord. On the night of the 18th the latter was in position to bring on an engagement in one hour's march. The former, from having a greater distance to march, and through the fault of a guide, was twenty miles back. On the 19th, by making a rapid march, hardy, well disciplined, and tried troops arrived within two miles of the place to be attacked. Unexpectedly, the enemy took the initiative and became the attacking party. The ground chosen was such that a large force on our side could not be brought into action; but the bravery and endurance of those brought in was such that, with the skill and presence of mind of the officer commanding, they were able to hold their ground till night closed the conflict. During the night the enemy fled, leaving our troops in possession of the field, with their dead to bury and wounded to care for. If it was the object of the enemy to make their way into Kentucky, they were defeated in that; if to hold their position until Van Dorn could come up on the south-west of Corinth and make a simultaneous attack, they were defeated in that. Our only defeat was in not capturing the entire army, or in destroying it, as I had hoped to do.
>
> It was a part of General Hamilton's command that did the fighting, directed entirely by that cool and deserving officer.
>
> I commend him to the President for acknowledgment for his services. * * * * I can not close this report without paying a tribute to all the officers and soldiers comprising this command. Their conduct on the march was exemplary and all were eager to meet the enemy. The possibility of defeat I do not think entered the mind of a single individual, and I believe this same feeling now pervades the entire army which I have the honor to command. * * * *   U. S. GRANT, *Major-General.*

In his account of the battle of Corinth, which took place

about two weeks after the action at Iuka, General Sherman is still more unjust to General Rosecrans. The battle was a brilliant and most decisive one, and General Rosecrans' conduct throughout, such as merited and secured the highest praise, and a few days after his return from a long pursuit of the enemy, he was relieved and promoted to the command of the Army of the Cumberland, in place of General Buell.

In regard to the affair at Corinth the Memoirs say:

"Still by the 1st of October, General Grant was satisfied that the enemy was meditating an attack in force on Boliver or Corinth; and on the 2d Van Dorn made his appearance near Corinth, with his entire army. On the 3d he moved down on that place from the north and north-west.

"General Rosecrans went out some four miles to meet him, but was worsted and compelled to fall back within the line of his forts. These had been begun under General Halleck, but were much strengthened by General Grant, and consisted of several detached redoubts bearing on each other, and inclosing the town and the depots of stores at the intersection of the two railroads. Van Dorn closed down on the forts by the evening of the 3d, and on the morning of the 4th assaulted with great vehemence.

"Our men, covered by good parapets, fought gallantly, and defended their posts well, inflicting terrible losses on the enemy, so that by noon the rebels were repulsed at all points and drew off, leaving their dead and wounded in our hands. * * * *

"Meantime, General Grant at Jackson, had dispatched Brigadier-General McPherson with a brigade directly for Corinth, which reached General Rosecrans after the battle; and in anticipation of his victory, had ordered him to pursue instantly, notifying him that he had ordered Ord's and Hurlbut's divisions rapidly across to Pocahontas, so as to strike the rebels in flank. On the morning of the 5th, General Ord reached Hatchie River at Davis' bridge, with four thousand men; crossed over and encountered the retreating army, captured a battery and several hundred prisoners, dispersing the rebel advance and forcing the main column to make a wide circuit by the south in order to cross the Hatchie River.

"Had General Rosecrans pursued promptly and been on the heels of this mass of confused and routed men, Van Dorn's army would surely have been utterly ruined; as it was, Van Dorn regained Holly Springs somewhat demoralized.

"General Rosecrans did not begin his pursuit till the next morning, the 5th, and it was then too late.

"General Grant was again displeased with him, and never became fully reconciled. General Rosecrans was soon after relieved, and transferred to the Army of the Cumberland in Tennessee, of which he afterward obtained the command in place of General Buell, who was removed.

"The effect of the battle of Corinth was very great. It was, indeed, a decisive blow to the Confederate cause in our quarter, and changed the whole aspect of affairs in West Tennessee. From the timid defensive, we were at once enabled to assume the bold offensive. In Memphis I could see its effects upon the citizens, and they openly admitted that their cause had sustained a death-blow."

The several insinuations against General Rosecrans (who had struck this death-blow), which the above extracts contain, are placed in their true light, through the telegrams sent by General Grant at the time of the movement, and his full report made later:

JACKSON, *October 5*, 1862.
General H. W. HALLECK, *Washington, D. C.*

Yesterday the rebels under Van Dorn, Price, and Lovell were repulsed from their attack on Corinth with great slaughter. The enemy are in full retreat, leaving their dead and wounded on the field. Rosecrans telegraphs that the loss is serious on our side, particularly in officers, but bears no comparison with that of the enemy. General Hackleman fell while gallantly leading his brigade. General Oglesby is dangerously wounded. McPherson reached Corinth with his command yesterday. Rosecrans pursued the retreating enemy this morning, and should he attempt to move toward Boliver, will follow him to that place. Hurlbut is at the Hatchie with five or six thousand men, and is no doubt, now with the pursuing column. From seven hundred to a thousand prisoners, beside wounded, are left on our hands.

U. S. GRANT, *Major-General.*

JACKSON, *October 5*, 1862.
General H. W. HALLECK, *Washington, D. C.*

General Ord, who followed Hurlbut and took command, met the enemy to day on the south side of the Hatchie, as I understand from a dispatch, and drove them across the stream and got possession of the heights with our troops. Ord took two batteries and about two hundred prisoners. A large portion of Rosecrans' forces were at Chewalla. At this distance every thing looks most favorable, and I can not see how the enemy are to escape without losing every thing but their small arms. I have strained every thing to take into the fight an adequate force, and to get them to the right place.

U. S. GRANT, *Major-General.*

JACKSON, *October 6*, 1862.
General H. W. HALLECK, *Washington, D. C.*

Generals Ord and Hurlbut came on the enemy's rear yesterday, Hurlbut having driven in small bodies the day before. After several hours hard fighting they drove the enemy five miles back across the Hatchie toward Corinth, capturing two batteries, about three hundred prisoners, and many small arms. I immediately apprised General Rosecrans of these facts, and directed him to urge on the good work. The following dispatch just received:

CHEWALLA, *October* 6, 1862.
" *To Major-General* GRANT.
"'The enemy are totally routed, throwing every thing away. We are following sharply.
W. S. ROSECRANS."

Under previous instructions, Hurlbut is also following. McPherson is in the lead of Rosecrans' column. Rebel General Martin said to be killed.
U. S. GRANT, *Major-General.*

JACKSON, *October* 8, 1862.
General H. W. HALLECK, *Washington, D. C.*
Rosecrans has followed rebels to Ripley. Troops from Bolivar will occupy Grand Juction to-morrow. With reënforcements rapidly sent in from the new lines, I can take any thing on the Mississippi Central road. I ordered Rosecrans back last night, but he is so adverse to returning that I have directed him to remain still, until you can be heard from.
U. S. GRANT, *Major-General.*

General Rosecrans' protest against giving up the pursuit, thus referred to by General Grant, was as follows:

HEADQUARTERS, JONESBORO, MISS., }
October 7, 1862, *midnight.* }
Major-General GRANT, *Jackson, Tenn.*
Yours, 8:30 P. M., received. I most deeply dissent from your views as to the policy of pursuit. We have defeated, routed, and demoralized the army which held the Lower Mississippi Valley. We have the two railroads leading south to the Gulf, through the most populous parts of this State, into which we can now pursue them by the Mississippi Central or Mobile & Ohio Road. The effect of returning to our old position will be to give them up the only corn they have in the country west of Alabama, including Tuscumbia Valley, and to permit them to recruit their forces, advance, and reoccupy their old ground, reducing us to the occupation of a defensive position, barren and worthless, on a long front, of which they can harass us until bad weather precludes any effectual advance, except along the railroads, where time, fortifications, and rolling stock will render them superior to us.

Our force, including what can be spared with Hurlbut, will garrison Corinth and Jackson, and enable us to push them. Our advance will cover even Holly Springs, which will be ours when we want it. All that is needful is to combine, push, and whip them. We have whipped, and should now push to the wall, all the forces in Mississippi, and capture the rolling stock of the railroads west of the Alabama & Mobile. Bragg's army alone could repair the damage we have it in our power to do them. But I beseech you to bend every thing to push them while they are broken, weary, hungry, and ill supplied. Draw every thing from Memphis to help move on Holly Springs. Let us concentrate, and appeal to the governors of the States to rush down some twenty or thirty new regiments to hold in our rear, and we can make a triumph of our start. Respectfully and truly,

W. S. ROSECRANS, *Major-General.*

In reply to this he received an order from the general commanding, directing him to desist from pursuit, and return with his command cautiously, but promptly, to Corinth.

WASHINGTON, 10 A M., *October 8, 1862.*
Major-General U. S. GRANT.

Why order a return of your troops? Why not reënforce Rosecrans, and pursue the enemy into Mississippi, supporting your army on the country?

H. W. HALLECK, *General-in-Chief.*

JACKSON, *October 8, 1862.*
General H. W. HALLECK, *Washington, D. C.*

An army can not subsist itself on the country except in forage. They did not start out to follow but a few days, and are much worn out; and I have information, not only that the enemy have reserves that are on their way to join the retreating column, but that they have fortifications to retreat to in case of need. The Mobile road is also open to the enemy to near Rienzi, and Corinth would be exposed by the advance. Although partial success might result from further pursuit, disaster would follow in the end. If you say so, however, it is not too late yet to go on, and I will join the moving column and go to the farthest extent possible. Rosecrans has been reënforced with every thing on hand, even at the risk of this road against raids.

U. S. GRANT, *Major-General.*

It was decided, however, to order General Rosecrans back, on the ground that he was not strong enough, or sufficiently prepared, for such a pursuit as he designed to make.

The following extract from orders issued by General Grant at Jackson, October 7th, shows that he then thought General Rosecrans had accomplished all possible for him to do in the place assigned him.

IUKA AND SECOND CORINTH.

HEADQUARTERS DEPARTMENT OF WEST TENNESSEE, }
JACKSON, TENN., *October* 7. }

[General Order No. 88.]

It is with heartfelt gratitude the General commanding congratulates the Armies of the West for another victory, won by them on the 3d, 4th, and 5th inst., over the combined armies of Van Dorn, Price, and Lovell. * * *
While one division of the army, under Major-General Rosecrans, was resisting and repelling the onslaught of the rebel hosts at Corinth, another from Bolivar, under Major-General Hurlbut, was marching upon the enemy's rear, driving in their pickets and cavalry, and attracting the attention of a large force of infantry and artillery. * * * *

To these two divisions of the army all praise is due, and will be awarded by a grateful country.

Between them there should be, and I trust is, the warmest bonds of brotherhood. Each was risking life in the same cause, and on this occasion risking it also to save and assist the other. No troops could do more than these separated armies. Each did all possible for it to do in the place assigned it. * * * *

By command of *Major-General* GRANT,

JOHN A. RAWLINS, A. A. G.

General Grant closed his formal report of this battle as follows:

As shown by the reports, the enemy was repulsed at Corinth, at 11 A. M. on the 4th, and not followed until next morning.

Two days' hard fighting without rest, probably, had so fatigued the troops as to make earlier pursuit impracticable. I regretted this as the enemy would have been compelled to abandon most of his artillery and transportation in the difficult roads of the Hatchie crossing had the pursuit commenced then.

The victory was most triumphant as it was however, and all praise is due officers and men for their undaunted courage and obstinate resistance against an enemy outnumbering them as three to two.

When it became evident that an attack would be made, I drew off from the guard along the line of the railroad all the troops that could possibly be spared (six regiments) to reënforce Corinth and Bolivar, as before stated; four of these were sent under General McPherson to the former place and formed the advance in the pursuit. Two were sent to Bolivar, and gave that much additional force to be spared to operate on the enemy's rear.

When I ascertained that the enemy had succeeded in crossing the Hatchie, I ordered a discontinuance of the pursuit. Before this order reached them, the advance infantry force had reached Ripley, and the cavalry had gone beyond possibly twenty miles. This I regarded, and yet regard, as absolutely necessary to the safety of our army. They could not have possibly caught the enemy before reaching his fortifications at Holly Springs, and where a garrison of several thousand troops was left that were not engaged in the battle of Corinth. Our own troops would have suffered for food, and suffered greatly from fatigue. Finding that the pursuit had followed so far, and that our forces were very much scattered, I immediately ordered an advance from Bolivar to be made, to cover the return of the Corinth forces. They went as far south as Davis' Mills, about seven miles south of Grand Junction, drove a small rebel garrison from there, and entirely destroyed the railroad bridges at that place.

The accompanying reports show fully all the casualties and other results of these battles.

I am, Colonel, very respectfully your obedient servant,

U. S. GRANT, *Major-General commanding.*

The following is the close of General Rosecrans' report of this battle:

Thus by noon ended the battle of the 4th of October.

After waiting for the enemy's return a short time, our skirmishers began to advance, and found that their skirmishers were gone from the field, leaving their dead and wounded. Having ridden over it and satisfied myself of the fact, I rode all over our lines, announcing the result of the fight in person; and notified our victorious troops that after two days of fighting, two almost sleepless nights of preparation, movement, and march, I wished them to replenish their cartridge boxes, haversacks, and stomachs, take an early sleep and start in pursuit by daylight. Returning from this I found the gallant McPherson with a fresh brigade on the public square, and gave him the same notice with orders to take the advance.

The results of the battle briefly stated are: We fought the combined rebel forces of Mississippi, commanded by Van Dorn, Price, Lovell, Villipigue, and Rust in person, numbering, according to their own authorities, thirty-eight thousand men.

We signally defeated them with little more than half their numbers, and they fled leaving their dead and wounded on the field. The enemy's loss in killed was fourteen hundred and twenty-three officers and men; their loss in wounded, taking the general average, amounts to fifty-six hundred and ninety-two.

We took twenty-two hundred and forty-eight prisoners, among whom are one hundred and thirty-seven field officers, captains, and subalterns, representing fifty-three regiments of infantry, sixteen regiments of cavalry, thirteen batteries of artillery, and seven battalions, making sixty-nine regiments, seven battalions, and thirteen batteries besides separate companies.

We took, also, fourteen stands of colors, two pieces of artillery, thirty-three hundred stands of small arms, forty-five hundred rounds of ammunition, and a large lot of accouterments.

The enemy blew up several ammunition wagons between Corinth and Chewalla, and beyond Chewalla many ammunition wagons and carriages were destroyed, and the ground was strewn with tents, officers' mess chests, and small arms.

We pursued them forty miles in force and sixty miles with cavalry. Our loss was only three hundred and fifteen killed, and eighteen hundred and twelve wounded, and two hundred and thirty-two prisoners and missing.

It is said the enemy was so demoralized and alarmed at our advance they set fire to the stores at Tupello, but finding we were not close upon them they extinguished the fire and removed the public stores, except two car loads of bacon which they destroyed. * * * *

W. S. ROSECRANS, *Major-General.*

Another report of General Rosecrans shows that General McPherson with his fresh troops, reached him just before sunset after the battle, and together with the whole command began the pursuit at daylight the next morning.

Rosecrans' force in the battle of Corinth was fifteen thousand seven hundred infantry, and two thousand five hundred cavalry, an aggregate of eighteen thousand two hundred against an enemy of thirty-eight thousand.

General Sherman admits that "beyond doubt the rebel army lost at Corinth fully six thousand men."

The records set forth with sufficient clearness the brilliant character of the battle, the energy of the pursuit, and the satisfaction felt by General Grant at the results. So far as the differences which arose between Generals Grant and Rosecrans about this time, grew out of these movements, they appear to have had their origin chiefly in General Rosecrans' insisting upon pursuing the enemy beyond where General Grant considered it prudent to do so, and persisting in expressing his opinions against those of his commanding officer. But whatever the causes of difference were, General Grant's report, setting forth that an earlier pursuit than the one made was probably impracticable, is a full answer to General Sherman's version of the cause of trouble.

CHAPTER V.

CHICKASAW BAYOU—PLUNGING AN ARMY THROUGH DEEP SWAMPS AGAINST IMPREGNABLE BLUFFS.

THE attack upon Vicksburg from the Yazoo River and Chickasaw Bayou in December, 1862, was under the sole direction of General Sherman.

The movement had been proposed by General Grant on the 4th of December, and the approval of the plan telegraphed by Halleck on the 5th. On the 8th Grant telegraphed that Sherman would be in command of the river expedition. To this Halleck replied:

WAR DEPARTMENT,
WASHINGTON, *December* 9, 1862.

Major-General GRANT, *Oxford, Miss.*

* * * The President may insist upon designating a separate commander, if not, assign such officers as you may deem best. Sherman would be my choice as the chief, under you.

H. W. HALLECK, *General-in-Chief.*

After General Sherman left Memphis and before his expedition failed, the President had acted as General Halleck surmised. The following telegram upon that point will also show from its date, that the subsequent removal of General Sherman had no connection with his failure:

WAR DEPARTMENT,
WASHINGTON, *December* 18, 1862.

Major-General GRANT, *Oxford, Miss.*

* * * * It is the wish of the President that General McClernand's corps shall constitute a part of the river expedition, and that he shall have the immediate command, under your direction.

H. W. HALLECK, *General-in-Chief.*

This campaign was the first after Shiloh, where General Sherman was entrusted with great responsibilities. General

Grant's order assigning him to the command, left both the details of the preparations and the plans of the movement entirely in his hands, as will appear from the first paragraph of that order:

HEADQUARTERS THIRTEENTH ARMY CORPS,
DEPARTMENT OF THE TENNESSEE, OXFORD, MISS., *December* 8, 1862.

Major-Gen. W. T. SHERMAN, *commanding Right Wing Army in the Field, present.*

GENERAL: You will proceed with as little delay as practicable to Memphis, Tennessee, taking with you one division of your present command. On your arrival at Memphis you will assume command of all the troops there, and that portion of General Curtis' forces at present east of the Mississippi River, and organize them into brigades and divisions in your own way.

As soon as possible move with them down the river to the vicinity of Vicksburg, and with the coöperation of the gun-boat fleet under command of Flag-Officer Porter, proceed to the reduction of that place in such manner as circumstances and your own judgment may dictate. * * * *

U. S. GRANT, *Major-General.*

On the same day Grant telegraphed to Halleck: "General Sherman will command the expedition down the Mississippi. He will have a force of about forty thousand men."

On the 22d of December this army rendezvoused at Friar's Point, ready to move up the Yazoo River to the rear of Vicksburg. On the 27th, the four divisions, Steele's, M. L. Smith's, Morgan's, and A. J. Smith's, aggregating over forty-two thousand men, were landed in front of the bluffs overlooking the swamps through which ran Chickasaw Bayou. To flounder through this boggy low land, cross the bayou, and storm the heights beyond, was the task Sherman laid out for his army. It was his first attempt to command more than a division in action, and he had not before directed a battle. Though the rebels had been reënforced in consequence of the failure of Grant's coöperative movement from Holly Springs, they were still far inferior in numbers to Sherman's army. Their position, however, was impregnable. The high bluffs were strengthened from base to summit with rifle-pits and heavier parapets, and to assault seemed madness then to many of the officers, and appears so still when all the facts can be coolly considered. But Sherman decided upon this manner of attack, and forty thousand men were moved through bogs and bayous to assault a position of which he now says in his Memoirs:

"The men of the Sixth Missouri actually scooped out with their hands caves in the bank, which sheltered them against the fire of the enemy, who, right over their heads, held their muskets outside the parapet vertically and fired down."

Extracts from General Sherman's own account show the nature and difficulties of the ground, and the character of the whole attack:

"The place of our disembarkation was, in fact, an island, separated from the high bluff known as Walnut Hills, on which the town of Vicksburg stands, by a broad and shallow bayou—evidently an old channel of the Yazoo. On our right was another wide bayou known as Old River, and on the left still another, much narrower, but too deep to be forded, known as Chickasaw Bayou. All the island was densely wooded, except Johnson's plantation, immediately on the bank of the Yazoo, and a series of old cotton-fields along Chickasaw Bayou. There was a road from Johnson's plantation directly to Vicksburg, but it crossed numerous bayous and deep swamps by bridges, which had been destroyed; and this road debouched on level ground at the foot of the Vicksburg bluff, opposite strong forts well prepared and defended by heavy artillery. On this road I directed General A. J. Smith's division, not so much by way of a direct attack as a diversion and threat.

"Morgan was to move to his left to reach Chickasaw Bayou, and to follow it toward the bluff, about four miles above A. J. Smith. Steele was on Morgan's left across Chickasaw Bayou, and M. L. Smith on Morgan's right. We met light resistance at all points, but skirmished on the 27th up to the main bayou that separated our position from the bluffs of Vicksburg, which were found to be strong by nature and by art, and seemingly well defended. On reconnoitering the front in person, during the 27th and 28th, I became satisfied that General A. J. Smith could not cross the intervening obstacles under the heavy fire of the forts immediately in his front, and that the main bayou was impassable, except at two points—one near the head of Chickasaw Bayou, in front of Morgan, and the other about a mile lower down, in front of M. L. Smith's division.

"During the general reconnoissance of the 28th, General Morgan L. Smith received a severe and dangerous wound in his hip, which completely disabled him and compelled him to go to his steamboat, leaving the command of his division to Brigadier-General D. Stuart; but I drew a part of General A. J.

Smith's division, and that General himself, to the point selected for passing the bayou, and committed that special task to his management.

"General Steele reported that it was physically impossible to reach the bluffs from his position, so I ordered him to leave but a show of force there, and to return to the west side of Chickasaw Bayou in support of General Morgan's left. He had to countermarch and use the steamboats in the Yazoo to get on the firm ground on our side of the Chickasaw.

"On the morning of December 29th all the troops were ready and in position. The first step was to make a lodgment on the foot-hills and bluffs abreast of our position, while diversions were made by the navy toward Haines' Bluff, and by the first division directly toward Vicksburg. I estimated the enemy's forces, then strung from Vicksburg to Haines' Bluff, at fifteen thousand men, commanded by the rebel Generals Martin Luther Smith and Stephen D. Lee. Aiming to reach firm ground beyond this bayou, and to leave as little time for our enemy to reënforce as possible, I determined to make a show of attack along the whole front, but to break across the bayou at the two points named, and gave general orders accordingly. I pointed out to General Morgan the place where he could pass the bayou, and he answered, 'General, in ten minutes after you give the signal I'll be on those hills.' He was to lead his division in person, and was to be supported by Steele's division. The front was very narrow, and immediately opposite, at the base of the hills, about three hundred yards from the bayou, was a rebel battery, supported by an infantry force posted on the spurs of the hill behind. To draw attention from this, the real point of attack, I gave instructions to commence the attack at the flanks.

"I went in person about a mile to the right-rear of Morgan's position, at a place convenient to receive reports from all other parts of the line, and about noon of December 29th gave the orders and signal for the main attack. A heavy artillery fire opened along our whole line, and was replied to by the rebel batteries, and soon the infantry fire opened heavily, especially on A. J. Smith's front and in front of General George W. Morgan. One brigade (DeCourcey's) of Morgan's troops crossed the bayou safely, but took to cover behind the bank, and could not be moved forward. Frank Blair's brigade, of Steele's division, in support, also crossed the bayou, passed over the space of level ground to the foot of the hills; but, being unsupported by Morgan, and meeting a very severe cross-fire of artillery, was staggered, and gradually fell back, leaving about five hundred men behind wounded and prisoners, among them Colonel Thomas Fletcher, afterward Governor of Missouri. Thayer's brigade, of Steele's division, took a wrong direction, and did not cross the bayou at all, nor did General Morgan cross in person. This attack failed, and I have always felt that it was due to the failure of General G. W. Morgan to obey his orders, or to fulfill his promise made in person. Had he used with skill and boldness one of his brigades, in addition to that of Blair's, he could have made a lodgment on the bluff, which would have opened the door for our whole force to follow. Meantime the Sixth Missouri Infantry, at heavy loss, had also crossed the bayou at the narrow passage lower down, but could not ascend the steep bank; right over their heads was a rebel battery, whose fire was in a measure kept down by our sharp-shooters (Thirteenth United States Infantry), posted behind logs, stumps, and trees, on our side of the bayou.

"The men of the Sixth Missouri actually scooped out with their hands caves in the bank, which sheltered them against the fire of the enemy, who, right over their heads, held their muskets outside the parapet vertically and fired down. So critical was the position that we could not recall the men till after dark, and then one at a time. Our loss had been pretty heavy, and we had accomplished nothing, and had inflicted little loss on our enemy. At first I intended to renew the assault, but soon became satisfied that, the enemy's attention having been drawn to the only two practicable points, it would prove too costly, and accordingly resolved to look elsewhere for a point below Haines' Bluff, or Blake's plantation." * * * *

Two succeeding efforts to secure a new position from which to attack failed, and two days afterward, as Pemberton was moving reënforcements into Vicksburg and out to Sherman's front, the expedition was abandoned, with a total loss of about two thousand men in killed and wounded. On returning to the mouth of the Yazoo, Sherman found McClernand there with orders to relieve him.

He thus concludes his account:

"Still my relief, on the heels of a failure, raised the usual cry at the North of 'repulse, failure, and bungling.' There was no bungling on my part, for I never worked harder, or with more intensity of purpose in my life; and General Grant, long after, in his report of the operations of the siege of Vicksburg, gave us all full credit for the skill of the movement, and described the almost impregnable nature of the ground; and although in all my official reports I assumed the whole responsibility, I have ever felt that, had General Morgan promptly and skillfully sustained the lead of Frank Blair's brigade on that day, we should have broken the rebel line, and effected a lodgment on the hills behind Vicksburg. General Frank Blair was outspoken and indignant against Generals Morgan and DeCourcey at the time, and always abused me for assuming the whole blame. But had we succeeded, we might have found ourselves in a worse trap, when General Pemberton was at full liberty to turn his whole force against us."

And so, according to General Sherman himself, bad as the assault at Chickasaw Bayou turned out to be, success might have proved still worse. But had an army of forty-two thousand men gained a position in rear of Vicksburg, it might, with the coöperation of the gun-boats, have held its own against Pemberton and all the forces he then could bring.

No amount of blame distributed among division commanders can conceal the recklessness with which an army was pushed through swamps and bayous against inaccessible bluffs, and the best answers to all Sherman's unjust attacks upon officers who fought with him there, are found in his own report of the action:

HEADQUARTERS RIGHT WING THIRTEENTH ARMY CORPS,
CAMP, MILLIKEN'S BEND, LA., *January* 3, 1863.

Colonel J. H. RAWLINS, *Assistant Adjutant-General to Major-General* GRANT, *Oxford, Miss., at last reliable accounts.*

SIR: * * * * As soon as we reached the point of debarkation DeCourcey's, Stuart's, and Blair's brigades were sent forward in the direction of Vicksburg about three miles, and on the 27th the whole army was disembarked and moved out in four columns: Steele's above the mouth of Chickasaw Bayou; Morgan, with Blair's brigade of Steele's division, below the same bayou; Morgan L. Smith on the main road from Johnson's plantation to Vicksburg, with orders to bear to his left, so as to strike the bayou about a mile south of where Morgan was ordered to cross it; and A. J. Smith's division keeping on the main road. All the heads of columns met the enemy's pickets and drove them toward Vicksburg. During the night of the 27th the ground was reconnoitered as well as possible, and it was found as difficult as it could possibly be from nature and art. Immediately in our front was a bayou, passable only at two points, on a narrow levee, or a sand bar, which was perfectly commanded by the enemy's sharp-shooters that lined the levee, or parapet, on its opposite bank.

Behind this was an irregular strip of bench, or table-land, on which were constructed a series of rifle pits and batteries, and behind that a high, abrupt range of hills, whose scarred sides were marked all the way up with rifle trenches, and the crowns of the principal hills presented heavy batteries.

The county road, leading from Vicksburg to Yazoo City, runs along the foot of these hills, and answered an admirable purpose to the enemy as a covered way, along which he moved his artillery and infantry promptly to meet us at any point at which we attempted to pass this difficult bayou. Nevertheless that bayou, with its levee parapets, backed by the lines of rifle pits, batteries, and frowning hills, had to be passed before we could reach *terra firma*, and meet our enemy on any thing like fair terms.

Steele, in his progress, followed substantially an old levee back from the Yazoo to the foot of the hills north of Thompson's Lake, but found that, in order to reach the hard land, he would have to cross a long corduroy causeway, with a battery enfilading it, others cross-firing it, with a similar line of rifle pits and trenches before decribed. He skirmished with the enemy on the morning of the 28th, whilst the other columns were similarly engaged, but on close and critical examination of the swamp and causeway in front, with the batteries and rifle pits well manned, he came to the conclusion that it was impossible for him to reach the county road without a fearful sacrifice. As soon as he reported this to me officially, and that he could not cross over from his position to the one occupied by our center, I ordered him to retrace his steps and cross back in steamboats to the south-west side of Chickasaw Bayou, and to support General Morgan, which he accomplished during the night of the 28th, arriving in time to support him and take part in the assault of the 29th.

General Morgan's division was evidently on the best of all existing roads from Yazoo River to the firm land. He had attached to his train the pontoons with which to make a bridge, in addition to the ford, or crossing, which I knew was in his front, the same by which the enemy's pickets had retreated. This pontoon bridge was, during the night, placed across a bayou supposed to be the main bayou, but which turned out to be an inferior one, and it was, therefore, useless; but the natural crossing remained, and I ordered him to cross over with his division, and carry the line of works to the summit of the hill by a determined assault. On the 28th a heavy fog, during the early part of the day, enveloped the whole country, but General Morgan advanced DeCourcey's brigade and engaged the enemy. Heavy firing of artillery and infantry were sustained, and his column moved on until he encountered the real bayou. This again checked his progress, and was not passed until the next day.

At the point where Morgan L. Smith's division reached the bayou was a narrow sand spit, with abattis thrown down by the enemy on our side, with the same deep and boggy bayou, with its levee parapet, and system of cross batteries and rifle pits on the other side. To pass it by the flank would have been utter destruction, for the head of column would have been swept away as fast as it presented itself above the steep bank. General M. L. Smith, whilst reconnoitering it early on the morning of the 28th, was, during the heavy fog, shot in the hip by a chance rifle bullet, which disabled him, and lost to me one of my best and most daring leaders, and to the Unites States the services of a practical soldier and enthusiastic patriot. I can not exaggerate the loss to me personally and officially of General Morgan L. Smith at that critical moment. His wound in the hip disabled him, and he was sent to the boat. General D. Stuart succeeded to his place and to the execution of his orders. General Stuart studied the nature of the ground in his front and saw all its difficulties, but made the best possible disposition to pass over his division, the Second, whenever he heard General Morgan engaged.

To his right, General A. J. Smith had placed Burbridge's brigade of his division next to Stuart, with orders to make rafts and cross over a portion of his men; to dispose his artillery so as to fire at the enemy across the bayou, and produce the effect of a diversion. His other brigade, Landrum's, occupied a key position on the main road, with pickets and supports pushed well forward into the tangled abattis, within three-fourths of a mile of the enemy's forts, and in plain view of the city of Vicksburg.

Our boats still lay at our place of debarkation, covered by the gun-boats and by four regiments of infantry, one of each division. Such was the disposition of our forces during the night of the 28th.

The enemy's right was a series of batteries or forts, seven miles above us on the Yazoo, at the first bluff, near Snyder's house, called Drumgould's Bluff; his left, the fortified city of Vicksburg; and his line connecting these was near fourteen miles in extent, and was a natural fortification, strengthened by a year's labor of thousands of negroes, directed by educated and skilled officers.

My plan was by a prompt and concentrated movement to break the center, near Chickasaw Creek, at the head of a bayou of the same name; and once in position to turn to the right (Vicksburg), or left (Drumgould's Bluff), according to information then obtained. I supposed their organized forces to amount to about fifteen thousand, which could be reënforced at the rate of about four thousand a day, provided General Grant did not occupy all the attention of Pemberton's forces at Grenada, or Rosecrans those of Bragg in Tennessee. Not one word could I hear from General Grant, who was supposed to be pushing south, or of General Banks, supposed to be ascending the Mississippi.

Time being every thing to us, I determined to assault the hills in front of Morgan on the morning of the 29th; Morgan's division to carry the position of the hills, Steele's division to support him and hold the county road. I had placed General A. J. Smith in command of his own division (First) and that of M. L. Smith (Second), with orders to cross on the sand spit, undermine the steep bank of the bayou on the further side, and carry at all events the levee parapets and first line of rifle pits to prevent a concentration on Morgan.

It was near twelve o'clock (noon) when Morgan was ready, by which time Blair's and Thayer's brigades of Steele's division were up with him and took part in the assault, and Hovey's brigade was close at hand. All the troops were massed as close as possible, and all our supports were well in hand.

The assault was made and a lodgment effected on the hard table-land near the county road, and the heads of the assaulting columns reached different points of the enemy's works, but then met so withering a fire from the rifle pits and cross-fire of grape and canister from the batteries, that the columns faltered and finally fell back to the point of starting, leaving many dead, wounded, and prisoners in the hands of enemy.

For a more perfect understanding of this short and desperate struggle I refer to the reports of Generals Morgan, Blair, Steele, and others inclosed.

General Morgan's first report to me was that the troops were not discouraged at all, though the losses in Blair's and DeCourcey's brigades were heavy, and he would renew the assault in half an hour; but the assault was not again attempted.

I urged General A. J. Smith to push his attack, though it had to be made across a narrow sand bar, and up a narrow path in the nature of a "breach," as a diversion in favor of Morgan, or real attack, according to its success.

During Morgan's progress he passed over the Sixth Missouri under circumstances that called for all the individual courage for which that admirable regiment is justly famous. Its crossing was covered by the United States regulars deployed as skirmishers up to the near bank of the bayou, covered as well as possible by fallen trees, and firing at any of the enemy's sharpshooters that showed a mark above the levee.

Before this crossing all the ground opposite was completely swept by our artillery, under the immediate supervision of Major Taylor, Chief of Artillery.

The Sixth Missouri crossed over rapidly by companies, and lay under the bank of the bayou, with the enemy's sharp-shooters over their heads within a few feet, so near that these sharp-shooters held out their muskets and fired down vertically upon our men.

The orders were to undermine this bank and make a road up it, but it was impossible; and after the repulse of Morgan's assault I ordered General A. J. Smith to retire this regiment under cover of darkness, which was successfully done. Their loss was heavy, but I leave to the brigade and division commanders to give names and exact figures.

Whilst this was going on Burbridge was skirmishing across the bayou at his front, and Landrum pushed his advance through the close abattis or entanglement of fallen timber close up to Vicksburg.

When the night of the 29th closed in we stood upon our original ground, and had suffered a repulse. The effort was necessary to a successful accomplishment of my orders, and the combinations were the best possible under the circumstances.

I assume all the responsibility and attach fault to no one, and am generally satisfied with the high spirit manifested by all * * * *

The naval squadron, Admiral Porter, now holds command of the Mississippi to Vicksburg and the Yazoo up to Drumgould's Bluff, both of which points must in time be reduced to our possession, but it is for other minds than mine to devise the way.

The officers and men comprising my command are in good spirits, disappointed of course at our want of success, but by no means discouraged. We reëmbarked our whole command in the sight of the enemy's batteries and army unopposed, remaining in full view a whole day, and then deliberately moved to Milliken's Bend.

I attribute our failure to the strength of the enemy's position, both natural and artificial, and not to his superior fighting; but, as we must all in the future have ample opportunities to test this quality, it is foolish to discuss it.

I will transmit with this detailed reports of division and brigade commanders, with statements of killed, wounded, and prisoners, and names as far as can be obtained.

The only real fighting was during the assault by Morgan's and Steele's divisions, and at the time of crossing the Sixth Missouri, during the afternoon of December 29th, by the Second Division.

Picket skirmishing and rifle practice across Chickasaw Bayou was constant for four days. This cost us the lives of several valuable officers and men, and many wounded. I have the honor to be,

Your obedient servant,

W. T. SHERMAN, *Major-General commanding.*

Accompanying this report is a list of casualties, which shows the following losses of each division:

	Killed.	Wounded.	Missing.
A. J. Smith's	1	1	......
M. L. Smith's	26	103	6
George W. Morgan's	62	447	386
F. Steele's	102	431	364
Total	191	982	756

An aggregate of nineteen hundred and twenty-nine, concerning which General Sherman made the following indorsement:

"My belief is that, of the missing, four hundred were taken prisoners after reaching the enemy's trenches, and the remainder will turn up on boats not their own."

From this report of General Sherman's it will be seen that the very divisions to which he now attributes his failure, and upon whose commanders he visits severe censure, were the identical troops and officers he reported at the time as having done his hardest fighting, and accomplished every thing it was possible to perform.

The reports of these division commanders, whom he then commended, in turn relieve the brigade officers he now abuses from the blame he attempts to fix upon them, and show that the conduct of Generals Morgan, DeCourcey, and Thayer, and the fighting of their troops were such as should have commanded high praise, even from General Sherman.

Immediately after this action General George Morgan was assigned to an equal command with General Sherman, namely, that of the First Corps, Army of the Mississippi, Sherman taking the Second Corps, while General McClernand succeeded him in command of the army.

It would be difficult to find material for more severe criticisms of the statements made in the Memoirs, concerning the failure at Chickasaw Bayou, than is contained in this report of Sherman's, written when the facts were vividly present to his mind.

CHAPTER VI.

CHATTANOOGA AND CHICKAMAUGA—INJUSTICE TO ROSE-CRANS, THOMAS, AND THE ARMY OF THE CUMBERLAND.

In a previous chapter it has been seen how coldly, unjustly, and almost contemptuously General Sherman's book treats of Buell and his army at Shiloh—a general and an army that, beyond all room for question, brought salvation to Grant's forces, to which sore disaster had come through a disgraceful surprise, for which Sherman was in person largely responsible.

Following him in his book through his excuses for bloody failure at Chickasaw Bayou, his protest against Grant's plan for capturing Vicksburg from the rear, and his assertion that it might have been taken six months earlier by another route, we find him again misrepresenting and sneering at the Army of the Ohio, under its successive commanders, Rosecrans and Thomas, then operating about Chattanooga under its new title, the Army of the Cumberland.

With the records of the war at his control, and at his very elbow, this is the version of Rosecrans' movement on, and capture of Chattanooga, which General Sherman puts forth:

"While we were thus lying idle in camp on the Big Black, the Army of the Cumberland, under General Rosecrans, was moving against Bragg at Chattanooga; and the Army of the Ohio, General Burnside, was marching toward East Tennessee.

"General Rosecrans was so confident of success that he somewhat scattered his command, seemingly to surround and capture Bragg in Chattanooga; but the latter, reënforced from Virginia, drew out of Chattanooga, concentrated his army at Lafayette, and at Chickamauga fell on Rosecrans, defeated him and drove him into Chattanooga.

"The whole country seemed paralyzed by this unhappy event; and the authorities in Washington were thoroughly stampeded. From the East the Eleventh Corps (Slocum) and the Twelfth Corps (Howard) were sent by rail to Nashville, and forward under command of General Hooker. Orders were also sent to General Grant by Halleck to send what reënforcements he could spare immediately toward Chattanooga.

"Bragg had completely driven Rosecrans' army into Chattanooga. The latter was in actual danger of starvation, and the railroad in his rear seemed inadequate to his supply. The first intimation which I got of this disaster was on the 22d of September, by an order from General Grant to dispatch one of my divisions immediately into Vicksburg to go toward Chattanooga, and I designated the First, General Osterhaus'—Steele, meantime, having been appointed to the command of the Department of Arkansas, and had gone to Little Rock. General Osterhaus marched the same day, and on the 23d I was summoned to Vicksburg in person, where General Grant showed me the alarming dispatches from General Halleck, which had been sent from Memphis by General Hurlbut, and said, on further thought, that he would send me and my whole corps. But, inasmuch as one division of McPherson's corps (John E. Smith's) had already started, he instructed me to leave one of my divisions on the Big Black, and to get the other two ready to follow at once. I designated the Second, then commanded by Brigadier-General Giles A. Smith, and the Fourth, commanded by Brigadier-General Corse."—Page 346, Vol. I.

Before considering General Sherman's story further, a statement of General Rosecrans' operations, which is sustained by the record, may properly be considered:

General Rosecrans, with his magnificent army, had, by his brilliant strategy, driven Bragg without serious battle out of Murfreesboro, out of Tullahoma, out of Wartrace, and finally across the Tennessee, here a deep and wide river, where he took post in the fortified city of Chattanooga.

The ojective point of Rosecrans' next campaign was the latter city. Two plans were open to him. He could cross the river above, in the face of Bragg's army, and assault the place. Had he done this, and at the cost of never so bloody a battle wrested that stronghold from Bragg, the whole nation would have applauded, and the movement been so plain that even General Sherman might have been compelled to write it correctly, notwithstanding his prejudices against the Army of the Cumberland.

The other course open to Rosecrans was the one he adopted, namely, to cross the Tennessee far below the city, and the three intervening mountain ranges, come down in the rear of Chattanooga, and force Bragg to evacuate it.

Long before the single line of railroad could bring him the needed supplies for such a campaign, Halleck, who knew nothing of the ground and its great difficulties, was telegraphing from Washington peremptory orders to move. But, waiting till he had twenty-five days' scant supplies, Rosecrans cut loose from his base and crossed the Tennessee under great disadvantages, one of his largest divisions actually crossing in canoes and upon rafts constructed by the men, many of the soldiers piling their clothes, guns, and cartridge-boxes on two or three rails, and pushing the whole over before them as they swam the half mile of deep water. The three ranges were all difficult in the extreme; but finally the main part of the army came down from Lookout Mountain into McLemore's Cove, in rear of Chattanooga, and Bragg, giving up the city without a blow, being unable to hold it and at the same time confront Rosecrans with any portion of his force, evacuated it and retreated to Lafayette, behind Pigeon Mountains. Here, he was virtually reënforced by Longstreet from Virginia, although the forces of the latter were still only within supporting distance, and not, as General Sherman writes, before he evacuated Chattanooga. And because he was thus reënforced he set out to re-occupy the city he had abandoned, and which he knew to be Rosecrans' objective point. Then occurred the widely misunderstood and misrepresented battle of Chickamauga.

Bragg, strengthened by Longstreet, started to interpose between Rosecrans and the stronghold he had lately evacuated. Rosecrans was also marching to occupy it as the objective point of his campaign. Thus marching, the heads of the two armies met where their respective roads to Chattanooga intersected, about six miles from the city, and facing toward each other and closing together like the blades of a pair of shears, these armies fought two days *for Chattanooga.*

The key positions of the whole movement were the passes in Missionary Ridge, which controlled the roads to Chattanooga, and these lay less than two miles from the field, and directly on the roads both armies were pushing over toward the city.

The history of the fighting is well known. The breaking of the right on the second day has been widely treated as if it were the rout of the Union forces. But Thomas, who remained with the largest part of the army intact, fought through to the close of the battle with his lines unbroken. The last divisions of our line to leave the field were in undisturbed possession of their ground, and withdrew quietly and unmolested. Thomas left the field mainly because the passes which controlled Chattanooga—the objective point of the campaign—were in his rear, and if he did not occupy them that night the chances were that the rebels would do so, and thus make successful their plan of battle, which was to turn the Union left and interpose between Rosecrans and Chattanooga.

The rebels did not follow till noon of the next day, and finding our army in the passes did not attack it. The following day Rosecrans' army marched undisturbed into Chattanooga, and Union troops held it till the close of the war.

Chickamauga, then, was the battle for Chattanooga; and at the end of a campaign which, when impartial history is written, will assuredly rank among the most brilliant for its strategy, the prize for which Rosecrans contended was won. The troops which fought longest and suffered most never looked upon the battle as a defeat, and were fully satisfied with the part they had played. To the Army of the Cumberland it was but the battle for, and the winning of Chattanooga. And this, though Sherman's readers would not dream of it, is how it came to pass that "Bragg had completely driven Rosecrans' army into Chattanooga."

General Rosecrans' movements which secured Chattanooga resembled in many of their main features those by which Sherman captured Atlanta. Rosecrans had successively flanked Bragg out of all positions from Murfreesboro to Chattanooga, and instead of assaulting this he moved to the rear, compelled its evacuation, fought for it in the open field, and occupied it. Sherman, chiefly by flanking Johnston, drove him back upon Atlanta. After many assaults, against the earnest advice of Thomas and others who wished him to go the rear and compel an evacuation, he finally yielded and marched to Lovejoy's and Jonesboro, leaving Slocum to watch for the evacuation of Atlanta, as Crittenden had watched for Rosecrans at Chattanooga.

The movement drew Hood out of Atlanta, and Slocum marched in, as Crittenden had passed into Chattanooga when Rosecrans' army flanked Bragg out of it. Sherman's army, at the moment of occupation, was quite as much scattered below Atlanta, as Rosecrans' had been south of Chattanooga. Suppose some story-teller of the war had then written: "Hood had completely driven Sherman's army into Atlanta!" If it be answered that Sherman marched back to his objective point without a fight, the scales may still settle even, for Sherman did not start to flank till after serious battle, while Rosecrans avoided assaulting a stronghold in the outset.

After these misrepresentations of the movement by which the Army of the Cumberland won this rebel stronghold on the Tennessee, the reader will be better prepared for the misstatements written in regard to the same army when it passed under the command of General Thomas, and took part in the battles of Lookout Mountain and Missionary Ridge. That army had well nigh starved in carrying out its purpose to hold the city it had taken. Thousands of horses and mules had died for want of food. There were brigade headquarters where the officers lived chiefly on parched corn; there were regimental headquarters where the daily food was mush or gruel; there were officers of high rank, who lived for days on sour pork and wormy and moldy bread. But the lofty spirit of these men was unbroken, and no army stood any where during the rebellion whose faith in final victory was stronger than the faith of these soldiers under George H. Thomas; and yet at this late day, and in the light of the immortal charge they, as an army, made up the heights of Missionary Ridge, the General of the armies affirms that General Grant doubted whether they would come out of their trenches for a fight.

But let General Sherman speak for himself as he does on page 361 of his first volume. Before perusing it let the reader bear in mind that the line of supplies of Thomas' army had been fully opened before Sherman arrived, through the coöperation of Generals Howard and Slocum, and without any help from him, and that the suffering for food was entirely at an end and not a present thing, as his words imply; that Chattanooga was no longer besieged, except as a rebel army was in front of it, while the communications to the rear, though not all that could be wished, were still ample to enable General Thomas to hold the place.

Says General Sherman, speaking of his arrival:

"Of course I was heartily welcomed by Generals Grant, Thomas, and all, who realized the extraordinary efforts we had made to come to their relief.

"The next morning we walked out to Fort Wood, a prominent salient of the defenses of the place, and from its parapet we had a magnificent view of the panorama. Lookout Mountain, with its rebel flags and batteries, stood out boldly, and an occasional shot fired toward Wauhatchee or Moccasin Point gave life to the scene. These shots could barely reach Chattanooga, and I was told that one or more shot had struck a hospital inside the lines. All along Missionary Ridge were the tents of the rebel beleaguering force; the lines of trench from Lookout up toward the Chickamauga were plainly visible, and rebel sentinels in a continuous chain were walking their posts in plain view, not one thousand yards off. 'Why,' said I, 'General Grant, you are besieged;' and he said, 'it is too true.' Up to that moment I had no idea that things were so bad. The rebel lines actually extended from the river below the town to the river above, and the Army of the Cumberland was closely held to the town and its immediate defenses. General Grant pointed out to me a house on Missionary Ridge where General Bragg's headquarters were known to be. He also explained the situation of affairs generally; that the mules and horses of Thomas' army were so starved that they could not haul his guns; that forage, corn, and provisions were so scarce that the men in hunger stole the few grains of corn that were given to favorite horses; that the men of Thomas' army had been so demoralized by the battle of Chickamauga that he feared they could not be got out of their trenches to assume the offensive; that Bragg had detached Longstreet with a considerable force up into East Tennessee to defeat and capture Burnside; that Burnside was in danger, etc.; and that he (Grant) was extremely anxious to attack Bragg in position, to defeat him, or at least to force him to recall Longstreet. The Army of the Cumberland had so long been in the trenches that he wanted my troops to hurry up to take the offensive *first;* after which, he had no doubt the Cumberland Army would fight well. Meantime the Eleventh and Twelfth Corps, under General Hooker, had been advanced from Bridgeport along the railroad to Wauhatchee, but could not as yet pass Lookout Mountain. A pontoon bridge had been thrown across the Tennessee River at Brown's Ferry, by which supplies were hauled into Chattanooga from Kelly's and Wauhatchee."

And this from a General whose own army alone, of the three engaged, failed in this very battle of Chattanooga to execute what was expected of it, and what it was ordered to do. It fought splendidly and persistently, but failed to gain a foothold on the main ridge upon Bragg's extreme right. Hooker carried Lookout, Thomas advancing and supporting his left as it swept around the mountain and reached downward toward the city. Thomas' men needed no example from Sherman; had not seen his army, saw none of his fighting, and knew very little of his movements, rose early from their bivouacks the day after Lookout, swung round over the plains and woods which the rebels had occupied, to make sure of their retreat to Missionary Ridge, then faced the ridge for two miles, formed that grand storming party, and, in the face of an army with sixty cannon in position, climbed those rugged heights and drove Bragg into sudden, unexpected, and rapid retreat. It was more than two hours after the battle was thus ended, by these men, who, forsooth, it was feared would not come out of their trenches to fight till Sherman had set them an example, before Sherman himself heard that the victory had been gained. And ten years after he assumes to sneer at the men who formed Thomas' storming army at Missionary Ridge. Let the official record answer him! General Grant, without waiting till Thomas' men could see Sherman fight and take courage, ordered an assault on the ridge. And, on this point, the records afford the means of correcting a common error in regard to this movement. The matter will be briefly presented here, although not mentioned in the Memoirs.

It has been frequently said that, after all, the Army of the Cumberland carried the ridge only by chance, and that no orders were given for going beyond the line of rifle pits at its base, but that the forward movement from that point was caused by a portion of the line starting on without orders, and thus leading the whole toward the summit.

General Grant, however, in his report states the character of the orders he gave General Thomas, and shows that the storming of the ridge was intended from the first:

"His (Hooker's) approach was intended as the signal for storming the ridge in the center with strong columns, but the time necessarily consumed in the construction of the bridge near Chattanooga Creek detained him to a later hour than was expected. * * * * Thomas was accordingly directed to move forward his troops, * * * * with a double line of skirmishers thrown out, followed in easy supporting distance by the whole force, and carry the rifle pits at the foot of Missionary Ridge, and when carried to reform his lines in the rifle pits, with a view of carrying the top of the ridge."

The form in which General Thomas communicated this order to his own troops, is shown by a paragraph from the report of General Baird who commanded his left division:

"I had just completed the establishment of my line, and was upon the left of it, when a staff officer from Major-General Thomas brought me verbal orders to move forward to the edge of the open ground which bordered the foot of Mission Ridge, within striking distance of the rebel rifle pits at its base, so as to be ready at a signal, which would be the firing of six guns from Orchard Knob, to dash forward and take those pits. He added this was preparatory to a general assault on the mountain; that it was doubtless designed by the Major-General commanding that I should take part in this movement; so that I would be following his wishes were I to push on to the summit."

"General Rosecrans was so confident of success that he somewhat scattered his command," say the Memoirs. There was another thing of which General Rosecrans was confident, and which a just or accurate writer should have mentioned when dealing out severe criticism. He had been notified from Washington, early in August, that Burnside would move through East Tennessee with an effective force of twelve thousand men upon his left, and was informed almost daily, before and after the battle of Chickamauga, that he would be on the ground for coöperative movements. The record history of this failure on the part of Burnside, is necessary to any fair review of Rosecrans' campaign against Chattanooga, and enough to show its real bearing will now be presented.

The dispatches which follow are from General Halleck at Washington, to Burnside on the march and in East Tennessee:

"*August 5th.*—You will immediately move with a column of twelve thousand men by the most practicable route on East Tennessee, making Knoxville or its vicinity your objective point. * * * * You will report by telegraph all the movements of your troops. As soon as you reach East Tennessee you will endeavor to connect with the forces of General Rosecrans, who has peremptory orders to move forward. The Secretary of War repeats his orders, that you move your headquarters from Cincinnati to the field, and take command of the troops in person."

"*September 5th.*—Nothing from you since August 31st. Keep General Rosecrans advised of your movements, and arrange with him for coöperation."

"*September 11th.*—Connect with General Rosecrans at least with your cavalry. * * * * General Rosecrans will occupy Dalton or some point upon the railroad, to close all access from Atlanta, also the mountain passes on the west. This being done it will be determined whether the moveable forces shall move into Georgia and Alabama, or into the Valley of Virginia and North Carolina."

"*September 13th.*—It is important that all the available forces of your command be pushed forward into East Tennessee. All your scattered forces should be centered there. As long as we hold Tennessee, Kentucky is perfectly safe. Move down as rapidly as possible toward Chattanooga to connect with Rosecrans. Bragg may hold the passes in the mountain to cover Atlanta, and move his main army through Northern Alabama to reach the Tennessee River, and turn Rosecrans' right and cut off his supplies. In that case he will turn Chattanooga over to you, and move to intercept Bragg."

"*September 11th.*—There are reasons why you should reënforce General Rosecrans with all possible dispatch. It is believed that the enemy will concentrate to give him battle. You must be there to help him."

"*September 15th.*—From information received here to-day it is very probable that three divisions of Lee's army have been sent to reënforce Bragg. It is important that all the troops in your department be brought to the front with all possible dispatch, so as to help General Rosecrans."

September 18th.— * * * * A part, at least, of Longstreet's corps is going to Atlanta. It is believed that Bragg, Johnston, and Hardee, with the exchanged prisoners from Vicksburg and Port Hudson are concentrating against Rosecrans. You must give him all the aid in your power."

"*September 9th.*

"*Major-General* BURNSIDE, *Knoxville.*

"General Rosecrans is on the Chickamauga River, twenty miles south of Chattanooga. He is expecting a battle, and wants you to sustain his left. Every possible effort must be made to assist him."

"*September 19th.*—General Meade is very confident that another part of Ewell's corps has gone to East Tennessee. The forces said to be collecting at Jonesboro are probably those that were at Wytheville, Newbern, etc., under Sam. Jones and Jackson."

"*September 20th.*—General Rosecrans had a severe battle yesterday, and expects another to-day. It is of vital importance that you move to his left flank."

"*September 21st.*—General Rosecrans telegraphed, at 9 o'clock this morning, that, if your troops do not join him immediately, they will be obliged to move down the north side of the Tennessee River. As the enemy has driven General Rosecrans back to near Chattanooga, Bragg may throw a force off into East Tennessee between you and General Rosecrans. The extent of the defeat and loss is not known here.

"General Rosecrans will require all the assistance you can give him to hold Chattanooga."

"*September 22d.*—Yours of yesterday is received. I must again urge you to move immediately to Rosecrans' relief. I fear your delay has already prompted Bragg to prevent your communication. Do not allow your troops to be caught by the enemy south of the Tennessee River. To all appearances your only safety is to move down on the north side. Sam. Jones is not likely to move from Danville unless reënforced. If the enemy should cross the Tennessee above Chattanooga you will be separated from Rosecrans, who may not be able to hold out on the south side."

"WASHINGTON, *September 27th,*
HEADQUARTERS OF THE ARMY.

"Your orders before leaving Kentucky, and frequently repeated telegrams after, were to connect your left on General Rosecrans' right, so that, if the enemy concentrated on one, the other would be able to assist. General Rosecrans was attacked on Chickamauga Creek and driven back to Chattanooga, which he holds, waiting for your assistance. Telegram after telegram has been sent to you to go to his assistance with all available force, you being the judge of what troops it was necessary, under the circumstances, to leave in East Tennessee. The route by which you were to reach General Rosecrans was also left to your discretion. When he was forced to fall back on Chattanooga you were advised, not ordered, to move on the north side of the Tennessee River, lest you might be cut up by the enemy on the south side. The danger of the latter movement being pointed out to you, you were left to decide for yourself. The substance of all telegrams from the President and from me was: you *must* go to General Rosecrans' assistance with all your available forces, by such route as, under the advice given you from us, and such information as you can get, you might deem most practicable. The orders are very plain, and you can not mistake their purport. It only remains for you to execute them. General Rosecrans is holding Chattanooga, and awaiting reënforcements from you. East Tennessee must be held at all hazards, if possible.

"The President has just signed his telegram, which is added, in which I fully concur."

"*October 1st.*—Yours of yesterday is received, the purport of all your instructions have been that you should hold some point near the upper end of the valley, and with all the remainder of your available force, march to the assistance of General Rosecrans. The route of march and all details were left to your own judgment. Since the battle of Chickamauga and the retreat of our forces to Chattanooga, you have been repeatedly informed that it would be dangerous to attempt to form a connection on the south side of the Tennessee River, and consequently that you ought to march on the northern side. General Rosecrans has now telegraphed to you that it is not necessary to join him at Chattanooga, but only to move down to such a position that you can come to his assistance if he should require it. You are in direct communication with him, and can learn his condition, and needs, sooner than I can.

"Distant expeditions into Georgia are not now contemplated. The object is to hold East Tennessee by forcing the enemy south of the mountains and barring the passes against his return."

"*October 3d.*—General Rosecrans reports that enemy's cavalry have crossed the river below Kingston, for a raid upon his connections. I can only repeat what I have so often urged, the importance of your communicating with General Rosecrans' army on the north side of the river, so far as to command the crossing."

"*October 5th.*—I can only repeat former instructions, to leave sufficient force in the upper end of the valley to hold Jones in check, and with the remainder to march down on the north side of the Tennessee River, guarding the fords, and connecting with General Rosecrans. I can not make them plainer."

"*October 14th.*—I have received no dispatch from you since the 7th until this morning, and have no information of the condition of affairs and the position of your troops. When you were urged to move down the river to General Rosecrans' assistance, that operation was deemed safe and of great importance. The condition of affairs may now be different. You certainly should hold Kingston, and as far below as may seem prudent.

"Hood will probably send a part of his army to the south-west. Whether to Bragg or by Abingdon is uncertain. I think your available force at Kingston and above should be held in readiness to move up the valley, should the enemy appear in force in south-west Virginia. A copy of this is sent to General Grant."

"*October* 18*th*.—General Rosecrans still calls for your coöperation with him at Chattanooga, and again suggests that Kingston should be made your main point of defense. In this I agree with him. If he can not hold Chattanooga, you can not hold East Tennessee, as that place threatens the gateway from Georgia. Why is it that you make no report of your position and movements? We are left entirely in the dark in regard to your army."

"*October* 24*th*.—It now appears pretty certain that Ewell's corps has gone to Tennessee, and its probable object is Abingdon. His force is estimated at from twenty to twenty-five thousand. It is reported that he left Lee's army on Monday last, but did not pass through Richmond. It is therefore most probable that he passed through Lynchburg taking the road to Abingdon."

The following telegrams were sent by Mr. Lincoln to General Burnside:

WASHINGTON, D. C., *September* 21*st.*, 2 A. M.

To General BURNSIDE, *Knoxville:*

Go to Rosecrans with your full force without a moment's delay.

A. LINCOLN.

September 21*st.*—If you are to do any good to Rosecrans, it will not do to waste time with Jonesboro. It is already too late to do the most good that might have been done, but I hope it will still do some good. Please do not wait a moment.
A. LINCOLN.

September 27.

To BURNSIDE, *at Knoxville.*

Your dispatch just received. My orders to you meant simply that you should save Rosecrans from being crushed out, believing if he lost his position you could not hold East Tennessee in any event, and that if he held his position East Tennessee was substantially safe in any event.

This dispatch is in no sense an order. General Halleck will answer you fully.

September 27.

To General BURNSIDE, *Knoxville.*

It was suggested to you, not ordered, that you move to Rosecrans on the north side of the river, because it was believed that the enemy would not permit you to join him if you should move on the south side. Hold your present position, send Rosecrans what you can spare in the quickest and safest way; in the meantime hold the remainder as nearly in readiness to go to him as you can consistently with the duty it is to perform while it remains.

East Tennessee can be no more than temporarily lost so long as Chattanooga is firmly held. A. LINCOLN.

It would be unjust to General Burnside to present these dispatches from the record without his excuses for never aiding Rosecrans. September 6th he telegraphed Halleck from Knoxville:

"We are making some movements to aid Rosecrans. A bearer of dispatches leaves here this evening or to-morrow with papers."

September 17th he telegraphed concerning a force which he had at Athens communicating with Rosecrans.

On the 19th:

"Am now sending on men that can be spared to aid Rosecrans. I shall go on to-day to Jonesboro. As soon as I learn the result of our movement to the east will go down by railroad and direct the movement of the reënforcements for Rosecrans. I have directed every available man in Kentucky to be sent down."

On the 20th, from Knoxville:

"Dispatch of 18th received. You may be sure that I will do all I can for Rosecrans. Arrived here last night, and am hurrying troops in his direction. I go up the road to-night for a day."

September 21st he telegraphed General Halleck from Morristown:

"Before I knew of the necessity of sending immediate assistance to Rosecrans I had sent a considerable portion of my force to capture or drive out a large force of the enemy under General Sam. Jones, stationed on the road from Bristol to Jonesboro, * * * * when the urgent dispatches from Rosecrans and yourself caused me to send back Brigadier-General Whick's division and Colonel Woolford's brigade of cavalry, with orders to move as rapidly as possible until they joined Rosecran's left flank. * * * When you remember the size of our forces, and amount of work we had to do, and the length of line occupied, you will not be surprised that I have not helped General Rosecrans, more particularly as I was so far impressed with the truth of the statement that Bragg was in full retreat. It has not seemed possible for me to successfully withdraw my forces from the presence of Jones, if he should be beaten back or captured. Yet, upon the receipt of your dispatch, if it were possible to get our force from there down to General Rosecrans within three or four days I should make the attempt, and shall, at the risk of being too late, order every available man in that direction. I am sure that I am disposed to give him every possible assistance. I sincerely hope that he will be able at least to check the enemy for seven or eight days, within which time I shall be able to make considerable diversion in his favor. I hope that my action will meet with the approval of the Department."

Thus it was that Burnside failed Rosecrans.

These dispatches throw a new light upon the difficulties with which General Rosecrans contended; and as this record was open to General Sherman, it would have been just to make it prominent in connection with his severe strictures. But there is another part of the record, with which even his memory must have been charged, that, had he written with fairness, would have been produced. Though no reader of the Memoirs would suspect it, General Sherman himself, when ordered from Vicksburg to Rosecrans' relief, was more than a month late with his troops. In fact, according to the notification sent Rosecrans by Halleck of the time named at Memphis for Sherman's arrival at Chattanooga, he was seven weeks behind, his command having reached only Memphis from Vicksburg at that date. At this point General Sherman in person was delayed by severe family affliction, but this did not retard the forward movement of his troops. While his book does not indicate that he was behind time, much stress is laid upon the statement that he was ordered to repair the railroad as he advanced, and no prominence is given to the fact that a most rapid advance, as well as a repair of the railroads, was repeatedly insisted upon. But it was not until General Grant himself had reached Chattanooga, and sent back word to Sherman to "drop all work on the Memphis and Charleston railroad, cross the Tennessee, and hurry eastward with all possible dispatch till you meet further orders from me," that any signs of haste were developed in his movements. General Grant had taken command, and relieved Rosecrans, and from that time forward General Sherman used almost superhuman efforts to reach Chattanooga.

The dispatches which set forth this most unfortunate delay are as follows:

HEADQUARTERS OF THE ARMY, }
WASHINGTON, D. C., *September* 13, 1863. }

Major-General GRANT or } *Vicksburg.*
Major-General SHERMAN, }

It is quite possible that Bragg and Johnston will move through Northern Alabama to the Tennessee River to turn General Rosecrans' right and cut off his communication. All of General Grant's available forces should be sent to Memphis, thence to Corinth and Tuscumbia, to coöperate with Rosecrans, should the rebels attempt that movement.

H. W. HALLECK, *General-in-Chief.*

WAR DEPARTMENT, *September* 14, 1863.
Major-General HURLBUT, *Memphis.*

There are good reasons why troops should be sent to assist General Rosecrans' right wing with all possible dispatch. Communicate with Sherman to assist you, and hurry forward reënforcements as previously directed.

H. W. HALLECK, *General-in-Chief.*

WAR DEPARTMENT, *September* 15, 1863.
Major-General HURLBUT, *Memphis.*

All troops that can possibly be spared in Western Tennessee and on the Mississippi River should be sent without delay to assist General Rosecrans on the Tennessee River. Urge General Sherman to act with all possible promptness. If you have boats send them down to bring up his troops. Information just received indicates that a part of Lee's army has been sent to reënforce Bragg.

H. W. HALLECK, *General-in-Chief.*

WAR DEPARTMENT, *September* 19, 1863.
Major-General ROSECRANS, *Chattanooga.*

* * * On the 15th Hurlbut says he is moving forward toward Decatur. I hear nothing of Sherman's troops ordered from Vicksburg. *
* * *

H. W. HALLECK, *General-in-Chief.*

WAR DEPARTMENT, *September* 19, 1863.
Major-General HURLBUT, *Memphis.*

Give me definite information of the number of troops sent toward Decatur, and where they are. Also what other troops are to follow, and when. Has nothing been heard from the troops ordered from Vicksburg? No effort must be spared to support Rosecrans' right and guard the crossings of the Tennessee River.

H. W. HALLECK, *General-in-Chief.*

Major-General HALLECK.

CAIRO, ILL., *September* 21, 12 M., 1863.

GENERAL-IN-CHIEF: I received your telegram of the 16th on the 18th, and forwarded it immediately to Sherman. I have sent twelve boats, and more will be sent to bring up his corps. The water is so low in the Ohio and Tennessee rivers that I think they must march from Corinth. I have ordered one million rations, and plenty of spare wagons to Corinth ready as they come up. * * * * I hold the cavalry of my corps to cover Sherman's movements. * * * * I have an abundance of rolling stock to Corinth, and from thence to Chattanooga should not take more than eight days of hard marching; * * * * with the best possible speed it will not be possible for Sherman to get into communication with General Rosecrans in less than fourteen days from this date at the best, and probably twenty days. * * * * S. E. HURLBUT, *Major-General*.

WAR DEPARTMENT, *September* 28, 1863.
Major-General ROSECRANS, *Chattanooga.*

Grant's forces were ordered to move by Memphis, Corinth, and Tuscumbia to Decatur, and thence as might be found necessary to coöperate with you. * * * * The order was received on the 18th, and steamers sent to Vicksburg to bring up the troops. They calculated to be able to communicate with you in fourteen days from that time. Since then nothing has been heard of them, there being no telegraph line. The troops from here will probably reach you first. H. W. HALLECK, *General-in-Chief*.

WAR DEPARTMENT, *September* 29, 1863.
Major-General GRANT, *Vicksburg.*

The enemy seems to have concentrated upon General Rosecrans all his available forces from every direction. To meet him it is necessary that all the forces that can be spared in your department be sent to General Rosecrans' assistance. He wishes them sent by Tuscumbia, Decatur, and Athens. As this requires the opening and running of the Memphis and Charleston Railroad east of Corinth, an able commander like Sherman or McPherson should be selected. H. W. HALLECK, *Major-General*.

On the 29th of September Hooker reported the head of his column passing from Cincinnati to Louisville, and on the 2d of October he telegraphed Mr. Stanton from Nashville: "The last of the infantry of the Eleventh Corps reached their destination yesterday. The Twelfth are now passing through this city."

WASHINGTON, *September* 30, 1863.
Major-General HURLBUT, *Memphis.*

* * * * All available forces must be pushed on toward General Rose-

crans as fast as possible. Your attention must be directed particularly to the repairing of the railroad and the transportation of supplies toward Decatur.

H. W. HALLECK, *General-in-Chief.*

October 2d, Hurlbut telegraphed Halleck:

"A supply train of four hundred wagons is ready at Corinth, and thirty days' rations for twenty thousand men."

WAR DEPARTMENT, *October* 4, 1863.

Major-General HURLBUT, *Memphis.*

As fast as troops arrive they should be pushed forward, first to Corinth and then to Tuscumbia, repairing the Memphis and Charleston Railroad. * * * * From there you will move by Florence on Athens or Decatur, on the north side of the river, or directly to Decatur, repairing the railroad according as it may be found most practicable or expeditious. Time is all important. The railroad must be kept up and guarded in order to secure the supplies of your army. * * * * Should General Sherman be assigned by General Grant to the command, you will furnish him with this and all other orders. H. W. HALLECK, *Major-General.*

On the 10th of October Sherman, then near Corinth, reported the situation to Halleck, and asked: "whether I shall give preference to securing this railroad or reaching the neighborhood of Athens with expedition. The latter I can surely accomplish, the former is problematical."

The troops from the Army of the Potomac having communicated with General Rosecrans by way of Bridgeport, General Sherman was instructed on the 14th, by Halleck in reply, to take care of his railroad.

General Grant, during all this time, had been absent in New Orleans. He reached Memphis on his return October 5th, proceeded to Cairo, and thence to Louisville to receive orders, where he was directed to take command at Chattanooga, relieving Rosecrans by Thomas. He started at once for the front, and shortly after his arrival, ordered Sherman to drop every thing on the railroad, and come on with dispatch.

He thus reported his action to Halleck:

CHATTANOOGA, *October* 26, 2 P. M.

Major-General HALLECK.

GENERAL-IN-CHIEF: I have sent orders to General Sherman to move east toward Stevenson, leaving every thing unguarded, except by way of the Army of the Cumberland east of Bear Creek. The possibility of the enemy breaking through our lines east of this, and the present inability to follow him from here if he should, is the cause of this order. Sherman's forces are the only troops I could throw in to head such a move.

U. S. GRANT, *Major-General.*

From these most urgent dispatches it is evident that a prompt movement of Sherman's relieving column, as well as the repair of the railroad, was expected by the authorities at Washington.

The railroad was in fair condition from the start as far as Corinth, as General Sherman says, and one of his divisions had reached that point on the 2d of October, as he also relates. On the 27th of that month he was at Bear Creek, only thirty miles east of Corinth, where he was "still busy in pushing forward the repairs to the railroad bridge," and "patching up the many breaks between it and Tuscumbia," when he received the dispatch from General Grant at Chattanooga, by way of Huntsville, to drop railroad work and hurry to Chattanooga with all possible speed.

All this time Rosecrans' army had been suffering for supplies—a suffering which Sherman, by prompt movement, might in great degree have prevented. But instead, before he could move his small command from Corinth, two corps had been sent from the Army of the Potomac, and, as Halleck surmised, had reached and relieved Rosecrans first; in fact had done so before Sherman began to exhibit any special activity in his advance. Thus Sherman failed Rosecrans. How much that was unfortunate in the situation, which he now treats as if it were altogether the fault of Rosecrans, might have been avoided had he then moved with due haste to his assistance!

Returning to Rosecrans' movement, and following him for a time, it will be seen that, with twenty-five days' supplies and ammunition for two great battles he had crossed the Tennessee, passed over three difficult mountain ranges, and coming down into the valley south of Chattanooga, compelled Bragg to evacuate the place. Crittenden's corps was left to observe the movements of Bragg, and pass round the point of Lookout into the city in case the enemy left it.

This, however, was in no sense a military occupation of the place, and Crittenden marched through to join Rosecrans below, where he was concentrating his flanking force to interpose it between the enemy and Chattanooga, and so occupy this city, which was the objective point of his campaign. The fact of one corps of his army having passed through Chattanooga, led to the general belief at the time that Rosecrans' army had taken the place, marched out to attack Bragg at Chickamauga, been defeated, and driven back into the city. This view was entertained at the time in Washington, although the Army of the Cumberland, with the exception of Crittenden's forces, never saw Chattanooga till two days after the battle of Chickamauga.

Upon receiving the news that Crittenden's corps had entered Chattanooga, General Halleck telegraphed:

WASHINGTON, *September* 11, 1863.
Major-General ROSECRANS, *Chattanooga*.

After holding the mountain passes in the west, and Dalton or some other point on the railroad to prevent the return of Bragg's army, it will be decided whether your army shall move further south into Georgia and Alabama. * * * * H. W. HALLECK, *General-in-Chief*.

This exploded view of the real situation General Sherman now revives.

In his next statement that Bragg reënforced from Virginia, drew out of Chattanooga, fell on Rosecrans at that place, defeated him and drove him into the city, the records are once more against him.

Bragg evacuated Chattanooga September 7th, and retreated to Lafayette. The reënforcements from Virginia were so near that point on the 15th it was resolved to march back toward Chattanooga and attack Rosecrans wherever found. A part of Longstreet's Virginia troops under Hood arrived at Dalton on the 18th, and participated in the first day's fight at Chickamauga, but Longstreet himself, with the rest of his command, did not arrive till midnight after the first day's battle. A brief extract from his official report is pertinent:

"HEADQUARTERS NEAR CHATTANOOGA, }
"October, 1863. }

"Our train reached Catoosa platform, near Ringgold, about two o'clock in the afternoon of the 19th of September. As soon as our horses came up, about four o'clock, I started with Colonel Sorrel and Colonel Manning of my staff to find the headquarters of the Commanding General. We missed our way and did not report until near eleven o'clock at night. * * * * As soon as the day of the 20th had dawned, I rode to the front to find my troops. The line was arranged from right to left as follows: Stewart's, Johnson's, Hinman's, and Preston's divisions, Hood's division (of which only three brigades were up), was in rear of Jackson, Kenshaw's and Humphries' brigades. McLaws' division was ordered forward from Ringgold the night before, but did not get up. General McLaws had not arrived from Richmond."

The impression sought to be created that Rosecrans' army was driven off the field is erroneous. Soon after four o'clock of the second day, General Thomas having received notice from General Rosecrans that rations and ammunition would be sent to meet him at Rossville, determined to hold the field until night and then withdraw and take possession of the passes there. At half after five he began the movement, and the divisions which commenced to withdraw at that time were attacked at the moment, but retired without confusion or serious losses. The last of the line maintained its position until after nightfall, and retired after the fighting for the day had ended.

Of the close of the battle and its results General Rosecrans in his official report, says:

"At nightfall the enemy had been repulsed along the whole line, and sunk into quietude, without attempting to renew the combat. General Thomas considering the excessive labors of the troops, the scarcity of ammunition, food, and water, and having orders from the General commanding to use his discretion, determined to retire on Rossville, where they arrived in good order, took post before morning, receiving supplies from Chattanooga, and offering the enemy battle during all the next day, and repulsing his reconnoissance. On the night of the 21st we withdrew from Rossville, took firm possession of the objective point of our campaign—Chattanooga—and prepared to hold it."

Coming down to the time when Rosecrans had been relieved, and General Thomas was in command in Chattanooga, General Sherman, in writing of his own arrival there on November 14th, and a conversation with General Grant the next day, represents the latter as informing him that forage and provisions were then extremely scarce, and that he feared Thomas' troops could not be drawn out of the trenches for a fight.

That General Grant could not have made such a statement about supplies is evident from the following dispatches sent more than two weeks before Sherman's arrival:

HEADQUARTERS MILITARY DIVISION OF THE MISSISSIPPI, CHATTANOOGA, *October* 26, 1863.

Major-General HALLECK, *Washington.*

* * * * General Thomas had also set on foot, before my arrival, a plan for getting possession of the river from a point below Lookout Mountain to Bridgeport. If successful, and I think it will be, the question of supplies will be fully settled. * * * *

U. S. GRANT, *Major-General.*

CHATTANOOGA, *October* 28, 1863.

Major-General HALLECK, *Washington.*

General Thomas' plan for securing the river and Southside road hence to Bridgeport has proved eminently successful. The question of supplies may now be regarded as settled. If the rebels give us one week more time I think all danger of losing territory now held by us will have passed away, and preparations may commence for offensive operations.

U. S. GRANT, *Major-General.*

That General Grant had no doubt of the capacity of General Thomas' troops to fight, is proved by the following telegram dated a week before Sherman arrived in person, and a fortnight before his troops came up:

CHATTANOOGA, *November* 7, 1863, 1:30 P. M.

To General HALLECK, *Washington.*

* * * * I have ordered Thomas to attack the enemy at the north end of Missionary Ridge, and when that is carried, to threaten or attack the enemy's line of communication between Cleveland and Dalton. This move will be made on Monday morning. I expect Sherman will reach Huntsville to-day. I have repeated orders to him to hurry forward with the Fifteenth Army Corps. U. S. GRANT, *Major-General.*

It will be noted that the point of attack thus assigned to General Thomas, before the arrival of Sherman, was that afterward committed to Sherman's troops, and which in spite of splendid fighting they failed to carry. Thus General Grant not only believed Thomas' men fully competent to do what was afterward assigned to Sherman, but felt so certain of their success that he ordered the movement before Sherman was even within supporting distance.

General Grant subsequently explained to Halleck why the attack ordered was not made:

CHATTANOOGA, *November 21, 1863.*
To General HALLECK, *Washington.*

I ordered an attack here two weeks ago, but it was impossible to move artillery. Now Thomas' chief of artillery says he has to borrow teams from Sherman to move a part of his artillery to where it is to be used. Sherman has used almost superhuman efforts to get up even at this time, and his force is really the only one that I can move. Thomas can take about one gun to each battery, and can go as far with his infantry as his men can carry rations to keep them and bring them back. I have never felt such restlessness before as I have at the fixed and immovable condition of the Army of the Cumberland. The Quartermaster-General states that the loss of animals here will exceed ten thousand. Those left are scarcely able to carry themselves. U. S. GRANT, *Major-General.*

And in his formal report of these operations he thus refers to the same matter:

"After a thorough reconnoitering of the ground however, it was deemed utterly impracticable to make the movement until Sherman could get up, because of the inadequacy of our force and the condition of the animals then at Chattanooga; and I was forced to leave Burnside for the present to contend against superior forces of the enemy, until the arrival of Sherman with his men and means of transportation."

Sherman's troops were delayed by the heavy roads and broken bridges, so that the orders for a general attack, first issued for the 21st, were suspended, also the subsequent orders for an attack on the 23d, as appears from the following letter to General Thomas:

> HEADQUARTERS MILITARY DIVISION OF THE MISSISSIPPI,
> CHATTANOOGA, *November* 22, 1863.
>
> GENERAL: The bridge at Brown's Ferry being down to-day, and the excessively bad roads since the last rain, will render it impossible for Sherman to get up either of his two remaining divisions in time for an attack to-morrow morning. With one of them up, and which would have been there now but for the accident to the bridge, I would still make the attack in the morning, regarding a day gained as of superior advantage to a single division of troops. You can make your arrangements for this delay.
>
> U. S. GRANT, *Major-General.*

Upon receiving this, General Thomas so far from considering the presence of Sherman's troops necessary to opening the battle, went to Grant, and urged that the attack on Lookout Mountain should begin at once. General Thomas gives this account of the matter in his official report:

> "Feeling as I did the necessity of avoiding delay, for fear the enemy should become advised of our plans, immediately upon the receipt of the above letter I went to General Grant, and advised against any further postponement of our movement, and suggested that, if needed, the Eleventh Corps, then between the two bridges, could be sent to General Sherman to take the place of the troops that could not join him, whilst these last, together with the troops already in Lookout Valley, would form a column to attack the enemy on Lookout Mountain, or at least divert his attention from Sherman's crossing above. This met the approbation of the Commanding General, and on it was based my order of the 23d to General Hooker, to demonstrate on Lookout, and if practicable to carry the position."

General Grant himself not only agreed to this attack on Lookout before Sherman came up, but on the next day, Sherman being still behind, ordered an attack by Thomas on the left in front of Missionary Ridge. This was made the day before Sherman got into position, and General Grant telegraphed the following report of it:

> CHATTANOOGA, *November* 23, 1863.
> To General HALLECK, *Washington.*
>
> General Thomas' troops attacked the enemy's left at 2 P. M. to-day, carried

the first line of rifle pits running over the knoll twelve hundred yards in front, taking about two hundred prisoners, besides killed and wounded. Our loss small. The troops moved under fire with all the precision of veterans on parade.

Thomas' troops will entrench themselves and hold their position until daylight, when Sherman will join in the attack from the mouth of Chickamauga, and a decisive battle will be fought   U. S. GRANT, *Major-General.*

General Grant in his formal report of the battle of Chattanooga, has this to say upon the point under consideration:

"Thomas having done on the 23d, with his troops in Chattanooga, what was intended for the 24th, bettered and strengthened his advanced positions during the day, and pushed the Eleventh Corps forward along the south bank of the Tennessee River, across Citico Creek, one brigade of which, with Howard in person, reached Sherman just as he had completed the crossing of the river."

General Sherman must have thought all this rather lively work for troops that could not be induced to leave their trenches till they had been persuaded by the inspiring spectacle of his men making a breakfast of the enemy.

The next day (24th) Hooker, acting under the orders of General Thomas, attacked and carried Lookout; Sherman attacked, but failed to carry the point he was ordered to occupy on the north end of Missionary Ridge. The day following this Sherman still struggled unsuccessfully to carry his objective point. Thomas' army, that up to this time had not even seen Sherman's troops, stormed Missionary Ridge, and "it was not till night closed in," as Sherman writes in his official report, "that I knew that the troops in Chattanooga had swept across Missionary Ridge and broken the enemy's center. Of course the victory was won, and pursuit was the next step."

The records which this chapter contains were accessible to General Sherman when he penned the statements which they so effectually refute.

CHAPTER VII.

THE MERIDIAN CAMPAIGN—UNJUST ARRAIGNMENT OF GENERAL W. SOOY SMITH.

GENERAL SHERMAN relates that in the Winter following the battle of Chattanooga, he conceived the idea of a movement eastward from the line of the Mississippi to penetrate the interior, and so break up railroads, and paralyze the rebel forces in that section, as to release a large body of troops for the coming campaign from Chattanooga.

Marching from Vicksburg February 3d, 1864, his columns reached Meridian on the 14th, remained there till the 20th, causing much destruction of roads, rolling-stock, stores, and manufacturing establishments of value to the enemy, and arrived at Canton, near Vicksburg, on his return, February 26th:

Much more had been expected at the North from the preparations made for the movement, and the statements circulated as to its object. It was the general belief that the expedition was to penetrate as far east as Selma, one of the interior points of greatest value to the enemy, and also turn upon Mobile. This impression was current at General Grant's headquarters and at Washington, and General Grant himself had written to Halleck, under date of January 15th, 1864, in the same letter which unfolded his plan for the general Spring campaign as follows:

"I shall direct Sherman, therefore, to move out to Meridian with his spare force—the cavalry going from Corinth, and destroy the railroads east and south of there so effectually that the enemy will not attempt to rebuild them during the rebellion. He will then return, unless the opportunity of going into Mobile with the force he has, appears perfectly plain."

And writing on the same subject to Thomas at Chattanooga, on the 19th of January, he said:

"He (Sherman) will proceed eastward as far as Meridian at least, and will thoroughly destroy the roads east and south from there, and, if possible, will throw troops as far east as Selma; or, if he finds Mobile so far unguarded as to make his force sufficient for the enterprise, will go there. To coöperate with this movement you want to keep up appearances of preparation of an advance from Chattanooga. It may be necessary even to move a column as far as Lafayette."

This, it will be observed, was written by the General who ordered the Meridian expedition to an officer whom he desired to coöperate with it.

So, while General Sherman insists that he had no intention of going through to Mobile, and that he wanted Banks to keep up a show of attack in that direction, it is evident that Grant had such a move in mind for him when the orders for the expedition were given.

The general verdict of failure which met Sherman on his return, called for prompt excuse, and the best at hand was found in the fact that the cavalry force from Memphis, under General Sooy Smith, had not reached Meridian as was intended.

The Memoirs give this version of General Smith's operations:

"At Memphis I found Brigadier-General W. Sooy Smith with a force of about twenty-five hundred cavalry, which he had, by General Grant's orders, brought across from Middle Tennessee, to assist in our general purpose as well as to punish the rebel General Forrest, who had been most active in harassing our garrisons in West Tennessee and Mississippi. * * * * * * A chief part of the enterprise was to destroy the rebel cavalry commanded by General Forrest, who were a constant threat to our railway communications in Middle Tennessee, and I committed this task to Brigadier-General W. Sooy Smith. General Hurlbut had in his command about seven thousand five hundred cavalry, scattered from Columbus, Kentucky, to Corinth, Mississippi, and we proposed to make up an aggregate cavalry force of about seven thousand 'effective' out of these and the twenty-five hundred which General Smith had brought with him from Middle Tennessee. With this force General Smith was ordered to move from Memphis straight for Meridian, Mississippi, and to start by February 1st. I explained to him personally the nature of Forrest as a man, and of his peculiar force; told him that in his route he was sure to encounter Forrest, who always attacked with a vehemence for which he must be prepared, and that, after he had repelled the first attack, he must, in turn, assume the most determined offensive, overwhelm him, and utterly destroy his whole force. I knew that Forrest could not have more than four thousand cavalry, and my own movement would give employment to every other man of the rebel army not immediately present with him, so that he (General Smith) might safely act on the hypothesis I have stated.

"Having completed all these preparations in Memphis, being satisfied that the cavalry force would be ready to start by the 1st of February, and having seen General Hurlbut with his two divisions embark in steamers for Vicksburg, I also reëmbarked for the same destination on the 27th of January. * * * * The object of the Meridian expedition was to strike the roads inland, so to paralyze the rebel forces, that we could take from the defense of the Mississippi River the equivalent of a corps of twenty thousand men, to be used in the next Georgia campaign; and this was actually done. At the same time I wanted to destroy General Forrest, who, with an irregular force of cavalry, was constantly threatening Memphis and the river above, as well as our routes of supply in Middle Tennessee. In this we failed utterly, because General W. Sooy Smith did not fulfill his orders, which were clear and specific, as contained in my letter of instructions to him of January 27th, at Memphis, and my personal explanations to him at the same time. Instead of starting at the date ordered, February 1st, he did not leave Memphis till the 11th, waiting for some regiment that was ice bound near Columbus, Kentucky; and then, when he did start, he allowed General Forrest to head him off and to defeat him with an inferior force near West Point, below Okalona, on the Mobile and Ohio Railroad.

"We waited at Meridian till the 20th to hear from General Smith, but hearing nothing whatever, and having utterly destroyed the railroads in and around that junction, I ordered General McPherson to move back slowly toward Canton. With Winslow's cavalry and Hurlbut's infantry I turned north to Marion, and thence to a place called 'Union,' whence I dispatched the cavalry farther north to Philadelphia and Louisville, to feel as it were for General Smith, and then turned all the infantry columns toward Canton, Mississippi.

"On the 26th we all reached Canton, but we had not heard a word of General Smith, nor was it until sometime after (at Vicksburg) that I learned the whole truth of General Smith's movement and of his failure. Of course I did not, and could not, approve of his conduct, and I know that he yet chafes under the censure. I had set so much store on his part of the project that I was disappointed, and so reported officially to General Grant. General Smith never regained my confidence as a soldier, though I still regard him as a most accomplished gentleman and a skillful engineer. Since the close of the war he has appealed to me to relieve him of that censure, but I could not do it, because it would falsify history."

It would not have falsified history, however, if General Sherman had said, that instead of waiting for a regiment which was ice bound near Columbus, Ky., General Smith, by General Sherman's personal and positive directions, was awaiting the arrival of Warring's entire brigade of cavalry, composed of the Fourth Missouri, Second New Jersey, Seventh Indiana, Nineteenth Pennsylvania, and a battery of the Second Illinois Cavalry.

Further than this, General Smith was distinctly informed by Sherman, before the departure of the latter, that it would be necessary to wait for this brigade in order to make up the requisite force with which to meet Forrest. General Sherman also assured him that his own movement on Meridian and the contemplated operations there did not of necessity depend upon a junction with the cavalry from Memphis. And this is shown to have been General Sherman's view, when he himself reached Meridian four days after the date he had fixed for his own and General Smith's arrival at that point, by the order he then issued. This was dated eight days after the time mentioned for a union of the forces there, and declares that all the objects of the expedition had been fully attained:

[Special Field Orders No. 20.]
HEADQUARTERS DEPARTMENT OF THE TENNESSEE,
MERIDIAN, MISS., *February* 18th, 1864.

1. Having fulfilled, and well, all the objects of the expedition, the troops will return to the Mississippi River to embark in another equally important movement.

2. * * * * The march will begin on the 20th instant, and the corps commanders will not pass Union and Decatur until they have communicated with each other by couriers across at these points. * * * *

4. The march should be conducted slow; about fifteen miles per day, and in good order. * * * * There is no seeming danger, but every precaution should be taken against cavalry dashes at our trains. * * * *

By order of *Major-General* W. T. SHERMAN,

L. M. DAYTON, *Aid-de-Camp.*

From General Smith's report, it appears that Warring's brigade did not reach him until the 8th. It had marched two hundred and fifteen miles, over a country covered with snow and ice, and been obliged to cross rivers, where in some instances it was necessary to build boats to ferry the command, and where at times the men were compelled to dismount and harness the horses to the artillery and the ammunition wagons in order to draw them through. Three days would seem scarcely enough to refit a brigade after such a march, but in that time it again started under General Smith.

A vigorous campaign was then made against Forrest, and pushed as far as was prudent or possible. The delay in starting had made it impracticable to reach General Sherman at Meridian, by the time he had set for returning, and so General Smith withdrew to Memphis. As a result of his expedition, he reported between one and two million bushels of corn destroyed, two thousand bales of cotton burned, thirty miles of railroad destroyed, three thousand horses and mules, and fifteen hundred negroes brought out of the enemy's country, besides the forage and subsistence taken for his mounted force of seven thousand.

General Sherman in his report of the Meridian expedition, made a few days after his return to Vicksburg, maintained that he had accomplished all he undertook, notwithstanding the delay in General Smith's movements.

This portion of his report is as follows:

"I inclose herewith my instructions to General Smith, with a copy of his report, and must say it is unsatisfactory. The delay in his starting to the 11th of February, when his orders contemplated his being at Meridian on the 10th, and when he knew I was marching from Vicksburg is unpardonable, and the mode and manner of his return to Memphis was not what I expected from an intended bold cavalry movement. * * * * I returned (to Canton) from Vicksburg, on the 6th inst., found all my army in, and learned that General Smith had not started from Memphis at all till the 11th of February, had only reached West Point, and turned back on the 22d, the march back to Memphis being too rapid for a good effect.

"Nevertheless, on the whole, we accomplished all I undertook."

General Smith, at the time of this expedition, was Grant's chief of cavalry, and when he was temporarily placed under the orders of Sherman for the Meridian campaign, he was engaged, in conjunction with other troops, in watching and operating against Forrest's command. He made full report to

General Grant of his operations under Sherman, and was commended for what he accomplished. As an evidence that General Sherman himself had lost no confidence in him, he was retained by that officer as chief-of-staff, when he succeeded Grant in command of the Military Division of the Mississippi, and was entrusted with the work of organizing the cavalry force for the Atlanta campaign, continuing active in the field during the first three months of that movement, when disabling sickness compelled him to leave the service. And yet General Sherman now writes: "General Smith never regained my confidence as a soldier."

The reports on file in the War Department regarding General Smith's movement are voluminous. His instructions contain no mention of February 1st being the day absolutely fixed for his starting, as now claimed in the Memoirs, and the reasons, both for the delay, and the subsequent return to Memphis, are of such a character as to fix no stain upon his record.

The Memoirs, in fixing the force with which he was to move at "about seven thousand," show that General Sherman expected General Smith to wait for Warring's brigade, since, without it, his force would only have numbered about five thousand. Instead of Forrest's strength being then estimated in Memphis at "not more than four thousand cavalry," it was believed to be, and in fact was, fully six thousand. Instead of being defeated at West Point "with an inferior force," General Smith was not defeated there at all; and further, he moved back from that place partly because the rebel cavalry force, which Sherman had not kept employed in his own front, was moving to join Forrest against him.

But aside from this expected reënforcement of the enemy the various reports disclose abundant reason for turning back from West Point. The force in General Smith's front was fully equal to his own, and was posted behind a river which became impassable when so held. The enemy's left was covered by a swamp and river, and a movement in that direction was impracticable, while his right was protected by the Tombigbee River which General Smith could not cross. His command was encumbered with a large body of negroes that he had gathered up in pursuance of orders and was in honor bound to protect. A rebel brigade was moving to the rear to occupy a strong point in his line of retreat. At this time General Sherman was retiring from Meridian, and had it been possible for General Smith to advance beyond West Point it would have been a move upon Polk's whole army, resulting in utter defeat.

General Smith penetrated further into the enemy's territory than General Sherman, and, in proportion to the strength of his command, inflicted heavier losses upon the enemy than Sherman.

CHAPTER VIII.

RESACA—THE FAILURE THERE ATTRIBUTED TO McPHERSON.

It is ungenerous in General Sherman to cast imputations upon General McPherson, the commander of the Army of the Tennessee, since this General and his army, often at sore cost, saved Sherman from himself, and won laurels for him to wear.

It is well known among many who participated in it, that the prominent officers of the three armies which began the Atlanta campaign, considered its opening moves at Dalton and Resaca as grave and needless failures. The feeling was that Sherman, with his one hundred thousand men, should have brought Johnston's forty-five thousand to decisive battle in front of Resaca.

General Sherman, in his book, labors to show first, that at the outset he fully intended to do this; and second, that the failure of his plan resulted from McPherson's timidity at a moment when this officer had an opportunity to insure brilliant success—such as does not occur twice in a single life.

As will be remembered, the enemy held a strongly fortified position in front of Dalton. The road from Chattanooga passed from the west through a deep gorge called Buzzard's Roost, in the mountain range which separated the two armies. Its sides were precipitous, finally taking the form of palisades. The range was Rocky Face. The gorge was partly commanded from the Union side by Tunnel Hill. About fifteen miles south, Snake Creek Gap, which had been almost entirely neglected by the enemy, opened through the ridge midway upon the roads leading from Dalton to Resaca.

Of the position, General Sherman writes as follows:

"The position was very strong, and I know that such a general as was my antagonist (Joseph Johnston), who had been there six months, had fortified it to the maximum.

"Therefore, I had no intention to attack the position seriously in front, but depended on McPherson to capture and hold the railroad to its rear, which would force Johnston to detach largely against him, or rather, as I expected, to evacuate his position at Dalton altogether.

"My orders to Generals Thomas and Schofield were merely to press strongly at all points in front, ready to rush in on the first appearance of 'let go,' and, if possible, to catch our enemy in the confusion of retreat."

And yet against this front, which he "had no intention of attacking seriously," he moved Thomas with over sixty thousand, and Schofield with over thirteen thousand, while McPherson with twenty-four thousand was sent to Johnston's rear through Snake Creek Gap, not with orders to remain on his line of communications, but to break his railroad and then retire to Snake Creek Gap, or return to the main army as he should deem best.

Which was the diversion? Were Thomas and Schofield making it in Buzzard Roost and upon impregnable Rocky Face, with over seventy-four thousand men, while McPherson was marching to the predetermined battle-field, in the rear of Dalton, with twenty-four thousand?

The attack began on the 7th of May. On that day Thomas carried Tunnel Hill. Of all the operations on the front during the 8th and 9th, when Thomas and Schofield were assaulting precipices, the Memoirs have nothing except the single sentence: "All the movements of the 7th and 8th were made exactly as ordered."

The history then proceeds:

"I had constant communication with all parts of the army, and on the 9th, McPherson's head of column entered and passed through Snake Creek perfectly undefended, and accomplished a complete surprise to the enemy. At its further *débouché* he met a cavalry brigade, easily driven, which retreated hastily north toward Dalton, and doubtless carried to Johnston the first serious intimation that a heavy force of infantry and artillery was to his rear, and within a few miles of his railroad. I got a short note from McPherson that day (written at 2 P. M., when he was within a mile and a halt of the railroad above and near Resaca), and we all felt jubilant. I renewed orders to Thomas and Schofield to be ready for the instant pursuit of what I expected to be a broken and disordered army, forced to retreat by roads to the east of Resaca, which were known to be very rough and impracticable.

"That night I received further notice from McPherson that he had found Resaca too strong for a surprise; that in consequence he had fallen back three miles to the mouth of Snake Creek Gap, and was there fortified. I wrote him next day the following letters, copies of which are in my letter-book; but his to me were mere notes in pencil, not retained."

The letters referred to are both dated May 11th. The material points affecting the question under discussion, are as follows:

"GENERAL: I received by courier (in the night) yours of 5 and 6:30 P. M. of yesterday. You now have your twenty-three thousand men, and General Hooker is in close support, so that you can hold all of Jos. Johnston's army in check should he abandon Dalton. He can not afford to abandon Dalton, for he has fixed it up on purpose to receive us, and he observes that we are close at hand waiting for him to quit. He can not afford a detachment strong enough to fight you, as his army will not admit of it.

"Strengthen your position; fight anything that comes; and threaten the safety of the railroad all the time. But, to tell the truth I would rather the enemy would stay in Dalton two more days, when he may find in his rear a larger party than he expects in an open field. At all events we can then choose our own ground, and he will be forced to move out of his works. I do not intend to put a column into Buzzard Roost Gap at present.

"McPherson had startled Johnston in his fancied security, but had not done the full measure of his work. He had in hand twenty-three thousand of the best men of the army, and could have walked into Resaca (then held only by a small brigade), or he could have placed his whole force astride the railroad above Resaca, and there have easily withstood the attack of all of Johnston's army, with the knowledge that Thomas and Schofield were on his heels. Had he done so, I am certain that Johnston would not have ventured to attack him in position, but would have retreated eastward by Spring Place, and we should have captured half his army and all his artillery and wagons at the very beginning of the campaign.

"Such an opportunity does not occur twice in a single life, but at the critical moment McPherson seems to have been a little timid. Still, he was perfectly justified by his orders, and fell back and assumed an unassailable defensive position in Sugar Valley, on the Resaca side of Snake Creek Gap. As soon as informed of this, I determined to pass the whole army through Snake Creek Gap, and to move on Resaca with the main army."

That McPherson moved promptly through Snake Creek Gap when ordered, is shown by the fact that he did not even wait for food for men or horses, as will appear from the following extract from the report of General G. M. Dodge, of the Sixteenth Army Corps, who had the advance in the movement on Resaca:

"During the entire day the command acted under the personal direction of Major-General McPherson, and promptly obeyed and executed all his orders. My transportation had not yet reached me. I had with the entire corps, since leaving Chattanooga, only seventeen wagons, and I had marched out in the morning without rations, most of the command having been without food since the day before at noon; thus a march of sixteen miles was made by the command, the men and animals whereof had had nothing to eat for a day and a half."

A report of General Dodge also shows that a detachment of his troops passed through the Gap, moved out to the railroad the night of the 8th, and found it clear of the enemy; that the next day his entire corps carried a hill close to Resaca, moved in force to the railroad, and from this point was withdrawn to the mouth of Snake Creek Gap. This was in accordance with the positive order of General Sherman to General McPherson.

After the slur upon McPherson's courage, the book relates that on the 11th, there being signs of the enemy evacuating Dalton, orders were given for the movement of all the army through Snake Gap, except the Fourth Corps and Stoneman's cavalry, which were left in front of Buzzard's Roost. During the 12th and 13th, the greater part of Thomas' and Schofield's army passed through the gap and were deployed against Resaca, where, now writes General Sherman, the enemy, "*as I anticipated*, had abandoned all his well-prepared defenses at Dalton, and was found inside of Resaca with the bulk of his army, holding his divisions well in hand, acting purely on the defensive, and fighting well at all points of conflict. * * * * On the 14th we closed in."

He thus closes the account of these opening operations of the Atlanta campaign:

"On the night of May 15th Johnston got his army across the bridges, set them on fire, and we entered Resaca at daylight. Our loss up to that time was about six hundred dead and thirty-three hundred and seventy-five wounded—mostly light wounds that did not necessitate sending the men to the rear for treatment. That Johnston had deliberately designed in advance to give up such a strong position as Dalton and Resaca, for the purpose of drawing us further south, is simply absurd. Had he remained in Dalton another hour it would have been his total defeat, and he only evacuated Resaca because his safety demanded it. The movement by us through Snake Creek Gap was a total surprise to him. My army about doubled his in size, but he had all the advantages of natural positions of artificial forts and roads, and of concentrated action. We were compelled to grope our way through forests, across mountains, with a large army, necessarily more or less dispersed. Of course I was disappointed not to have crippled his army more at that particular stage of the game; but, as it resulted, these rapid successes gave us the initiative, and the usual impulse of a conquering army. Johnston having retreated in the night of May 15th, immediate pursuit was begun."

Thus, seven days after the movement began, General Sherman had finally accomplished what General Thomas, who, assisted by General Schofield, had thoroughly reconnoitered the position in February, had urged should be done at the first, as will now appear from the record history of Buzzard Roost and Resaca.

On the 28th of February, 1864, before General Sherman had succeeded General Grant in the command of the Military Division of the Mississippi, General Thomas, who was in command of the Army of the Cumberland at Chattanooga, telegraphed General Grant at Nashville, proposing the following plan for a Spring campaign:

"I believe if I can commence the campaign with the Fourteenth and Fourth Corps in front, with Howard's corps in reserve, that I can move along the line of the railroad and overcome all opposition as far, at least, as Atlanta."

In a subsequent report upon the campaign, dated March 10, 1864, General Thomas thus speaks of this proposition:

"The above proposition was submitted to General Grant for his approval, and if obtained, it was my intention (having acquired by the reconnoissance of February 23d, 24th, and 25th, a thorough knowledge of the approaches direct upon Dalton, from Ringgold and Cleveland), to have made a strong demonstration against Buzzard Roost, attracting Johnston's whole attention to that point, and to have thrown the main body of my infantry and cavalry through Snake Creek Gap upon his communications, which I had ascertained from scouts he had, up to that time, neglected to observe or guard. With this view I had previously asked for the return to me of Granger's corps and my cavalry from East Tennessee, and had already initiated preparations for the execution of the above movement as soon as the Spring opened sufficiently to admit of it."

On the 17th of March General Grant was made Lieutenant-General, and was succeeded in command at Nashville by General Sherman. In the same report General Thomas continues:

"Shortly after his assignment to the command of the Military Division of the Mississippi, General Sherman came to see me at Chattanooga, to consult as to the position of affairs, and adopt a plan for a Spring campaign. At that interview I proposed to General Sherman that if he would use McPherson and Schofield's armies to demonstrate on the enemy's position at Dalton, by the direct roads through Buzzard Roost Gap, and from the direction of Cleveland, I would throw my whole force through Snake Creek Gap, which I knew to be unguarded, fall upon the enemy's communications between Dalton and Resaca, thereby turning his position completely, and force him either to retreat toward the east, through a difficult country, poorly supplied with provisions and forage, with a strong probability of total disorganization of his force, or attack me; in which latter event I felt confident that my army was sufficiently strong to beat him, especially as I hoped to gain a position on his communications before he could be made aware of my movement. General Sherman objected to this plan for the reason that he desired my army to form the reserve of the united armies, and to serve as a rallying point for the two wings, the Army of the Ohio and that of the Tennessee, to operate from.

"(Later, when the campaign in Georgia was commenced, the Army of the Tennessee was sent through Snake Creek Gap to accomplish what I had proposed doing with my army, but not reaching Snake Creek Gap before the enemy had informed himself of the movement, McPherson was unable to get upon his communications before Johnston had withdrawn part of his forces from Dalton, and had made dispositions to defend Resaca.")

Such is General Thomas' brief account of this movement.

Below will be found its history as presented in General Sherman's own dispatches, to which scarcely any allusion is made in his book.

On the 24th of April General Sherman wrote as follows to General Grant, informing him of the intention to attack Johnston in position at Dalton:

"At Lafayette all our armies will be together, and if Johnston stands at Dalton we must attack him in position."

HEADQUARTERS MILITARY DIVISION OF THE MISSISSIPPI, }
IN THE FIELD, CHATTANOOGA, *May* 1, 1864. }
General GRANT, *Culpepper, Va.*

* * * * The first move will be Thomas, Tunnel Hill; Schofield, Catoosa Springs; and McPherson, Villanow. Next move will be battle.
* * * * W. T. SHERMAN, *Major-General.*

HEADQUARTERS MILITARY DIVISION OF THE MISSISSIPPI, }
IN THE FIELD, CHATTANOOGA, *May* 4, 1864. }
General GRANT, *Culpepper, Va.*

Thomas' center is at Ringgold, left at Catoosa, right at Leets' tan-yard. Dodge is here, Fifteenth corps at Whiteside, Schofield closing up on Thomas. All move to-morrow, but I hardly expect serious battle till the 7th. Every thing very quiet with the enemy. Johnston evidently awaits my initiative. I will first secure Tunnel Hill, then throw McPherson rapidly on his communications, attacking at the same time in front, cautiously, and in force.
W. T. SHERMAN, *Major-General commanding.*

May 5th, he notified General McPherson of the move which Thomas and Schofield were directed to make against Rocky Face, and directed him to march to Snake Creek Gap, secure it, attack the enemy boldly from it, attempt to so break the railroad that it would require some days to repair it, and then "withdraw to Snake Creek Gap and come to us, or wait the developments according to your judgment and the information you may receive." In the same order General Sherman expresses the hope that "the enemy will fight at Dalton."

In the forenoon of May 7th, he directed General Schofield to "see if Rocky Face Ridge can be reached from your position," and at two o'clock, "reconnoiter the ridge to-night and make a lodgment to-morrow morning, but don't be drawn into battle."

On the 8th, General Thomas was ordered "to get, if possible, a small force on Rocky Face Ridge," and General Schofield "to follow from Lee's along down Rocky Face to the enemy's signal station, if possible."

On the same day, the 8th, he telegraphed from Tunnel Hill, in front of Buzzard Roost, to General Halleck, at Washington:

"I have been all day reconnoitering the mountain range through whose gap the railroad and common road pass. By to-night McPherson will be in Snake Creek Gap threatening Resaca, and to-morrow all will move to the attack. Army in good spirits and condition. I hope Johnston will fight here instead of drawing me far down into Georgia."

On the 9th he telegraphed General J. D. Webster, at Nashville:

"Have been fighting all day against rocks and defiles. General McPherson was at 2 P. M. within two miles of Resaca, and will there break the road, and leave Johnston out of rations. To-morrow will tell the story."

And on the 9th, at 8 P. M., from Tunnel Hill, to General Halleck as follows:

"We have been fighting all day against precipices and mountain gaps to keep Johnston's army busy, while McPherson could march to Resaca to destroy the railroad behind him. I heard from McPherson up to 2 P.M., when he was within a mile and a half of the railroad.

"After breaking the road good, his orders are to retire to the mouth of Snake Creek Gap and be ready to work on Johnston's flank in case he retreats south. I will pitch in again early in the morning."

Which shows conclusively that Sherman ordered McPherson back to Snake Gap, and that the charge of timidity is gratuitous. It also shows that on the night of the 9th, Sherman was still expecting to attack by Rocky Face and Buzzard Roost.

On the 9th, General Thomas, from his headquarters at Tunnel Hill, sent to General Sherman the following statement of Captain Merril, Chief Engineer of the Department of the Cumberland, who had just returned from Geary's camp:

"He says that Geary attempted to carry Mill Gap by assault, but was repulsed with a loss probably of two hundred to three hundred killed and wounded; that the enemy were still in force (only infantry), but strongly posted; that it is impossible to obtain possession of the gap by direct assault, or only at the expense of fearful loss; that Geary's last orders were to withdraw into the valley, and encamp beyond artillery range. Geary was not making an attempt to turn the position. The only way to do so is to get a force upon the mountain "somewhere" where the enemy can not defend it so strongly."

On the 10th he wrote from Tunnel Hill to General Thomas: "I think you are satisfied that your troops can not take Rocky Face Ridge, and also the attempt to put our columns into the jaws of Buzzard Roost would be fatal to us."

And later in the same day:

"I propose to leave hereabouts one of your corps, say Howard's, the cavalry of Colonel McCook, and the cavalry of General Stoneman, to keep up the feint of a direct attack on Dalton, through Buzzard Roost, as long as possible; and with all the remainder of the three armies to march to, and through, Snake Creek Gap, and to attack the enemy in force from that quarter. * * * * we will calculate all to go to Snake Creek and close up on General McPherson during the day after to-morrow."

At 7 A. M. of the 10th this telegram was sent to Halleck:

"I am starting for the extreme front in Buzzard Roost Gap, and make this dispatch that you may understand Johnston acts purely on the defensive. I am attacking him on his strongest fronts, viz.: west and north, till McPherson breaks his line at Resaca, when I will swing round through Snake Creek Gap and interpose between him and Georgia. I am not driving things too fast, because I want two columns of cavalry that are rapidly coming up to me from the rear—Stoneman on my left and Garrard on my right, both due to-day.

"Yesterday I pressed hard to prevent Johnston detaching against McPherson, but to-day I will be more easy, as I believe McPherson has destroyed Resaca, when he is ordered to fall back to the mouth of Snake Creek Gap, and act against Johnston's flank when he does start. All are in good condition."

On the 10th of May, for the first time, he notified General

McPherson of his intention to attack in force, through Snake Creek Gap, as follows: "The Buzzard Roost Gap is so well defended, and naturally is so strong, that I will undertake to attack Johnston through Snake Creek Gap. * * * * we may not be able to put our project in operation by the day after to-morrow, but we will all get ready. * * * * Do you think Johnston has yet discovered the nature of your forces?"

On the 10th he also telegraphed General Halleck as follows:

"General McPherson reached Resaca, but found the place strongly fortified and guarded, and did not break the road. According to his instructions, he drew back to the *débouché* of the gorge, where he has a strong defensive position, and guards the only pass into the valley of the Oostanaula available to us. Buzzard Roost Gap, through which the railroad passes, is naturally and artificially too strong to be attempted. I must feign on Buzzard Roost, but pass through the Snake Creek Gap and place myself between Johnston and Resaca, where we will have to fight it out. I am making the preliminary move. Certain that Johnston can make no detachments, I will be in no hurry."

So it was not until some days after the attack began that he came to the conclusion, as he tells Halleck, that he "must feign on Buzzard Roost," but attack through Snake Creek Gap, which statement—as well as several dispatches already quoted—conflicts pointedly with the assertion that, from the first he "had no intention to attack the position seriously in front."

General Sherman having refrained from hurrying, and Johnston having virtually escaped him, he telegraphed to General Halleck on the 14th: "By the flank movement on Resaca we have forced Johnston to evacuate Dalton, and are on his flank and rear; but the parallelism of the valleys and mountains does not give us all the advantages of an open country; but I will press him all that is possible." And on the 15th: "We intend to fight Joe Johnston until he is satisfied, and I hope he will not attempt to escape; if he does, my bridges are down, and we will be after him." And on the 16th : " We are in possession of Resaca. * * * * Generals Stoneman's and Garrard's cavalry are trying to get into the rear of the enemy, and I hope will succeed. Our difficulties will increase beyond the Etowah, but if Johnston will not fight us behind such works as we find here, I will fight him on any open ground he may stand at."

It is easy to see what good ground there was for the opinion which prevailed in the Army of the Cumberland, that the failure of these first movements of the Atlanta campaign resulted from General Sherman's refusal to accept the advice of General Thomas, and persisting, instead, in pushing two armies for three days against " precipices," only to be obliged, when it was too late, to try the plan of Thomas, and failing solely because of delay.

The injustice of the attempt to lay the responsibility of the failure upon General McPherson can also be clearly seen in the light of these records.

CHAPTER IX.

KENESAW—UNGENEROUS TREATMENT OF THOMAS—INACCU-
RATE STATEMENTS.

THERE was no military movement made by Sherman, from the time he began the Atlanta campaign till the end of the war, which brought such severe criticism upon him from the armies which he commanded as the assault upon Kenesaw Mountain. By the almost universal verdict along the lines, it was adjudged an utterly needless move, and so an inexcusable slaughter. Before the assault he had Thomas, with sixty thousand men, in front of the enemy's center. That enemy was not over forty-five thousand strong, and he had Schofield and McPherson, with over thirty-five thousand, to operate on the flank, and force the evacuation of Kenesaw without a battle, exactly as was done a few days after the assault. And these three armies, which had been fighting for three years, did not appreciate then, and have never appreciated Sherman's reasons for hurling two of them against an impregnable mountain, which were mainly, as he wrote, to teach his own army that it was sometimes necessary to assault fortified lines, and show the enemy that, on occasion, "he would assault, and that boldly."

And it cost over two thousand veterans killed and wounded to teach those who survived such a lesson as this!

Those who read Sherman's Memoirs from the stand-point of the three armies then operating under him, will naturally look for his account of Kenesaw, and all material points are hereby given in full:

"During the 24th and 25th of June, General Schofield extended his right as far as prudent, so as to compel the enemy to thin out his lines correspondingly, with the intention to make two strong assaults at points where success would give us the greatest advantage. I had consulted Generals Thomas, McPherson, and Schofield, and we all agreed that we could not, with prudence, stretch out any more; and, therefore, there was no alternative but to attack 'fortified lines,' a thing carefully avoided up to that time. I reasoned, if we could make a breach any where near the rebel center, and thrust in a strong head of column, that with the one moiety of our army we could hold in check the corresponding wing of the enemy, and with the other sweep in flank and overwhelm the other half. The 27th of June was fixed as the day for the attempt, and in order to oversee the whole, and to be in close communication with all parts of the army, I had a place cleared on the top of a hill to the rear of Thomas' center, and had the telegraph wires laid to it. The points of attack were chosen, and the troops were all prepared with as little demonstration as possible. About 9 A. M. of the day appointed the troops moved to the assault, and all along our lines for ten miles a furious fire of artillery and musketry was kept up. At all points the enemy met us with determined courage and in great force. McPherson's attacking column fought up the face of the lesser Kenesaw, but could not reach the summit. About a mile to the right, just below the Dallas road, Thomas' assaulting column reached the parapet, where Brigadier-General Harker was shot down mortally wounded, and Brigadier-General Daniel McCook (my old law partner) was desperately wounded, from the effects of which he afterward died.

"By 11:30 the assault was, in fact, over, and had failed. We had not broken the rebel line at either point, but our assaulting columns held their ground within a few yards of the rebel trenches, and there covered themselves with parapet. McPherson lost about five hundred men and several valuable officers, and Thomas lost nearly two thousand men. * * * *

"While the battle was in progress at the center, Schofield crossed Olley's Creek on the right, and gained a position threatening Johnston's line of retreat; and to increase the effect, I ordered Stoneman's cavalry to proceed rapidly still further to the right to Sweetwater. Satisfied of the bloody cost of attacking intrenched lines, I at once thought of moving the whole army to the railroad at a point (Fulton) about ten miles below Marietta, or to the Chattahoochee River itself, a movement similar to the one afterward so successfully practiced at Atlanta. All the orders were issued to bring forward supplies enough to fill our wagons, intending to strip the railroad back to Allatoona, and leave that place as our depot, to be covered as well as possible by Garrard's cavalry. General Thomas, as usual, shook his head, deeming it risky to leave the railroad; but something had to be done, and I had resolved on this move, as reported in my dispatch to General Halleck on July 1st:

"General Schofield is now south of Olley's Creek, and on the head of Nickajack. I have been hurrying down provisions and forage, and to-morrow night propose to move McPherson from the left to the extreme right, back of

General Thomas. This will bring my right within three miles of the Chattahoochee River, and about five miles from the railroad. By this movement I think I can force Johnston to move his whole army down from Kenesaw to defend his railroad and the Chattahoochee, when I will (by the left flank) reach the railroad below Marietta; but in this I must cut loose from the railroad with ten days' supplies in wagons. Johnston may come out of his intrenchments to attack Thomas, which is exactly what I want, for General Thomas is well intrenched on a line parallel with the enemy south of Kenesaw. I think that Allatoona and the line of the Etowah are strong enough for me to venture on this move. The movement is substantially down the Sandtown road straight for Atlanta.

"McPherson drew out his lines during the night of July 2d, leaving Garrard's cavalry, dismounted, occupying his trenches, and moved to the rear of the Army of the Cumberland, stretching down the Nickajack; but Johnston detected the movement, and promptly abandoned Marietta and Kenesaw. I expected as much, for by the earliest dawn of the 3d of July I was up at a large spy-glass, mounted on a tripod, which Colonel Poe, United States Engineers, had at his bivouac close by our camp. I directed the glass on Kenesaw, and saw some of our pickets crawling up the hill cautiously. Soon they stood upon the very top, and I could plainly see their movements as they ran along the crest just abandoned by the enemy. In a minute I roused my staff, and started them off with orders in every direction for a pursuit by every possible road, hoping to catch Johnston in the confusion of retreat, especially at the crossing of the Chattahoochee River. * * * *

"As before explained, on the 3d of July, by moving McPherson's entire army from the extreme left, at the base of Kenesaw, to the right, below Olley's Creek, and stretching it down the Nickajack toward Turner's Ferry of the Chattahoochee, we forced Johnston to choose between a direct assault on Thomas' intrenched position, or to permit us to make a lodgment on his railroad below Marrietta, or even to cross the Chattahoochee. Of course, he chose to let go Kenesaw and Marietta, and fall back on an intrenched camp, prepared by his orders in advance, on the north and west bank of the Chattahoochee, covering the railroad crossing and his several pontoon bridges."

The points of this narrative are very clearly made, but most contradictory of each other, as even a causual reading will reveal, and wholly at variance in important particulars with the official record, as will shortly be made to appear. They may be fairly summed up as follows:

1. During the 25th of June, the assault being on the morning of the 27th, General Schofield had extended his right as far as prudent.

2. After a consultation with Thomas, McPherson, and Schofield, it was agreed, because the line was then extended

as far as prudent, that there was no alternative but to assault the mountain.

3. Notwithstanding it was so imprudent to stretch out any more, that an assault was necessary instead, still Schofield, while the assault was in progress, moved off to the right, across Olley's Creek, while the cavalry extended his line still further, to the Sweetwater.

4. Satisfied of the bloody cost of assaulting the position at Kenesaw, General Sherman concluded to flank it by extending his lines to the right as far as Fulton, and possibly to the Chattahoochee River, still further beyond.

5. "General Thomas, as usual, shook his head, deeming it risky to leave the railroad," but something had to be done, and so he (Sherman) decided to extend his lines as above.

6. The moment Johnston detected this movement, he promptly, and as a matter of course, let go Kenesaw and Marietta without a fight.

In answer to the contradictions implied by the third point above, it may be claimed that it was the assault which fixed Johnston's attention, and required help from his flanks, that made it possible for Schofield to extend his lines. But the official records show that Schofield was actually prolonging his lines the whole day preceding the battle—that is, during the 26th—in spite of the statements in the text that, "during the 24th and 25th, he had extended his right as far as prudent." If, on the other hand, it be claimed that Schofield's movement on the 26th was to compel the enemy to withdraw part of his force from Kenesaw to strengthen the flank in front of Schofield, and thus make the assault practicable, it would appear that a stronger flanking movement might have caused the enemy to withdraw entirely, without the necessity of an assault, exactly as did occur a few days after.

The records have much to say about Kenesaw that is not even referred to in the Memoirs.

The following field dispatches from General Sherman to General Schofield, who was operating on the right, will be sufficient to show that the latter was extending his lines during the 26th and also during the 27th, the day of the assault:

Sherman to Schofield, June 26: "Is the brigade across Olley's Creek above the Sandtown road, or at the road?"

Sherman to Schofield, June 26: "All right. Be careful of a brigade so exposed, but I am willing to risk a good deal."

Sherman to Schofield, June 26: "Good bridge should be made to-night across Olley's Creek, where the brigade is across, and operations resumed there in the morning early."

Sherman to Schofield, June 27, 11:45 A. M.: "Neither McPherson nor Thomas has succeeded in breaking through, but each has made substantial progress at some cost. Push your operations on the flank and keep me advised."

The following parts of dispatches to General Thomas bear upon the same point:

Sherman to Thomas, June 27, 1:30 P. M.: "Schofield has one division close up on the Powder Spring road, and the other (division) across Olley's Creek, about two miles to his right and rear."

Sherman to Thomas, June 27, 4:10 P. M.: "Schofield has gained the crossing of Olley's Creek on the Sandtown road, the only advantage of the day."

Sherman to Thomas, June 27, evening: "Schofield has the Sandtown road, within eleven miles of the Chattahoochee, and we could move by that flank."

As will be seen from the extracts quoted from the Memoirs, General Sherman claims that the assault was the result of a consultation and agreement between himself and Generals Thomas, McPherson, and Schofield. As a matter of fact the latter did not favor an assault but earnestly discouraged it. Two of these officers are now dead, but the field orders of General Thomas are accessible, and the whole tenor of these disputes General Sherman's claim, as will now appear.

From his telegraph station, on a hill in rear of Thomas'

center, General Sherman communicated with him throughout the day. Of these dispatches the following bear upon the question at issue:

Thomas to Sherman, 8 A. M., June 27: "The movement of my troops against the enemy's work has commenced."

Which was answered as follows:

"Every thing moving well on this flank, and Schofield reports the same. Push your troops with all the energy possible. W. T. S."

Thomas to Sherman, in the field, 9 A. M., June 27: "General Howard reports that he has advanced and is doing well. I have not yet received report from Palmer."

Answered as follows:

"All well. Keep things moving.
"9:50 A. M. W. T. S."

Thomas to Sherman, 10:45 A. M., June 27: "Yours received. General Harker's brigade advanced to within twenty paces of the enemy's breastworks, and was repulsed with canister at that range, General Harker losing an arm. General Wagner's brigade of Newton's division, supporting General Harker, was so severely handled that it is compelled to reorganize. Colonel Mitchell's brigade of Davis' division captured one line of rebel breastworks, which they still hold. McCook's brigade was also very severely handled, nearly every colonel being killed or wounded. Colonel McCook wounded. It is compelled to fall back and reorganize. The troops are all too much exhausted to advance, but we hold all we have gained."

General Sherman upon receiving this urged another attempt to break the line, as follows:

Sherman to Thomas, June 27, 11:45 A. M.: "McPherson's column marched to the top of the hill through very tangled brush, but was repulsed; it is found almost impossible to deploy, but they still hold the ground. I wish you to study well the positions, and if it be possible to break the line do it; it is easier now than it will be hereafter. I hear Leggett's guns well behind the mountain."

A little later Sherman again urged Thomas to make a second assault, as the following dispatch shows:

Sherman to Thomas, June 27, 1:30 p. m.: "McPherson and Schofield are at a dead-lock? Do you think you can carry any of the enemy's main line to-day? McPherson's men are up to the abattis, and can't move without the direct assault. I will order the assault if you think you can succeed at any point. Schofield has one division close up on the Powder Spring road, and the other across Olley's Creek, two miles to his right and rear."

To both of these dispatches General Thomas sent the following reply, expressing himself decidedly against a second assault:

Thomas to Sherman, 1:40 p. m., 27th June: "Your dispatches 11:45 a. m. and 1:30 p. m. received. Davis' two brigades are now within sixty yards of the enemy's intrenchments. Davis reports that he does not think he can carry the works by assault on account of the steepness of the hill, but he can hold his position, put in one or two batteries to-night, and probably drive them out to-morrow morning. General Howard reports the same. Their works are from six to seven feet high and nine feet thick. In front of Howard they have a very strong abattis. Davis' loss in officers has been very heavy. Nearly all the field officers of McCook's brigade, with McCook have been killed or wounded. From what the officers tell me I do not think we can carry the works by assault at this point to-day, but they can be approached by saps and the enemy driven out.

"Very respectfully, GEORGE H. THOMAS, *Major-General*."

General Sherman replied as follows, still suggesting another assault by intimating that the difficulties were not sufficient to warrant the use of time enough for regular approaches:

Sherman to Thomas, June 27, 2:25 p. m.; "Secure what advantageous ground you have gained; but is there any thing in the enemy's present position that if we should approach by regular saps, he could not make a dozen new parapets before our saps were completed? Does the nature of the ground warrant the time necessary for regular approaches?"

To this Thomas returned the following very decided answer:

Thomas to Sherman, June 27: "Your dispatch of 2:25 received. We still hold all the ground we have gained, and the division commanders report their ability to hold. They also report the enemy's works exceedingly strong; in fact, so strong that they can not be carried by assault, except by immense sacrifice, even if they can be carried at all. I think, therefore, the best chance is to approach them by regular saps, and if we can find a favorable approach to batter them down. We have already lost heavily to-day without gaining any material advantage. One or two more such assaults would use up this army. G. H. THOMAS, *Major-General.*"

Sherman to Thomas, June 27, 4:10 P. M.: "Schofield has gained the crossing of Olley's Creek, on the Sandtown road, the only advantage of the day. You may order all ground of value gained to-day to be secured, and prepare batteries in the manner proposed by Davis. I doubt if we can resort to regular approaches."

Thomas to Sherman, June 27, 6 P. M: "The assault of the enemy's works in my front was well arranged, and the officers and men went to their work with the greatest coolness and gallantry. The failure to carry them is due only to the strength of the works, and to the fact that they were well manned, thereby enabling the enemy to hold them securely against the assault. We have lost nearly two thousand officers and men, among them two brigade commanders, General Harker, commanding a brigade in Newton's division, and Colonel Dan. McCook, commanding a brigade in Jeff. Davis' division, both reported to be mortally wounded, besides some six or eight field officers killed. Both General Harker and Colonel McCook were wounded on the enemy's breastworks, and all say that had they not been wounded we would have driven the enemy from his works. Both Generals Howard and Palmer think that they can find favorable positions on their lines for placing batteries for enfilading the enemy's works. We took between ninety and one hundred prisoners."

Sherman to Thomas, June 27, evening: "Let your troops fortify as close up to the enemy as possible. Get good positions for artillery, and group your command as conveniently as you can by corps and divisions, keeping reserves. Schofield has the Sandtown road within eleven miles of the Chattahoochee, and we could move by that flank. The question of supplies will be the only one. I regret beyond measure the loss of two such young and dashing officers, as Harker and Dan. McCook. McPherson lost two or three of his young and dashing officers, which is apt to be the case in unsuccessful assaults. Had we broken the line to-day it would have been most decisive; but, as it is, our loss is small compared with some of those East. It should not in the least discourage us. At times assaults are necessary and inevitable. At Arkansas Post we succeeded; at Vicksburg we failed. I do not think our loss to-day greater than Johnston's when he attacked Hooker and Schofield the first day we occupied our present ground."

The excuses made to General Thomas for the assault in the last part of the above dispatch are significant.

The same evening he telegraphed Halleck, intimating as a

reason for the assault that the position could not well be turned without abandoning the railroad:

"I can not well turn the position of the enemy without abandoning my railroad, and we are already so far from our supplies that it is as much as the road can do to feed and supply the army. There are no supplies of any kind here. I can press Johnston and keep him from reënforcing Lee, but to assault him in position will cost us more lives than we can spare."

And yet at 9 o'clock the same evening he telegraphed General Thomas:

"Are you willing to risk the move on Fulton, cutting loose from our railroad? It would bring matters to a crisis, and Schofield has secured the way."

But his excuses to Generals Halleck and Grant a few days later cap the climax of all which the records contain in regard to Kenesaw. Witness the following:

Sherman to Halleck, July 9: "The assault I made was no mistake. I had to do it. The enemy, and our own army and officers, had settled down into the conviction that the assault of lines formed no part of my game, and the moment the enemy was found behind any thing like a parapet, why, every body would deploy, throw up counter-works and take it easy, leaving it to the 'Old Man' to turn the position. Had the assault been made with one-fourth more vigor, mathematically, I would have put the head of George Thomas' whole army right through Johnston's deployed line, on the best ground for 'go-ahead,' while my whole forces were well in hand on roads converging to my then object, Marietta."

And the following:

Sherman to Grant, July 12: "I regarded an assault on the 27th June necessary, for two good reasons: first, because the enemy, as well as my own army, had settled down into the belief that 'flanking' alone was my game; and second, that on that day and ground, had the assault succeeded, I could have broken Johnston's center and pushed his army back in confusion and with great loss to his bridges over the Chattahoochee. We lost nothing in *morale* in the assault, for I followed it up on the extreme right, and compelled him to quit the very strong lines of Kenesaw, Smyrna camp ground, and the Chattahoochee in quick succession."

But Sherman states that the enemy lost only eight hundred

and eight in killed and wounded during the attack. So it could not have been the assault that finally induced him to leave, but the "flanking." And this was just as practicable before the assault as after it, and was subsequently made without the cost of a battle.

The above dispatches and extracts suggest all needed comment.

In the extract from the Memoirs quoted above, there is a slur upon General Thomas, which deserves notice.

Says General Sherman:

"Satisfied of the bloody cost of attacking intrenched lines, I at once thought of moving the whole army to a point (Fulton) about ten miles below Marietta. * * * * General Thomas, as usual, shook his head, deeming it risky to leave the railroad." * * * *

For this insinuation there is no excuse. The following is the telegram from Sherman to Thomas, proposing this very move to the latter:

HEADQUARTERS, *June* 27, 9 P. M.

General THOMAS:

Are you willing to risk the move on Fulton, cutting loose from our railroad? It would bring matters to a crisis, and Schofield has secured the way.

W. T. SHERMAN, *Major-General commanding.*

In the first place, as General Sherman communicated with General Thomas upon this subject by telegraph and in cipher, it is evident that Thomas could not have shaken his head through that medium; and second, while a figurative shaking might have been communicated in very plain terms, the dispatches show not only that this indication of dissent was wholly wanting, but that on the contrary, Thomas approved the plan in the following exceedingly suggestive and emphatic manner:

HEADQUARTERS DEPARTMENT OF THE CUMBERLAND, *June* 27.

General SHERMAN:

What force do you think of moving with? If with the greater part of the army I think it decidedly better than butting against breastworks twelve feet thick and strongly abattised.

GEO. H. THOMAS, *Major-General U. S. V.*

Immediately after the above, Thomas telegraphed the following inquiry, having in view, evidently, the possibility that his pontoons might be needed:

General SHERMAN. June 27.
How far is Fulton from the crossing of Olley's Creek? Will we have to cross any other streams of much size? When do you wish to start?
GEO. H. THOMAS, *Major-General.*

And yet with these telegrams in the record, showing prompt approval of his move, and a disposition to coöperate in it immediately, General Sherman ventures the above fling at General Thomas.

These last dispatches were answered as follows, Sherman to Thomas, June 27th, 9:30 P. M.: "According to Merrill's map it is about ten miles. Nickajack the only stream to cross. Time for starting day after to-morrow."

Sherman to Thomas, June 27, 9:45 P. M.: "If we move on Fulton, we must move with the whole army, leaving our railroad on the chance of success. Go where we may, we will find the breastworks and abattis, unless we move more rapidly than we have heretofore."

The dispatches thus far quoted, have been at all times accessible to General Sherman, and they are quite sufficient to show that the correct history of the battle at Kenesaw is not set forth in his Memoirs.

Of the immediate effect of the flanking movement on Kenesaw, begun on the night of the 2d of July following the assault, General Sherman says:

"As before explained, on the 3d of July, by moving McPherson's entire army from the extreme left, at the base of Kenesaw to the right, below Olley's Creek, and stretching it down the Nickajack toward Turner's Ferry of the Chattahoochee, we forced Johnston to choose between a direct assault on Thomas' intrenched position, or to permit us to make a lodgment on his railroad below Marietta, or even to cross the Chattahoochee. Of course he chose to let go Kenesaw and Marietta, and fall back on an intrenched camp prepared by his orders in advance on the north and west bank of the Chattahoochee, covering the railroad crossing and his several pontoon bridges. I confess I had not learned beforehand of the existence of this strong place.

in the nature of a *tête-du-pont*, and had counted on striking him an effectual blow in the expected confusion of his crossing the Chattahoochee, a broad and deep river then to his rear. Ordering every part of the army to pursue vigorously on the morning of the 3d of July, I rode into Marietta, just quitted by the rebel rear guard, and was terribly angry at the cautious pursuit by Garrard's cavalry, and even by the head of our infantry columns. But Johnston had in advance cleared and multiplied his roads; whereas ours had to cross at right angles from the direction of Powder Springs toward Marietta, producing delay and confusion. By night Thomas' head of column ran up against a strong rear guard intrenched at Smyrna camp ground, six miles below Marietta, and there, on the next day, we celebrated our Fourth of July, by a noisy but not a desperate battle, designed chiefly to hold the enemy there till Generals McPherson and Schofield could get well into position below him, near the Chattahoochee crossings. It was here that General Noyes, late Governor of Ohio, lost his leg. * * * * During the night Johnston drew back all his army and trains inside the *tête du-pont* at the Chattahoochee, which proved one of the strongest pieces of field fortification I ever saw."

This "noisy but not desperate battle" of July 4th was nothing less than an attack upon the strong works at Smyrna camp ground by the Sixteenth Corps under General Dodge, who pressed close up, and then sent a storming party of two brigades over them. It was one of the most gallant and successful fights of the Atlanta campaign, and one of the very few instances where heavy intrenchments were carried by direct assault. General Sherman ordered General McPherson to attack these lines, and he in turn, forwarded the order to General Dodge, directing the latter to move against the works if he thought he could carry them. They were stormed, General Noyes of Ohio, having prominent command in the charging column, and carried. As a consequence, the rebels let go the strong line of Smyrna camp ground and retreated.

CHAPTER X.

THE BATTLE OF ATLANTA AND ITS POLITICAL GENERALS.

GENERAL SHERMAN'S recollections fail to supply the interesting and significant inside history of the battle of Atlanta, by which name the action of July 22d was usually known in his army.

Speaking of two of the prominent actors in that battle, he says:

> "I regarded both Generals Logan and Blair as 'volunteers,' that looked to personal fame and glory as auxiliary and secondary to their political ambition, and not as professional soldiers."

And again:

> "Both were men of great courage and talent, but were politicians by nature and experience, and it may be that for this reason they were mistrusted by regular officers like Generals Schofield, Thomas, and myself."

The first of these paragraphs suggests the reflection whether it is any more reprehensible for volunteer generals to be actuated by "political ambition," than for professional soldiers to look upon "personal fame and glory" as their chief incentive—for such is the position in which General Sherman leaves his friends. The public will not judge them so harshly. These two brief extracts form a portion of General Sherman's comments upon the battle of Atlanta.

At the very opening of this action, McPherson then commanding the Army of the Tennessee was killed, and the desperate battle was fought through from noon till after night by his troops, commanded by these same political Generals and volunteers, Logan and Blair, assisted by that other well known politcian and volunteer, General Dodge, then commanding the Sixteenth Corps.

It was preëminently a battle fought and won by the class of officers and men thus pointed out by General Sherman. These saved one of his armies that day from the results of a surprise as great as fell upon him at Shiloh. Under these circumstances it would be natural to expect that high soldierly sentiment, if possessed by him, would not only have prompted a full acknowledgment of such services, unaccompanied by any questioning of motives, but would also have led him to assume the responsibility for a surprise which belonged solely to himself. But the reader of these Memoirs will look in vain for the key with which to unlock the mysteries of the situation on that day. The official record, however, supplies it.

Ten pages of the Memoirs are devoted to this action.

The situation was as follows: On the night of the 21st of July Sherman's army had fought its way close up to the outer lines of the rebels, established at an average of a little over three miles from Atlanta, and north and east of the city. Thomas was on the right, with the Army of the Cumberland; Schofield, with the Army of the Ohio, occupied the center, and McPherson's Army of the Tennessee held the left.

It had been ascertained three days before—that is, on the 18th—that Hood had relieved Johnston, and what was expected of the former is shown by the following statement in the Memoirs:

> "I immediately inquired of General Schofield, who was his classmate at West Point, about Hood—as to his general character, etc., and learned that he was bold, even to rashness, and courageous in the extreme. I inferred that the change of commanders meant 'fight.' Notice of this important change was at once sent to all parts of the army, and every division commander was cautioned to be always prepared for battle in any shape."

It would have been fortunate, as the sequel will show, if General Sherman had heeded his own cautions.

On the 20th, Hood made a "furious sally" on the right.

The Union loss was about two thousand, and General Sherman thus states the result:

"We had, however, met successfully a bold sally, had repelled it handsomely, and were also put on our guard; and the event illustrated the future tactics of our enemy." After this the reader would not expect to read of a great surprise. Nor will the traces of it be found very clearly marked in the book, as will now appear:

"During the night" (of the 21st) "I had full reports from all parts of our line, most of which was partially intrenched as against a sally, and finding that McPherson was stretching out too much on his left flank, I wrote him a note early in the morning" (of the 22d) "not to extend so much by his left; for we had not troops enough to completely invest the place, and I intended to destroy utterly all parts of the Augusta Railroad to the east of Atlanta, then to withdraw from the left flank and add to the right. In that letter I ordered McPherson not to extend any further to the left, but to employ General Dodge's corps (Sixteenth), then forced out of position, to destroy every rail and tie of the railroad from Decatur up to his skirmish line, and I wanted him (McPherson) to be ready, as soon as General Garrard returned from Covington (whither I had sent him) to move to the extreme right of Thomas, so as to reach, if possible, the railroad below Atlanta, viz.: the Macon road.

"In the morning we found the strong line of parapet, 'Peach-tree line,' to the front of Schofield and Thomas, abandoned, and our lines were advanced rapidly close up to Atlanta. For some moments I supposed the enemy intended to evacuate, and in person was on horseback at the head of Schofield's troops. * * * * Schofield was dressing forward his lines, and I could hear Thomas further to the right engaged, when General McPherson and his staff rode up. We went back to the Howard House, a double frame building, with a porch, and sat on the step discussing the chances of battle and of Hood's general character. McPherson had also been of the same class at West Point with Hood, Schofield, and Sheridan. We agreed that we ought to be unusually cautious, and prepared at all times for sallies and for hard fighting, because Hood, though not deemed much of a scholar, or of great mental capacity, was undoubtedly a brave, determined, and rash man; and the change of commanders at that particular crisis argued the displeasure of the Confederate Government with the cautious but prudent conduct of General Joe. Johnston. McPherson was in excellent spirits, well pleased at the progress of events so far, and had come over purposely to see me about the order I had given him to use Dodge's corps to break up the railroad, * * * * saying that before receiving my order he had diverted Dodge's two divisions (then in motion) from the main road, along a diagonal one that led to his extreme left flank, then held by Giles A. Smith's division (Seventeenth Corps), for the purpose of strengthening that flank. * * * * Of course I assented at once. * * * * While we sat there we could hear lively skirmishing going on near us (down about the distillery), and occasionally round shot from twelve or twenty-four pound guns came through the trees in reply to those of Schofield, and we could hear similar sounds all along down the lines of Thomas to our right, and his own to the left, but presently the firing appeared a little more brisk (especially over about Giles A. Smith's division), and then we heard an occasional gun back toward Decatur. I asked him what it meant. We took my pocket compass (which I always carried), and by noting the direction of the sound, we became satisfied that the firing was too far to our left rear to be explained by known facts, and he hastily called for his horse, his staff, and his orderlies, * * * * jumped on his horse, saying he would hurry down his line and send me back word what these sounds meant. * * * * (Soon after)—one of McPherson's staff, with his horse covered with sweat, dashed up to the porch, and reported that General McPherson was either 'killed or a prisoner.' He explained that when they had left me, a few minutes before, they had ridden rapidly across to the railroad, the sounds of battle increasing as they neared the position occupied by General Giles A. Smith's division, and that McPherson had sent first one, then another of his staff to bring some of the reserve brigades of the Fifteenth Corps over to the exposed left flank; that he had reached the head of Dodge's corps (marching by the flank on the diagonal road as described), and had ordered it to hurry forward to the same point; that then, almost, if not entirely alone, he had followed this road leading across the wooded valley behind the Seventeenth Corps, and had disappeared in these woods, doubtless with a sense of absolute security. The sound of musketry was there heard and McPherson's horse came back, bleeding, wounded, and riderless. I ordered the staff officer who brought this message to return at once, to find General Logan (the senior officer present with the Army of the Tennessee), to report the same facts to him, and to instruct him to drive back this supposed small force, which had evidently got around the Seventeenth Corps through the blind woods in rear of our left flank. I soon dispatched one of my own staff (McCoy, I think) to General Logan, with similar orders, telling him to refuse his left flank, and to fight the battle (holding fast to Leggett's Hill) with the Army of the Tennessee; that I would personally look to Decatur and to the safety of his rear, and would reënforce him if he needed it." * * * *

After explaining how Hood had first withdrawn from his outer line on the night of the 21st, occupied the fortified line next to Atlanta, and then sallied out with part of his force, passed entirely around the left of the Army of the Tennessee, and struck it in flank and rear while a portion of it was in motion, General Sherman continues:

"The enemy was, therefore, enabled, under cover of the forest, to approach quite near before he was discovered; indeed, his skirmish line had worked through the timber and got into the field to the rear of Giles A. Smith's division of the Seventeenth Corps unseen, had captured Murray's battery of regular artillery, moving through these woods entirely unguarded, and had got possession of several of the hospital camps.

"The right of this rebel line struck Dodge's troops in motion; but, fortunately, this corps (Sixteenth) had only to halt, face to the left, and was in line of battle; and this corps not only held in check the enemy, but drove him back through the woods. About the same time this same force had struck General Giles A. Smith's left flank, doubled it back, captured four guns in position and the party engaged in building the very battery, which was the special object of McPherson's visit to me, and almost enveloped the entire left flank. The men, however, were skillful and brave, and fought for a time with their backs to Atlanta. They gradually fell back, compressing their own line, and gaining strength by making junction with Leggett's division of the Seventeenth Corps, well and strongly posted on the hill. One or two brigades of the Fifteenth Corps, ordered by McPherson, came rapidly across the open field to the rear, from the direction of the railroad, filled up the gap from Blair's new left to the head of Dodge's column—now facing to the general left—thus forming a strong left flank at right angles to the original line of battle. The enemy attacked, boldly and repeatedly, the whole of this flank, but met an equally fierce resistance, and on that ground a bloody battle raged from little after noon till into the night. * * * *

"I rode over the whole of it" (the field) "the next day, and it bore the marks of a bloody conflict. The enemy had retired during the night inside of Atlanta, and we remained master of the situation outside. I purposely allowed the Army of the Tennessee" [then in the hands of three political generals] "to fight this battle almost unaided, save by demonstrations on the part of Generals Schofield and Thomas against the fortified lines to their immediate fronts, and by detaching, as described, one of Schofield's brigades to Decatur, because I knew that the attacking force could only be a part of Hood's army, and that, if any assistance were rendered by either of the other armies, the Army of the Tennessee would be jealous. Nobly did they do their work that day, and terrible was the slaughter done to our enemy, though at sad cost to ourselves."

In reporting upon the battle to General Halleck, General Sherman telegraphed:

"McPherson's sudden death, and Logan succeeding to the command, as it were, in the midst of battle, made some confusion on our extreme left; but it soon recovered, and made sad havoc with the enemy, who had practiced one of his favorite games of attacking our left when in motion, and before it had time to cover its weak flank."

Following this, among some general observations upon the battle, and the question of a successor, the extracts given at the opening of this chapter are found.

From the above fair outlines of General Sherman's account, the reader would conclude that some of the warnings received in regard to Hood's methods were disregarded, and that the new Confederate commander had sallied against, and passed entirely around our left, finding it unprepared and partly in motion by the flank, and that some confusion resulted, and a bloody battle, which was not particularly unexpected by General Sherman, and did not, in a great degree, disturb him.

The real reason for this confusion on the left does not appear in the Memoirs. The key to unlock the bloody mysteries of the 22d of July, where the Union loss was thirty-five hundred men, with General McPherson, and ten pieces of artillery, lies deeply covered under the sentence: "For some moments I supposed the enemy intended to evacuate."

Some omitted leaves from the official record will show how long these "moments" were.

In a report made by General Sherman to General Halleck, dated August 15, 1864, this paragraph occurs, though it is not mentioned in his book:

"On the morning of the 22d, somewhat to my surprise, this whole line was found abandoned, and I confess I thought the enemy had resolved to give us Atlanta without further contest. But General Johnston had been relieved of the command, and General Hood substituted. A new policy seemed resolved upon, of which a bold attack upon our right was an index, * * * * About 10 A. M. I was in person with General Schofield examining the appearance of the enemy's line opposite the distillery, where we attracted enough of the enemy's fire of artillery and musketry to satisfy me the enemy was in Atlanta in force, and meant to fight."

The last order recorded in General McPherson's field letter

book, in the morning of the day he was killed, furnishes a further commentary upon those "moments," during which General Sherman thought the enemy "intended to evacuate:"

THREE AND A HALF MILES EAST OF ATLANTA, GEORGIA, }
July 22, 1864. }

Major-General JOHN A. LOGAN, *Commanding Fifteenth Army Corps:*

The enemy having evacuated their works in front of our lines, the supposition of Major-General Sherman is that they have given up Atlanta, and are retreating in the direction of East Point.

You will immediately put your command in pursuit to the south and east of Atlanta, without entering the town. You will keep a route to the left of that taken by the enemy, and try to cut off a portion of them while they are pressed in the rear and on our right by Generals Schofield and Thomas.

Major-General Sherman desires and expects a vigorous pursuit.

Very respectfully, your obedient servant,

JAMES B. MCPHERSON, *Major-General.*

The following telegram also furnishes testimony to the same end:

CAMP ON RAILROAD, FOUR MILES FROM ATLANTA, }
9 P. M., *July* 22, 1864. }

Major THOMAS T. ECKERT, *Washington.*

At daylight to-day it was found that the rebels had gone from our entire front, and General Sherman announced the occupation of Atlanta by Schofield, and ordered pursuit by Thomas and McPherson. Vigorous pursuit was made, and the enemy found in the fortifications of Atlanta, and not Schofield. We hold the railroad to within two and a half miles of the center of the place; that is about the average distance of the whole line, though Schofield and Dodge are nearer. The fighting has been severe, and we lose McPherson, killed by a shot through the lungs while on a reconnoissance. It is thought that the enemy will be gone in the morning, as they have attacked and been repulsed since dark. Hood fights his graybacks desperately.

J. C. VAN DUZEN, *Cipher Operator, U. S. M. T.*

One of the political generals however had informed himself very early in the morning that the rebels had not evacuated Atlanta, as General Sherman supposed; but instead, held the inner lines, near the city, in force. This appears from General Dodge's report of the operations of the Sixteenth Corps on the Atlanta campaign, in which he says:

"At 4 o'clock A. M. of the 22d of July, General Sweeney, commanding the

Second Division, reported to me that the enemy had disappeared from his front, and I immediately ordered him to push forward a heavy skirmish line, which he did promptly, and reported the enemy in force in the works surrounding Atlanta."

Upon this corps, a few hours later, fell the chief brunt of the battle, as it was hastening to defend the left, and the character of its fighting is sufficiently shown by the facts that it first held its ground, then repulsed the enemy, and that every field officer engaged appears to have been on the list of the killed or wounded.

The character of the surprise upon the left is shown by the following extract from General Blair's report of the battle:

"In the morning of the 22d the enemy came in on my rear and left in very heavy force, with the intention of overpowering and destroying this corps. Although we had no warning of his approach, and although attacked immediately in rear, the men and officers behaved with unparalleled gallantry, repulsing every assault, changing front repeatedly with a coolness and courage which can not be too highly praised."

The account given in the above narrative, of the early note to McPherson not to extend so far to the left, certainly needs further explanation in the light of the order, also an early one, to pursue the rebels well to the left, past Atlanta even, and on toward East Point.

The question also arises, if Hood, in his sally, was practising one of his "favorite games," why he was allowed to succeed so well in his play.

But the one point that will stand out in bolder relief than any other, is the flippancy with which the terms "volunteers" and "political generals" are used against those who, in the midst of grave surprise, brought on by the order of the commanding general, rallied their three corps in the face of an army that had outflanked them, and burst upon them in reverse as well, and fought for hours with the rebel line—sometimes from one face of abandoned Confederate works, sometimes from the other, through that long Summer afternoon and far into the night, and against every disadvantage finally achieved victory, and retrieved the one great mistake with which the commanding general began the day; namely, announcing the evacuation of Atlanta and starting two of his armies by the flank in pursuit.

CHAPTER XI.

THE MARCH TO THE SEA—DID GRANT OR SHERMAN PLAN IT?

DID General Sherman originate the idea of the March to the Sea? This is a question which he makes very prominent in his Memoirs, and answers at length and most decidedly in the affirmative. But here, as in other instances which have been brought to the attention of the public, the distinguished author and historian ignores some important portions of the official records which others may find interesting.

The following is the version of the origin of this movement given in Volume II of the Memoirs:

"I have often been asked by well-meaning friends, when the thought of that march first entered my mind. I knew that an army which had penetrated Georgia as far as Atlanta could not turn back. It must go ahead; but when, how, and where, depended on many considerations. As soon as Hood had shifted across from Lovejoy's to Palmetto I saw the move in my "mind's eye;" and, after Jeff. Davis' speech at Palmetto, of September 26, I was more positive in my conviction, but was in doubt as to the time and manner. When General Hood first struck our railroad above Marietta we were not ready, and I was forced to watch his movements further till he had "caromed off" to the west of Decatur. Then I was perfectly convinced, and had no longer a shadow of doubt. The only possible question was as to Thomas' strength and ability to meet Hood in the open field."—Page 166.

Hood shifted to Palmetto September 21st; Davis' speech was on the 26th of September, and Hood moved to the west of Decatur October 26th; so that Sherman's account fixes the following points for himself:

The move was in his "mind's eye," September 21, 1864.
He was in doubt as to time and manner after September 26.

(128)

He had no doubt about the move October 26.

The points of the narrative, in the chapter devoted to the question of planning the March to the Sea, are these:

Hood having moved upon Sherman's railroad communications, General Thomas returned to Chattanooga with a considerable force, and on the 29th of September Sherman telegraphed the condition of affairs to Halleck, saying, among other things, "I prefer for the future to make the movement on Milledgeville, Millen, and Savannah."

On that day (October 1) he telegraphed Grant:

* * * * "Why will it not do to leave Tennessee to the forces which Thomas has, and the reserves soon to come to Nashville, and for me to destroy Atlanta and march across Georgia to Savannah or Charleston, breaking railroads and doing irreparable damage? We can not remain on the defensive."

On the 9th (October) he telegraphed General Thomas at Nashville:

"I want to destroy all the road below Chattanooga, including Atlanta, and to make for the sea-coast. We can not defend this long line of road."

On that same day he telegraphed to General Grant at City Point:

"It will be a physical impossibility to protect the roads, now that Hood, Forrest, Wheeler, and the whole batch of devils are turned loose without home or habitation. * * * * I propose that we break up the railroad from Chattanooga forward, and that we strike out with our wagons for Milledgeville, Millen, and Savannah. * * * * I can make this march, and make Georgia howl!"

October 10th he telegraphed Thomas as follows:

"He (Hood) is now crossing the Coosa River below Rome, looking west. Let me know if you can hold him with your forces now in Tennessee and the expected reënforcements, as, in that event, you know what I propose to do."

And on the same day to General Grant:

"Hood is now crossing the Coosa twelve miles below Rome, bound west.

If he passes over to the Mobile & Ohio Railroad, had I better not execute the plan of my letter sent you by Colonel Porter, and leave General Thomas with the troops now in Tennessee to defend the State? He will have an ample force when the reënforcements ordered reach Nashville. * * * *

"From General Corse, at Rome, I learned that Hood's army had disappeared, but in what direction he was still in doubt; and I was so strongly convinced of the wisdom of my proposition to change the whole tactics of the campaign, to leave Hood to General Thomas, and to march across Georgia to Savannah or Charleston, that I again telegraphed to General Grant:

"'KINGSTON, GA., *October* 11, 11 A. M.

"'*Lieutenant-General* GRANT.

"'We can not now remain on the defensive. With twenty-five thousand infantry, and the bold cavalry he has, Hood can constantly break my road. I would infinitely prefer to make a wreck of the road and of the country from Chattanooga to Atlanta, including the latter city, send back all my wounded and unserviceable men, and with my effective army move through Georgia, smashing things to the sea. * * * * I can make Savannah, Charleston, or the mouth of the Chattahoochie (Appalachicola). Answer quick, as I know we will not have the telegraph long.'

"I received no answer to this at the time. * * * *

"It was at Ship's Gap that a courier brought me the cipher message from General Halleck which intimated that the authorities in Washington were willing I should undertake the march across Georgia to the sea. The translated dispatch named 'Horse-i-bar Sound' as the point where the fleet would await my arrival. After much time I construed it to mean 'Ossabaw Sound,' below Savannah, which was correct. [General Sherman gives none of the dispatches which passed in regard to the matter.]

"On the 16th I telegraphed General Thomas at Nashville:

"'Send me Morgan's and Newton's old divisions. Reëstablish the road, and I will follow Hood wherever he may go.' * * * *

"General Thomas' reply was (October 17):

* * * * "'Mower and Wilson have arrived and are on their way to join you. I hope you will adopt Grant's idea of turning Wilson loose, rather than undertake the plan of a march with the whole force through Georgia to the sea, inasmuch as General Grant can not coöperate with you as at first arranged.'

"So it is clear that at that date neither General Grant nor General Thomas heartily favored my proposed plan of campaign. * * * *

"On the 26th of October I learned that Hood's whole army had made its appearance about Decatur, Alabama, and at once caused a strong reconnoissance to be made down the Coosa to near Gadsden, which revealed the truth that the enemy was gone, except a small force of cavalry, commanded by

General Wheeler, which had been left to watch us. I then finally resolved on my future course, which was to leave Hood to be encountered by General Thomas, while I should carry into full effect the long-contemplated project of marching for the sea-coast, and thence to operate toward Richmond. But it was all-important to me and to our cause that General Thomas should have an ample force, equal to any and every emergency.

"He then had at Nashville about eight or ten thousand new troops, and as many more civil employés of the quartermaster's department, which were not suited for the field, but would be most useful in manning the excellent forts that already covered Nashville. At Chattanooga he had General Steedman's division, about five thousand men, besides garrisons for Chattanooga, Bridgeport, and Stevenson; at Murfreesboro he also had General Rousseau's division, which was full five thousand strong, independent of the necessary garrisons for the railroad. At Decatur and Huntsville, Alabama, was the infantry division of General R. S. Granger, estimated at four thousand, and near Florence, Alabama, watching the crossings of the Tennessee, were General Edward Hatch's division of cavalry, four thousand; General Croxton's brigade, twenty five hundred, and Colonel Capron's brigade, twelve hundred. Besides which General J. H. Wilson had collected in Nashville about ten thousand dismounted cavalry, for which he was rapidly collecting the necessary horses for a remount. All these aggregated about forty-five thousand men.

"General A. J. Smith at that time was in Missouri with the two divisions of the Sixteenth Corps which had been diverted to that quarter to assist General Rosecrans in driving the rebel General Price out of Missouri. This object had been accomplished, and these troops, numbering from eight to ten thousand, had been ordered to Nashville. To these I proposed at first to add only the Fourth Corps (General Stanley), fifteen thousand, and that corps was ordered from Gaylesville to march to Chattanooga and thence to report for orders to General Thomas; but subsequently, on the 30th of October, at Rome, Georgia, learning from General Thomas that the new troops promised by General Grant were coming forward very slowly, I concluded to further reënforce him by General Schofield's corps (Twenty-third), twelve thousand, which corps accordingly marched for Resaca, and there took the cars for Chattanooga. I then knew that General Thomas would have an ample force with which to encounter General Hood any where in the open field, besides garrisons to secure the railroad to his rear, and as far forward as Chattanooga. * * * *

"On the 1st of November I telegraphed very fully to General Grant [General Sherman does not give this dispatch], and on the 2d of November received (at Rome) this dispatch:

"'City Point, *November* 1, 1864, 6 P. M.

"'*Major-General* Sherman.

"'Do you not think it advisable, now that Hood has gone so far north, to entirely ruin him before starting on your proposed campaign? With Hood's army destroyed you can go where you please with impunity. I believed, and still believe, if you had started south while Hood was in the neighborhood of you, he would have been forced to go after you. Now that he is far away he might look upon the chase as useless, and he will go in one direction while you are pushing in the other. If you can see a chance of destroying Hood's army, attend to that first and make your other move secondary.

"' U. S. GRANT, *Lieutenant-General.*'

"My answer is dated:

"' ROME, GA., *November* 2, 1864.

"' *General* GRANT.

"' Your dispatch is received. If I could hope to overhaul Hood I would turn against him with my whole force; then he would retreat to the south-west, drawing me as a decoy away from Georgia, which is his chief object. If he ventures north of the Tennessee River, I may turn in that direction and endeavor to get below him on his line of retreat; but, thus far, he has not gone above the Tennessee River. General Thomas will have a force strong enough to prevent his reaching any country in which we have an interest, and he has orders, if Hood turns to follow me, to push for Selma, Alabama. No single army can catch Hood, and I am convinced the best results will follow from our defeating Jeff. Davis' cherished plan of making me leave Georgia by maneuvering.

"' Thus far I have confined my efforts to thwart this plan, and have reduced baggage so that I can pick up and start in any direction; but I regard the pursuit of Hood as useless. Still, if he attempts to invade Middle Tennessee, I will hold Decatur, and be prepared to move in that direction; but, unless I let go of Atlanta, my force will not be equal to his.'

"From that place, on the same day (November 2), [I] again telegraphed to General Grant:

"'If I turn back the whole effect of my campaign will be lost. By my movements I have thrown Beauregard (Hood) well to the west, and Thomas will have ample time and sufficient troops to hold him until the reënforce-ments from Missouri reach him. We have now ample supplies at Chattanooga and Atlanta, and can stand a month's interruption to our communications. I do not believe the Confederate army can reach our railroad lines, except by cavalry raids, and Wilson will have cavalry enough to checkmate them. I am clearly of opinion that the best results will follow my contemplated movement through Georgia.'

"That same day I received, in answer to the Rome dispatch, the following:

"' CITY POINT, VA., *November* 2, 1864, 11:30 A. M.

"' *To Major-General* SHERMAN.

"' Your dispatch of 9 A. M. yesterday is just received. I dispatched you the same date, advising that Hood's army, now that it had worked so far north, ought to be looked upon now as the object. With the force, however, you have left with General Thomas, he must be able to take care of Hood and destroy him. I do not see that you can withdraw from where you are to follow Hood without giving up all we have gained in territory. I say, then, go on as you propose. U. S. GRANT, *Lieutenant-General.*'

"This was the first time that General Grant assented to the March to the Sea, and, although many of his warm friends and admirers insist that he was the author and projector of that march, and that I simply executed his plans, General Grant has never, in my opinion, thought so or said so. The truth is fully given in an original letter of President Lincoln, which I received at Savannah, Georgia, and have at this instant before me, every word of which is in his own familiar handwriting. It is dated:

"'WASHINGTON, D. C., *December* 26, 1864.
* * * * "'When you were about leaving Atlanta for the Atlantic coast, I was anxious, if not fearful; but, feeling that you were the better judge, and remembering 'nothing risked, nothing gained,' I did not interfere. Now, the undertaking being a success, the honor is all yours; for I believe none of us went further than to acquiesce; and, taking the work of General Thomas into account, as it should be taken, it is indeed a great success. * * * *   A. LINCOLN.'"

Following this, in General Sherman's narrative, is the extract from page 167, given in the opening of this letter. A few brief extracts will close the account:

"On the 6th of November, at Kingston, I wrote and telegraphed to General Grant [General Sherman does not give these papers] reviewing the whole situation, gave him my full plan of action, stated that I was ready to march as soon as the election was over, and appointed November 10th as the day for starting. On the 8th I received this dispatch:

"'CITY POINT, VA., *November* 7, 1864, 10:30 P. M.
"'*Major-General* SHERMAN.

"'Your dispatch of this evening received. I see no present reason for changing your plan. Should any arise, you will see it, or if I do I will inform you. I think every thing here is favorable now. Great good fortune attend you! I believe you will be eminently successful, and at worst can only make a march less fruitful of results than hoped for.
"'U. S. GRANT, *Lieutenant-General.*'

"On the 10th of November the movement may be said to have fairly begun."

The above is a full and fair summary of the account in the Memoirs of the discussion attending Sherman's starting for

Savannah. It is in brief an extended argument to show that General Sherman planned the March to the Sea, and that General Grant and the authorities at Washington opposed his plan for several weeks, but finally gave a reluctant consent to its execution. This view has been impressed upon the country ever since the close of the war.

It is doubtful whether a more skillful misuse of official records has ever before been made to uphold an erroneous history of a military movement, and this will now be made to appear.

The question under discussion between the parties named was *not* whether General Sherman should make a campaign to the sea, but whether he should begin it by abandoning Atlanta and the line of the railroad, and especially *before* he destroyed Hood's army. A campaign to the sea to cut the Confederacy in two, was decided upon by General Grant during the previous January, when he was in command at Nashville, and eight months before the time when General Sherman claims to have had such a move in his "mind's eye." General Thomas, General Halleck, and General Sherman were each notified at that time of this plan of General Grant.

The first idea of the latter, as expressed in January, 1864, was to march through to Mobile, holding Atlanta and Montgomery as intermediate points, but the Union forces having occupied Mobile Bay on the 23d of August, just before the capture of Atlanta, General Grant, immediately after the fall of the latter place, telegraphed General Sherman that, as our forces had now secured the control of Mobile, he thought Sherman had better move on Augusta as soon as his men were rested, while Canby acted on Savannah. The following letters and telegrams are sufficiently explicit upon these points:

HEADQUARTERS MILITARY DIVISION OF THE MISSISSIPPI,
NASHVILLE, TENN., *January* 15, 1864.
[Confidential.]

Major-General HALLECK, *Washington.*

* * * * I look upon the next line for me to secure, to be that from Chattanooga to Mobile, Montgomery and Atlanta being the important intermediate points. To do this, large supplies must be secured on the Tennessee River, so as to be independent of the railroad from here to the Tennessee for a considerable length of time. Mobile would be a second base. The destruction which Sherman will do the roads around Meridian will be of material importance to us in preventing the enemy from drawing supplies and in clearing that section of all large bodies of rebel troops. I do not look upon any points except Mobile in the south and the Tennessee River in the north as presenting practical starting points from which to operate against Atlanta and Montgomery. They are objectionable as starting points to be all under one command, from the fact that the time it will take to communicate from one to the other will be so great. But, Sherman or McPherson, one of whom would be entrusted with the distant command, are officers of such experience and reliability, that all objections on that score, except that of enabling the two armies to act as an unit, would be removed. * * *

The same objection will exist probably not to so great an extent, however, if the movement is made in more than one column. This will have to be with an army of the size we will be obliged to use.

Heretofore I have refrained from suggesting what might be done in other commands than my own, in coöperation with it, or even to think much over the matter. But, as you have kindly asked me in your letter of the 8th of January, only just received, for an interchange of views on our present situation, I will write you again in a day or two, going outside of my own operations. U. S. GRANT, *Major-General.*

Afterward, when General Grant was made Lieutenant-General and ordered East, turning over his command at Nashville to General Sherman, he sent the latter a copy of the above letter for his guidance.

Four days after thus unfolding his plan for the Atanta and Gulf campaign to General Halleck, and while General Sherman was on the Mississippi preparing his Meridian campaign, General Thomas, who was then in command at Chattanooga, was made acquainted with General Grant's design by the following letter:

HEADQUARTERS MILITARY DIVISION OF THE MISSISSIPPI,
NASHVILLE, *January* 19, 1864.

Major-General GEORGE H. THOMAS, *Chattanooga.*

Owing to the presence of Longstreet in East Tennessee it will be impossible to attempt any movement from your present position while he remains.

The great number of veterans now absent and yet to be furloughed will be another difficulty in the way of any movement this Winter. Sherman, however, will be able to collect about twenty thousand men from that part of his command now along the Mississippi River available for a movement eastward from Vicksburg. He expects to have these ready to start about the 24th inst. He will proceed eastward as far as Meridan, at least, and will thoroughly destroy the roads east and south from there, and, if possible, will throw troops as far east as Selma; or if he finds Mobile so far unguarded as to make his force sufficient for the enterprise, will go there. To coöperate with this movement, you want to keep up appearances of preparation of an advance from Chattanooga. It may be necessary even to move a column as far as Lafayette.

The time for the advance, however, would not be before the 30th inst., or when you might learn the enemy were contemplating an attack. Logan will also be instructed to move, at the same time, what force he can from Bellefontaine toward Rome. We will want to be ready at the earliest possible moment in the Spring for the advance. I look upon the line for this army to secure in the next campaign to be that from Chattanooga to Mobile, Atlanta and Montgomery being the important intermediate points.

I look upon the Tennessee River and Mobile as being the most practicable points from which to start, and to hold as bases of supplies if the line is secured. I have so written to the General-in-Chief, only giving my views more fully, and shall write him to-day, giving my views of the coöperation we should have from the Eastern armies.

I shall recommend that no attempt be made toward Richmond by any of the routes heretofore operated upon, but that a moving force of sixty thousand men be thrown into Newbern or Suffolk, favoring the latter place; and move out, destroying the road as far toward Richmond as possible. Then move toward Raleigh as rapidly as possible, hold that point, and open communication with Newbern, even Wilmington. From Raleigh the enemy's most important line would be so threatened as to force them to keep on it a guard that would reduce their armies in the field much below our own. Before any part of this programme can be carried out, Longstreet must be driven from East Tennessee.

To do this it may be necessary to send more force from your command.

I write this to give you an idea of what I propose, and at the same time to hear such suggestions as you may have to propose.

U. S. GRANT, *Major-General.*

By the last of February, General Sherman having been meantime in the depths of his raid to Meridian, the preparations for the campaign thus marked out by General Grant had progressed so far that General Thomas was sending in estimates of the number of troops needed to guard the roads and bridges from Nashville south, both by way of Decatur and of Stevenson, on to Chattanooga, and south to

Atlanta. This appears clearly enough from the following telegram:

[By telegraph from Chattanooga, February 28, 1864.]
Major-General GRANT, *Nashville.*

General Butterfield, by my direction, has recently examined the line between here and Nashville, and reports that he thinks six thousand men will be sufficient to guard that line, two regiments of which force should be cavalry.

From what I know of the road between Nashville and Decatur, two thousand infantry and two thousand cavalry will be sufficient to protect that line. One thousand infantry will be sufficient to protect the line from Athens to Stevenson. Probably both lines of communication can be guarded by six thousand infantry and two thousand cavalry, a great portion of which should be made up from the local militia of Tennessee, or troops organized especially for the preservation of order in the State.

I believe if I can commence the campaign with the Fourteenth and Fourth Corps in front, with Howard's corps in reserve, that I can move along the line of the railroad and overcome all opposition as far, at least, as Atlanta. I should want a strong division of cavalry in advance. As soon as Captain Merrill returns from his reconnoissance along the railroad lines, I can give you a definite estimate of the number of troops required to guard the bridges along the road. GEO. H. THOMAS, *Major-General U. S. Volunteers.*

General Grant having been made Lieutenant General, and ordered to Washington, summoned General Sherman, who had returned from Meridian, to Nashville, which latter point he reached on the 17th of March, 1864. On that day he was assigned to the command of the Military Division of the Mississippi, and immediately afterward left with General Grant, accompanying the latter, then on his way to Washington, as far as the Burnet House, in Cincinnati, where about the 20th of March, a further consultation was held in regard to the forthcoming campaign.

Immediately upon arriving at his headquarters in the East, General Grant notified Halleck of the orders he had given Banks for a move on Mobile, to coöperate with Sherman, as is indicated in the following extract:

HEADQUARTERS IN THE FIELD,
CULPEPPER, VA., 4 P. M., *March* 25, 1864.
Major-General H. W. HALLECK, *Chief of Staff.*

I sent a letter to General Banks before leaving Nashville, directing him to finish his present expedition and assemble all his available force at New Orleans as soon as possible, and prepare to receive orders for the taking of Mobile.

If Shreveport is carried, about eight thousand (8,000) troops can be spared from Steele and Rosecrans to join Banks, and, if necessary, to insure success against Mobile, they can be taken from Sherman. * * * *

U. S. GRANT, *Lieutenant-General.*

The letter to General Banks thus referred to, coupled with further instructions to the same end, was published at length in General Grant's final report dated July 22, 1865:

Major-General N. P. Banks, then on an expedition up the Red River against Shreveport, Louisiana, (which had been organized previous to my appointment to command), was notified by me on the 15th of March, of the importance it was that Shreveport should be taken at the earliest possible day, and that if he found that the taking of it would occupy from ten to fifteen days more time than General Sherman had given his troops to be absent from their command, he would send them back at the time specified by General Sherman, even if it led to the abandonment of the main object of the Red River expedition, for this force was necessary to movements east of the Mississippi; that should his expedition prove successful, he would hold Shreveport and the Red River with such force as he might deem necessary, and return the balance of his troops to the neighborhood of New Orleans, commencing no move for the further acquisition of territory, unless it was to make that then held by him more easily held; that it might be a part of the Spring campaign to move against Mobile; that it certainly would be, if troops enough could be obtained to make it without embarrassing other movements; that New Orleans would be the point of departure for such an expedition; also, that I had directed General Steele to make a real move from Arkansas as suggested by him (General Banks), instead of a demonstration, as Steele thought advisable. On the 31st of March, in addition to the foregoing notification and directions, he was instructed as follows:

1st. If successful in your expedition against Shreveport, that you turn over the defense of the Red River to General Steele and the navy.

2d. That you abandon Texas entirely, with the exception of your hold upon the Rio Grande. This can be held with four thousand men, if they will turn their attention immediately to fortifying their positions. At least one-half of the force required for this service might be taken from the colored troops.

3d. By properly fortifying on the Mississippi River, the force to guard it from Port Hudson to New Orleans can be reduced to ten thousand men, if not to a less number. Six thousand more would then hold all the rest of the territory necessary to hold until active operations can again be resumed west of the river. According to your last return, this would give you a force of over thirty thousand effective men with which to move against Mobile. To this I expect to add five thousand men from Missouri. If, however, you think the force here stated too small to hold the territory regarded as necessary to hold possession of, I would say concentrate at least twenty-five thousand men of your present command for operations against Mobile. With these and such additions as I can give you from elsewhere, lose no time in making a demonstration, to be followed by an attack upon Mobile. Two or more iron-clads will be ordered to report to Admiral Farragut. This gives him a strong naval fleet with which to coöperate.

You can make your own arrangements with the Admiral for his coöperation, and select your own line of approach.

My own idea of the matter is, that Pascagaula should be your base; but, from your long service in the Gulf Department, you will know best about the matter. It is intended that your movements shall be coöperative with movements elsewhere, and you can not now start too soon. All I would now add is, that you commence the concentration of your forces at once. Preserve a profound secresy of what you intend doing, and start at the earliest possible moment. U. S. GRANT, *Lieutenat-General*.

Major-General N. P. Banks.

In addition to sending General Sherman a copy of the letter to Halleck, dated Nashville, January 15th, General Grant, a few days after sending the above letter to General Banks, again wrote the outlines of his plans to General Sherman, as will be seen by the letters which follow:

HEADQUARTERS ARMIES OF THE UNITED STATES, }
WASHINGTON, D. C., *April* 4, 1864. }

Major-General W. T. SHERMAN, *Commanding Military Division of the Mississippi.*

GENERAL: It is my design, if the enemy keep quiet and allow me to take the initiative in the Spring campaign, to work all parts of the army together, and somewhat towards a common center. For your information I now write you my programme as at present determined upon.

I have sent orders to Banks by private messenger to finish up his present expedition against Shreveport with all dispatch; to turn over the defense of the Red River to General Steele and the navy, and return your troops to you and his own to New Orleans; to abandon all of Texas except the Rio Grande, and to hold that with not to exceed four thousand men; to reduce the number of troops on the Mississippi to the lowest number necessary to hold it, and to collect from his command not less than twenty-five thousand (25,000) men. To this I will add five thousand (5,000) from Missouri. With this force he is to commence operations against Mobile as soon as he can. It will be impossible for him to commence too early.

Gilmore joins Butler with ten thousand (10,000) men, and the two operate against Richmond from the south side of James River. This will give Butler thirty three thousand (33,000) men to operate with; General W. F. Smith commanding the right wing of his forces, and Gilmore the left wing. I will stay with the Army of the Potomac, increased by Burnside's corps of not less than twenty-five thousand (25,000) effective men, and operate directly against Lee's army wherever it may be found.

Sigel collects all his available force in two columns—one, under Ord and Averill, to start from Beverly, Virginia; and the other, under Crooke, to start from Charleston, on the Kanawha, to move against the Virginia & Tennessee Railroad. Crooke will have all cavalry, and will endeavor to get in about Saltville and move east from there to join Ord. His force will be all cavalry, while Ord will have from ten to twelve thousand men of all arms.

You I propose to move against Johnston's army, to break it up, and to get into the interior of the enemy's country as far as you can, inflicting all the damage you can against their war resources.

I do not propose to lay down for you a plan of campaign, but simply to lay down the work it is desirable to have done, and leave you free to execute in your own way. Submit to me, however, as early as you can, your plan of operations.

As stated Banks is ordered to commence operations as soon as he can. Gilmore is ordered to report at Fortress Monroe by the 18th inst., or as soon thereafter as practicable. Sigel is concentrating now. None will move from their places of rendezvous until I direct except Banks. I want to be ready to move by the 25th inst. if possible; but all I can now direct is that you get ready as soon as possible. I know you will have difficulties to encounter getting through the mountains to where supplies are abundant, but I believe you will accomplish it.

From the expedition from the Department of West Virginia I do not calculate on very great results, but it is the only way I can take troops from there. With the long line of railroad Sigel has to protect he can spare no troops except to move directly to his front. In this way he must get through to inflict great damage on the enemy, or the enemy must detach from one of his armies a large force to prevent it. In other words, if Sigel can't skin himself, he can hold a leg whilst some one else skins.

I am, General, very respectfully, your obedient servant,

U. S. GRANT, *Lieutenant-General.*

General Grant had assumed command of all the armies on the 17th of March, and before the month closed matured his general plans for the Spring campaign and sent to all army commanders a map, which he thus describes in his final report of operations:

"The accompanying map, a copy of which was sent to General Sherman and other comanders in March, 1864, shows by red lines the territory occupied by us at the beginning of the rebellion and at the opening of the campaign of 1864, while those in blue are the lines which it was proposed to occupy."

General Sherman thus acknowledges its receipt:

HEADQUARTERS MILITARY DIVISION OF THE MISSISSIPPI,
NASHVILLE, TENN., *April 5, 1864.*

Colonel C. B. COMSTOCK, *General* GRANT'S *Staff, Washington, D. C.*

DEAR COLONEL: Your letter of March 26th came to me on the 2d inst., and the mail brought me the map yesterday. The parcel had evidently been opened and the postmaster had marked some additional postage on it. I will cause inquiries to be made lest the map has been seen by some eye intelligent enough to read the meaning of the blue and red lines. We can not be too careful in these matters.

That map to me contains more information and ideas than a volume of printed matter. Keep your retained copies with infinite care, and if you have occasion to send out to other commanders any more I would advise a special courier. From that map I see *all*, and glad am I that there are minds now at Washington able to devise; and for my part, if we can keep our counsels, I believe I have the men and ability to march square up to the position assigned me, and to hold it. Of course, it will cost us many a hard day, but I believe in fighting in a double sense—first, to gain physical results, and next, to inspire respect on which to build up our nation's power.

Of course, General Grant will not have time to give me the details of movements East, and the *times*. Concurrent action is the thing. It would be wise if the General, through you or some educated officer, should give me timely notice of all contemplated movements, with all details that can be foreseen. I now know the results aimed at, I know my base and have a pretty good idea of my lines of operation. No time shall be lost in putting my forces in mobile condition, so that all I ask is notice of time, that all over the grand theater of war there shall be simultaneous action. We saw the beauty of time in the battle of Chattanooga, and there is no reason why the same harmony of action should not pervade a continent.

I am well pleased with Captain Poe, and would not object to half a dozen thoroughly educated young engineer officers.

I am, with respect, your friend,

W. T. SHERMAN, *Major-General commanding.*

In reply to further letters from General Grant, setting forth his plans, Sherman wrote:

HEADQUARTERS MILITARY DIVISION OF THE MISSISSIPPI,
NASHVILLE, TENN., *April 10, 1864.*

Lieutenant-General U. S. GRANT, *Commander-in-Chief, Washington, D. C.*

DEAR GENERAL: Your two letters of April 4 are now before me, and afford me infinite satisfaction. That we are now all to act on a common plan, converging on a common center, looks like enlightened war.

Like yourself, you take the biggest load, and from me you shall have thorough and hearty coöperation. I will not let side issues draw me off from your main plans in which I am to knock Joe Johnston, and do as much damage to the resources of the enemy as possible. I have heretofore written to General Rawlins and Colonel Comstock, of your staff, somewhat of the method in which I propose to act. I have seen all my army, corps, and division commanders, and signified only to the former, viz.: Schofield, Thomas, and McPherson, our general plans, which I inferred from the purport of our conversations here and at Cincinnati. * * * *

Should Johnston fall behind Chattahoochee, I would feign to the right, but pass to the left and act on Atlanta or its eastern communications according to developed facts.

This is about as far ahead as I feel disposed to look, but I would ever bear in mind that Johnston is at all times to be kept so busy that he can not in any event send any part of his command against you or Banks.

If Banks can at the same time carry Mobile and open up the Alabama River, he will in a measure solve the most difficult part of my problem—*provisions*. But in that I must venture. Georgia has a million of inhabitants. If they can live we should not starve. If the enemy interrupt my communications I will be absolved from all obligations to subsist on our own resources, but will feel perfectly justified in taking whatever and whenever I can find.

I will inspire my command if successful, with my feelings that beef and salt are all that is absolutely necessary to life, and parched corn fed General Jackson's army once on that very ground.

As ever, your friend and servant,

W. T. SHERMAN, *Major-General*.

Under date of Nashville, April 16th, 1864, General Sherman wrote General McPherson as follows:

"I take it for granted that, unless Banks gets out of Red River and attacks Mobile (which is a material part of General Grant's plan), we will have to fight Polk's army as well as Johnston's."

Mobile Bay having been captured a few weeks before the fall of Atlanta, General Grant, a few days after General Sherman had occupied the latter place, suggested the following modification of his plan:

CITY POINT, VA., *September* 10, 1864.

Major-General SHERMAN:

As soon as your men are properly rested, and preparations can be made, it is desirable that another campaign should be commenced.

We want to keep the enemy continually pressed to the end of the war. If we give him no peace while the war lasts, the end can not be far distant. Now that we have all of Mobile Bay that is valuable, I do not know but it will be the best move for Major-General Canby's troops to act upon Savannah, while you move on Augusta. I should like to hear from you, however, on this matter. U. S. GRANT, *Lieutenant-General.*

To the above suggestion Sherman replied that it would risk his whole army to move as suggested by Grant, unless the latter could capture the Savannah River up to Augusta, or the Chattahoochee up to Columbus. The following is this reply, dated September 10, 8 P. M.:

General GRANT.

I have your dispatch of to-day. My command need some rest and pay. Our roads are also broken back near Nashville, and Wheeler is not yet disposed of. Still I am perfectly alive to the importance of pushing our advantage to the utmost. I do not think we can afford to operate further, dependent on the railroad. It takes so many men to guard it, and even then it is nightly broken by the enemy's cavalry that swarms about us. Macon is distant one hundred and three miles and Augusta one hundred and seventy-five miles. If I could be sure of finding provisions and ammunition at Augusta or Columbus, Georgia, I can march to Milledgeville and compel Hood to give up Augusta or Macon, and could then turn on the other. The country will afford forage and many supplies, but not enough in any one place to admit of a delay. In scattering for forage we have a great many men picked up by the enemy's cavalry.

If you can manage to take the Savannah River as high as Augusta, or the Chattahoochee as far up as Columbus, I can sweep the whole State of Georgia, otherwise I would risk our whole army by going too far from Atlanta.

W. T. SHERMAN, *Major-General.*

In reply to this telegram holding that there would be great risk in moving far beyond Atlanta, Grant wrote at length, under date of September 12th, stating his own plans for movements East, and telling Sherman that he plainly saw the difficulties in supplying his army, except when it should be constantly moving beyond. The following extract is sufficient to show its bearing upon the question now under discussion:

"What you are to do with the forces at your command, I do not exactly see. The difficulties of supplying your army, except when they are constantly moving beyond where you are, I plainly see. If it had not been for Price's movement, Canby could have sent twelve thousand more men to Mobile. From your command on the Mississippi an equal number could have been taken. With these forces, my idea would have been to divide them, sending one-half to Mobile and the other half to Savannah. You could then move as proposed in your telegram, so as to threaten Macon and Augusta equally. Whichever one should be abandoned by the enemy you could take and open up a new base of supplies." * * * *

General Sherman's letter, in reply to the above, was dated September 20th, and contains these extracts:

"Now that Mobile is shut out to the commerce of our enemy, it calls for no further effort on our part, unless the capture of the city can be followed by the occupation of the Alabama River and the railroad to Columbus, Georgia, when that place would be a magnificent auxiliary to my further progress into Georgia. * * * *

"If successful, I suppose that Fort Caswell will be occupied, and the fleet at once sent to the Savannah River. Then the reduction of that city is the next question. It once in our possession, and the river open to us, I would not hesitate to cross the State of Georgia with sixty thousand men, hauling some stores and depending on the country for the balance. Where a million of people find subsistence, my army won't starve. * * * *

"I will, therefore, give it as my opinion that your army and Canby's should be reënforced to the maximum; that, after you get Wilmington, you should strike for Savannah and its river; that General Canby should hold the Mississippi River, and send a force to take Columbus, Georgia, either by way of the Alabama or Appalachicola River; that I should keep Hood employed, and put my army in fine order for a march on Augusta, Columbia, and Charleston, and start as soon as Wilmington is sealed to commerce, and the city of Savannah is in our possession. * * * *

"If you will secure Wilmington and the city of Savannah from your center, and let General Canby have command over the Mississippi River and the country west of it, I will send a force to the Alabama and Appalachicola, provided you give me one hundred thousand of the drafted men to fill up my old regiments; and if you will fix a day to be in Savannah I will insure our possession of Macon and a point on the river below Augusta." * * *

This last is sufficiently explicit as to the conditions upon which General Sherman was willing to undertake a march to the sea.

On the 4th of October, while the subject of Sherman's further movement from Atlanta was under consideration, and three weeks before the time he now claims in his Memoirs that he had fully made up his mind in regard to the march to Savannah, General Grant wrote the following letter to General Halleck, both in regard to the nature of the original plan and the modifications suggested by the success in Mobile Bay:

HEADQUARTERS ARMIES OF THE UNITED STATES,
CITY POINT, VA., October 4, 1864.

Major-General HALLECK, *Chief of Staff of the Army, Washington, D. C.*

GENERAL: Your letter of the 2d inst., in relation to the movements of the Western armies and the preparations ordered by the staff officers of General Canby, is received. When this campaign was commenced nothing else was in contemplation but that Sherman, after capturing Atlanta, should connect with Canby at Mobile. Drawing the Nineteenth Corps, however, from Canby, and the movements of Kirby Smith demanding the presence of all of Canby's surplus forces in another direction, has made it impossible to carry out the plan as early as was contemplated. Any considerable force to coöperate with Sherman on the sea-coast must now be sent from here. The question is whether, under such circumstances, Augusta and Savannah would not be a better line than Selma, Montgomery, and Mobile. I think Savannah might be taken by surprise with one corps from here and such troops as Foster could spare from the Department of the South. This is my view, but before giving positive orders I want to make a visit to Washington and consult a little on the subject. All Canby can do with his present force is to make demonstrations on Mobile and up the Appalachicola toward Columbus. He can not positively have the force to require the transportation your letters would indicate he has called for, or to consume the supplies. Either line indicated would cut off the supplies from the rich districts of Georgia, Alabama and Mississippi equally well. Whichever way Sherman moves he will undoubtedly encounter Hood's army, and in crossing to the sea-coast will sever the connection between Lee's army and this district of country. I wrote to Sherman on this subject, sending my letter by a staff officer. He is ready to attempt (and feels confident of his ability to succeed) to make his way to either the Savannah River or any of the navigable streams emptying into the Atlantic or Gulf, if he is only certain of finding a base open for him when he arrives. The supplies Canby was ordering, I presume, were intended for the use of Sherman's army. I do not deem it necessary to accumulate them in any great quantity until the base to which he is to make his way is secured.

Very respectfully your obedient servant,

U. S. GRANT, *Lieutenant-General.*

That General Sherman had heard nothing of the plan for the Spring campaign up to the time of his arrival in Nashville, about the 17th of March, 1864, is quite evident from the following extracts from one of his own letters:

HEADQUARTERS DEPARTMENT OF THE TENNESSEE,
MEMPHIS, *March 14th, 1864.*

Major-General McPHERSON, *commanding, etc., Vicksburg.*

DEAR GENERAL: * * * * I am summoned by General Grant to be in Nashville on the 17th, and it will keep me moving night and day to get there by that date. * * * *

I don't know, as yet, the grand strategy of the next campaign, but on arrival at Nashville I will soon catch the main points, and will advise you of them. * * * * I am truly your friend,

W. T. SHERMAN, *Major-General commanding.*

These various extracts from the records show conclusively that a campaign from Chattanooga through to the Gulf, originated with General Grant, and that he subsequently modified it on account of the control of Mobile having been secured before Atlanta was captured. It will now be made to appear that the discussion which took place between General Sherman and General Grant was *not* over the question whether a march to the sea should be made, but whether it should be undertaken before Hood's army was overthrown, this army having passed to General Sherman's rear. As soon as the last move of the enemy had developed itself, and Thomas had been sent back to shoulder the responsibility of taking care of him, General Sherman became strongly possessed with the idea of marching through to the sea without first destroying Hood. He saw no risk in leaving Atlanta, and no longer seemed to think it necessary for Grant to first take Savannah, and Canby to take Columbus. Any route through Georgia, in the absence of Hood, was, as General Sherman expressed it in a telegram to Grant (not given in the Memoirs), "all open, with no serious enemy to oppose at present."

Then the discussion between Sherman and Grant already alluded to began.

Finally, by underestimating Hood's forces, and largely

overestimating those proposed to be left with Thomas, Sherman obtained the desired permission, and when Grant had thus been made to believe that Thomas would have ample force to meet Hood in the field and destroy him, and not till then, did he allow Sherman to go.

The overestimates of Thomas' forces, and underestimates of Hood's were as follows:

November 1st Sherman telegraphed Grant (the dispatch not being given in the Memoirs), that Hood's force was thirty thousand infantry, and from seven to ten thousand cavalry, and that General Thomas would have (according to a summary of General Sherman's figures, as given in detail in this dispatch), from fifty-three to sixty thousand, beside a large force of cavalry—now stated in the Memoirs to have been about ten thousand—thus representing to General Grant that Hood's whole force was only from thirty-seven to forty thousand, while Thomas had from sixty-three to seventy thousand. In the same dispatch he informed Grant that he had retained only fifty thousand men for his March to the Sea, when, as the official returns now printed in his Memoirs (Vol. II, page 172), show, he retained over sixty-two thousand.

No wonder General Grant was finally persuaded to give up that part of his plan which, for its first step, involved the destruction of Hood.

General Sherman, in his book (Vol. II, page 162), as already quoted, now that he deems it necessary for history to vindicate his march away from the very enemy that for five months had so stoutly resisted his combined forces, thus allowing Hood to turn upon the fragments left for General Thomas to gather up, states the forces available to General Thomas for a fight at Nashville at from sixty-five to seventy-one thousand, beside seventeen thousand seven hundred cavalry, or a total force of from eighty-two thousand seven hundred to eighty-eight thousand seven hundred. This appears from a summary of his figures and not in direct terms.

The official returns of the forces actually available for the battle of Nashville, which returns were at General Sherman's service when he prepared the above figures, are as follows: Infantry, forty-one thousand eight hundred and fifteen; cavalry, ten thousand five hundred and ninety-six; artillery, three thousand and sixty-one; total, fifty-five thousand four hundred and seventy-two, or twenty-seven thousand two hundred and twenty-eight less than Sherman's lowest estimate.

A few extracts from General Thomas' report of his campaign will test all the above statements of Sherman:

"At this time I found myself confronted by the army which, under General J. E. Johnston, had so skillfully resisted the advance of the whole active army of the Military Division of the Mississippi, from Dalton to the Chattahoochee, reënforced by a well equipped and enthusiastic cavalry command of over twelve thousand (12,000), led by one of the boldest and most successful commanders in the rebel army. My information from all sources confirmed the reported strength of Hood's army to be from forty to forty-five thousand infantry, and from twelve to fifteen thousand cavalry. My effective force, at this time, consisted of the Fourth Corps, about twelve thousand (12,000), under Major-General D. S. Stanley; the Twenty-third Corps, about ten thousand (10,000), under Major-General J. M. Schofield; Hatch's division of cavalry, about four thousand (4,000); Croxton's brigade, twenty-five hundred (2,500), and Capron's brigade, of about twelve hundred (1,200). The balance of my force was distributed along the railroad, and posted at Murfreesboro, Stevenson, Bridgeport, Huntsville, Decatur, and Chattanooga, to keep open our communications, and hold the posts above named, if attacked, until they could be reënforced, as up to this time it was impossible to determine which course Hood would take—advance on Nashville, or turn toward Huntsville. Under the circumstances, it was manifestly best to act on the defensive until sufficiently reënforced to justify taking the offensive. * * * *

"It was therefore with considerable anxiety that we watched the forces at Florence to discover what course they would pursue with regard to General Sherman's movements, determining thereby whether the troops under my command, numbering less than half those under Hood, were to act on the defensive in Tennessee, or to take the offensive in Alabama. * * * * The possibility of Hood's forces following General Sherman was now at an end, and I quickly took measures to act on the defensive. Two divisions of infantry, under Major-General A. J. Smith, were reported on their way to join me from Missouri, which, with several one-year regiments then arriving in the Department, and detachments collected from points of minor importance, would swell my command when concentrated to an army nearly as large as that of the enemy. * * * *

"My only resource then was to retire slowly toward my reënforcements, delaying the enemy's progress as much as possible to gain time for reënforcements to arrive and concentrate. * * * * Since the departure of General Sherman about seven thousand (7,000) men belonging to his column had collected at Chattanooga, comprising convalescents returning to their commands and men returning from furlough.

"These men had been organized into brigades to be made available at such points as they might be needed. My command had also been reënforced by twenty (20) new one-year regiments, most of which, however, were absorbed in replacing old regiments whose term of service had expired."

The very dispatch which General Sherman quotes as Grant's assent to the march, shows that he gave it upon the ground that Thomas, with the force Sherman said he had left him, could destroy Hood. This telegram was in reply to one of November 1st, given just above, mis-stating Thomas' available force. After saying he had telegraphed Sherman on the same day that Hood's army should be looked upon as the "object," the dispatch continued:

"With the force, however, that you have left with General Thomas, he must be able to take care of Hood and destroy him. * * * * I say, then, go on as you propose."

General Sherman interprets the last clause of this order as if it read: "Go on and execute the March to the Sea, which you have originated," when, in fact, he should have interpreted it: "You propose to march without first destroying Hood. As Thomas can now take care of him, I say go."

There is an expression in the congratulatory order issued by General Sherman to his army, after reaching Savannah, which can not well be explained in accordance with his theory that he planned the March to the Sea. Speaking of Hood's movement to his rear as an attempt to decoy him out of Georgia, General Sherman in that order wrote:

"But we were not thus to be led away by him, and preferred to lead and control events ourselves. Generals Thomas and Schofield, commanding the departments to our rear, returned to their posts and prepared to decoy General Hood into their meshes, while we came on to complete the *original* journey." * * * *

When General Sherman wrote of our "original journey," he may have had in mind a letter he sent General Banks, then in Louisiana, dated Nashville, April 3, 1864. It contained the following paragraph:

> "All is well in this quarter, and I hope by the time you turn against Mobile our forces will again act toward the same end, though from distant points. General Grant, now having lawful control, will doubtless see that all minor objects are disregarded, and that all the armies act on a common plan."

Two weeks before this he had returned from the Cincinnati conference with General Grant, where the latter communicated to him the plan of the Atlanta campaign and the movement beyond to Mobile, as he had in the previous January made them known to Generals Halleck and Thomas. As will be seen these letters were written about a month before the opening of the Atlanta campaign, and over five months before the date claimed by General Sherman as the earliest time when he had the March to the Sea in his "mind's eye."

There are some singular and important omissions in General Sherman's story. On page 166, after quoting Grant's dispatch of November 2d, given above, he says: "This [November 2d] was the first time that General Grant assented to the March to the Sea."

And yet, on November 1st, as appears in a dispatch to General Grant, given in one of General Sherman's published reports, he said:

> "Hood's cavalry may do a good deal of damage, and I have sent Wilson back with all dismounted cavalry, retaining only about four thousand five hundred. This is the best I can do, and shall therefore, when I get to Atlanta the necessary stores, move south as soon as possible."

Was he going without the permission which he here says he did not receive until November 2d?

The fact is, however, that, notwithstanding the statement that Grant's dispatch of November 2d was his first assent to the March, he had really given such assent three weeks before, in the following answer to Sherman's telegram of October 11th, heretofore quoted:

        CITY POINT, VA., *October* 11, 1864, 11:30 P. M.

Major-General SHERMAN.

Your dispatch of to-day received. If you are satisfied the trip to the sea-coast can be made, holding the line of the Tennessee River firmly, you may make it, destroying all the railroad south of Dalton or Chattanooga, as you think best.   U. S. GRANT, *Lieutenant-General.*

In this permission also, the condition of holding Tennessee firmly against Hood is prominent.

The next day General Grant again telegraphed as follows:

        CITY POINT, *October* 12, 1864, 1 P. M.

General SHERMAN, *Kingston.*

On reflection I think better of your proposition. It will be much better to go south than to be forced to come north. You will, no doubt, clear the country where you go of railroad tracks and supplies.   *   *   *   *

      U. S. GRANT, *Lieutenant-General.*

General Sherman, on page 154, says he received no answer to his Kingston dispatch "at the time." The reason is obvious. It was dated 11:30 P. M. of the 11th, and the next day Sherman left for Rome. His telegraphic communications with Kingston and with Washington, however, remained perfect, and it is not likely that a dispatch from the Lieutenant-General, directing the march of an army through to the sea-coast, would be long delayed. If he had never received it in the field, however, he need not now have made the above mistake of three weeks in so important a date, since General Grant's reply of October 11th was printed in full in his final report of the operations of the armies.

On page 157 Sherman says: "So it is clear that at that date [October 17] neither General Grant nor General Thomas heartily favored my proposed plan of campaign." And yet the day before this he had telegraphed Halleck:

"I got the dispatch in cipher about providing me a place to come out on salt water, but the cipher is imperfect, and I can not make out whether

Savannah or Mobile be preferred; but I also want to know if you are willing that I should destroy Atlanta and the railroad."

And on this very date (October 17) he had received the following from General Grant:

"The moment I know you have started south, stores will be shipped to Hilton Head, where there are transports ready to take them to meet you at Savannah. In case you go south I would not propose holding any thing south of Chattanooga, certainly not south of Dalton. Destroy in such case all of military value in Atlanta."

As early as October 13th, two weeks before General Sherman claims that he finally decided on this march, General Grant had ordered coöperating forces to proceed to the coast below Savannah and move inland against the Gulf Railroad. This appears in the following from Halleck to Grant, dated Washington, October 22d:

"I had prepared instructions to General Canby to move all available forces in Mobile Bay and elsewhere to Brunswick and up the Savannah and Gulf Railroad, as directed by you on the 13th, but on learning that Sherman's operations were uncertain I withheld the order."

October 19th Sherman telegraphed Thomas:

* * * * "I propose with the Armies of Ohio, Tennessee, and two corps of this, to sally forth and make a hole in Georgia and Alabama that will be hard to mend. I will, probably, about November 1st, break up the railroads and bridges, destroy Atlanta, and make a break for Mobile, Savannah, or Charleston." * * * *

Under date of October 19, 1864, General Sherman wrote General Halleck as follows:

"I must have alternatives; else, being confined to one route, the enemy might so oppose, that delay and want would trouble me; but, having alternatives, I can take so eccentric a course that no general can guess my objective. Therefore, when you hear I am off, have lookouts at Morris Island, S. C., Ossabaw Sound, Ga., Pensacola and Mobile Bays. I will turn up somewhere, and, believe me, I can take Macon, Milledgeville, Augusta, and Savannah, Ga., and wind up with closing the neckband of Charleston so that they will ctarve out.

"This movement is not purely military or strategic, but it will illustrate the vulnerability of the South."

Colonel Bowman, in his "Sherman and his Campaigns," a work written in the interest of Sherman, commenting upon the above letter, says:

"General Grant promptly authorized the proposed movement, indicating, however, his preference for Savannah as the objective, and fixing Dalton as the northern limit for the destruction of the railway."

To this alternative letter Halleck replied, under date of October 31:

"The alternatives mentioned in your letter of October 19th will be prepared for by boats at Hilton Head and Pensacola, with means of transportation to any point where required."

Certain correspondence, which passed between General Sherman before Atlanta and General Canby before Mobile, has a forcible bearing upon the questions under consideration. It will be noticed that this correspondence began some weeks before the capture of Atlanta, and related to a move beyond upon Montgomery:

Major-General CANBY, *Mobile.*
NEAR ATLANTA, *August* 17, 1864.

Dispatch of the 6th received. * * * * If possible the Alabama River should be possessed by us in connection with my movement. I could easily open communication to Montgomery, but I doubt if you will have troops enough until the September draft. I can press on Atlanta good, but I do not want Kirby Smith here. * * * *
W. T. SHERMAN, *Major-General.*

NEW ORLEANS, *August* 27th. By way of CAIRO, *September 9th,*
Received at HEADQUARTERS, *September* 29, 1864.

Major-General SHERMAN.

* * * * I have a reserve of twelve thousand men up the river to watch Kirby Smith. I do not think he can cross in any force without being discovered in time to prevent it, but I can not use this force against Mobile and prevent a passage.

The route you suggested has been considered, and with twenty thousand men we could control the Alabama River from Mobile to Montgomery. *

* * * I will keep the enemy about Mobile uneasy, and will act against the city and river the moment I can gather a sufficient force.

Ed. R. Canby, *Major-General.*

Headquarters Military Division of the Mississippi. In the Field, Atlanta, Georgia, September 10, 1864.

General Canby, *New Orleans.*

Dispatch of the 27th received. I got to Atlanta by a couple of good moves. You succeeded at Fort Morgan sooner than I expected. We must have the Alabama River now, and also the Appalachicola at the old arsenal, and up to Columbus. My line is so long now that it is impossible to protect it against cavalry raids; but if we can get Montgomery and Columbus, Georgia, as bases in connection with Atlanta, we have Georgia and Alabama at our feet. You ought to have more men, and it is a burning shame that at this epoch we should need men, for the North is full of them.

They can raise a political convention any time of fifty to one hundred thousand men, and yet they pretend they can not give us what we want. But keep at it, and I only want to express my idea that I would not bother with the city of Mobile, which will simply absorb a garrison for you, but would use the Tensas channel and notify General Gardner, of the rebel army, to maintain good order, etc., in the now useless streets of Mobile.

I will be ready to sally forth again in October, but ought to have some assurance that, in case of necessity, I can swing into Appalachicola or Montgomery, and find friends.

W. T. Sherman, *Major-General commanding.*

By telegraph from New Orleans, 17th *September*, via Cairo, 24th.

Major-General Sherman.

Your dispatch of the 10th has just been received. The plans you suggested have been under consideration, and preparations are now in progress.

I think I can give you the assurance that you will find friends in Mobile, if the trouble in Arkansas River should be soon ended, how far east of that will depend upon the reënforcements that can be spared for this command?

Ed. R. Canby, *Major-General.*

Kingston, Georgia, *November* 7, 1864.

General Canby, *New Orleans.*

Beauregard has left Georgia altogether and shifted across to the neighborhood of Florence, Alabama, threatening to invade Tennessee. We are all ready for him there, and I have still an army with which to go on. If you hear I have destroyed Atlanta and marched south, be prepared with boats to send me supplies from Ponchartrain, and have the navy look out for my fires and rocket signals along the east side of Mobile Bay, as high up as Old Blakely.

W. T. Sherman, *Major-General.*

The last letter written by General Sherman to General Grant before cutting loose from Atlanta, was dated November 6th. It is referred to in the Memoirs, but not quoted. It contains the following significant passages:

"The only question in my mind is whether I ought not to have dogged him [Hood] far over into Mississippi, * * * * but then I thought that by so doing I would play into his hands by being drawn or decoyed too far away from our original line of advance."

And again, he argues for a movement on Pensacola and Mobile as follows:

"Admitting this reasoning to be good, that such a movement [to the sea] per se be right; still there may be reasons why one route would be better than another. There are three from Atlanta—south-east, south, and south-west—all open, with no serious enemy to oppose at present.

"*The first* would carry me across the only east and west railroad remaining to the Confederacy, which would be destroyed, and thereby the communications between the armies of Lee and Beauregard severed. Incidentally I might destroy the enemy's depots at Macon and Augusta, and reach the sea-shore at Charleston or Savannah, from either of which points I could reënforce our armies in Virginia.

"*The second* and easiest route would be due south, following substantially the valley of Flint River, which is very fertile and well supplied, and fetching up on the navigable waters of the Appalachicola, destroying *en route* the same railroad, taking up the prisoners of war still at Andersonville, and destroying about four hundred thousand (400,000) bales of cotton near Albany and Fort Gaines.

"This, however, would leave the army in a bad position for future movements.

"*The third*, down the Chattahoochee to Opelika and Montgomery, thence to Pensacola or Tensas Bayou, in communication with Fort Morgan.

"This latter route would enable me at once to coöperate with General Canby in the reduction of Mobile, and occupation of the line of the Alabama.

"In my judgment the first would have a material effect upon your campaign in Virginia; the second would be the safest of execution; but the third would more properly fall within the sphere of my own command, and have a direct bearing upon my own enemy, 'Beauregard.' If, therefore, I should start before I hear further from you, or before further developments turn my course, you may take it for granted that I have moved *via* Griffin to Barnesville; that I break up the road between Columbus and Macon *good*; and then, if I feign on Columbus, will move *via* Macon and Millen to Savannah; or, if I feign on Macon, you may take it for granted that I have shot off toward Opelika, Montgomery and Mobile Bay or Pensacola."

The following extracts from the final report of General Grant, dated Washington, July 22, 1865, bear pointedly upon the questions under consideration. In describing the combined movements ordered for the Spring of 1864, he says:

"General Sherman was instructed to move against Johnston's army, break it up, and to go into the interior of the enemy's country as far as he could, inflicting all the damage he could upon their war resources. If the enemy in his front showed signs of joining Lee, to follow him up to the full extent of his ability, while I would prevent the concentration of Lee upon him, if it was in the power of the Army of the Potomac to do so. More specific instructions were not given, for the reason that I had talked over with him the plans of the campaign, and was satisfied that he understood them and would execute them to the fullest extent possible."

And again:

"It was the original design to hold Atlanta, and by getting through to the coast, with a garrison left on the southern railroads, leading east and west through Georgia, to effectually sever the East from the West.

"In other words, cut the would-be Confederacy in two again, as it had been cut once by our gaining possession of the Mississippi River. General Sherman's plan virtually effected this object."

That part of Sherman's plan here referred to, is his proposition to march through Georgia without holding Atlanta.

The above citations from the official records, and chiefly from those in General Sherman's possession, are quite sufficient to show that the correct history of the March to the Sea is not given in the Memoirs.

There was this important difference between Grant's plan and Sherman's: Grant's contemplated a prior destruction of Hood's army. Sherman's was a march away from an enemy. This branch of the subject will be treated at length in a subsequent chapter.

The records thus far produced are sufficient to show that General Grant, while still in command at Nashville, and two months before his promotion as Lieutenant-General, had planned a movement from Chattanooga through to Mobile, and that he then had in mind a coöperation on the part of the Eastern armies. There are records to show, further, that in the preceding November he was contemplating a concert of action between these armies, and his idea was to secure a commander for the Army of the Potomac who would act in full accord with him. He settled upon W. F. Smith as that officer, and thus urged his promotion:

HEADQUARTERS MILITARY DIVISION OF THE MISSISSIPPI,
CHATTANOOGA, TENN., *November* 12, 1863.

Hon. E. M. STANTON, *Secretary of War.*

I would respectfully recommend that Brigadier-General W. F. Smith be placed first on the list for promotion to the rank of Major-General. He is possessed of one of the clearest heads in the army, is very practical and industrious. No man in the service is better qualified than he for our largest commands. I have the honor, etc.,

U. S. GRANT, *Major-General.*

HEADQUARTERS MILITARY DIVISION OF THE MISSISSIPPI,
CHATTANOOGA, TENNESSEE, *November* 30, 1863.

His Excellency, A. LINCOLN, *President of the United States.*

In a previous letter addressed to the Secretary of War, I recommended Brigadier-General W. F. Smith for promotion. Recent events have entirely satisfied me of his great capacity and merits, and I hasten to renew the recommendation and to urge it. The interests of the public service would be better subserved by this promotion than the interests of General Smith himself. My reason for writing this letter now is to ask that W. F. Smith's name be placed first on the list for promotion of all those previously recommended by me. I have the honor, etc.,

U. S. GRANT, *Major-General.*

His object in making these recommendations appears from further correspondence.

Early in December he wrote General Halleck expressing the opinion that East Tennessee and his immediate front were safe; that the roads were such that extensive movements in that latitude were impossible for either army, and so a small force could hold his lines while he should move on Mobile, and thus greatly advance the Spring operations. In this letter his intention of including Mobile in his plan of a movement in the Spring from Chattanooga, also appears. Omitting the description of the general situation, it is as follows:

CHATTANOOGA, *December* 7, 1863.
Major-General HALLECK, *Washington.*

* * * * I feel unwilling, or rather desirous to avoid keeping so large a force idle for many months. I take the liberty of suggesting a plan of campaign that I think will go far toward breaking down the rebellion before Spring. It will at least keep the enemy harassed, and prevent that reorganization which could be effected by Spring if left unimpeded.

I propose, with the concurrence of higher authority, to move by way of New Orleans and Pascagoula on Mobile. I would hope to secure that place, or its investment by the last of January. Should the enemy make an obstinate resistance at Mobile, I would fortify outside and leave a garrison sufficient to hold the garrison of the town, and with the balance of the army make a campaign into the interior of Alabama and possibly Georgia. The campaign of course would be suggested by the movements of the enemy. It seems to me this move would secure the entire States of Alabama and Mississippi, and a part of Georgia, or force Lee to abandon Virginia and North Carolina. Without his force the enemy have not got army enough to resist the army I can take.

I am General, your obedient servant,
U. S. GRANT, *Major-General.*

The Assistant Secretary of War having visited General Grant, and talked over the question of this campaign, returned to Washington and reported fully to the authorities.

General Halleck then telegraphed General Grant as follows:

WASHINGTON, *December* 21, 1863, 4:30 P. M.
Major-General U. S. GRANT.

As I understand from your dispatch of the 7th, and from conversation with Mr. Dana, you propose:

1. To expel the enemy from East Tennessee, and to provide against his return into that valley.
2. To either force the rebels further back into Georgia or to provide against their return by that line into Tennessee.
3. To clean out West Tennessee.
4. To move a force down the Mississippi and operate against Mobile.

The importance of these objects is considered to be in the order above stated. It is thought that the fourth should not be definitely determined upon till the other three are accomplished, or their accomplishment made reasonably certain. Moreover, circumstances may be such by the time that your spare forces reach Port Hudson or New Orleans as to require their services west of the Mississippi. If so, the latter part of the plan would be somewhat varied, or its execution delayed.

H. W. HALLECK, *General-in-Chief.*

The communication of the Assistant Secretary which presented the matter at greater length, shows that the question of putting General W. F. Smith in command of the Army of the Potomac had been thoroughly discussed, and Grant, the President, the Secretary of War, and General Halleck agreed that it would be better to select Smith than General Sherman:

WASHINGTON, *December* 21, 1863, 6 P. M.

Major-General U. S. GRANT, *Chattanooga.*

I have had detailed conversations with the President, the Secretary of War, and General Halleck, with respect to your project of a campaign in Alabama. It meets the full approval of them all in every respect, not only because it keeps your army active during the otherwise useless weather of the Winter, but because it appears to them well conceived and as certain of producing the desired effect as any plan can be. "If it succeed" said the Secretary of War, "Bragg's army become prisoners of war without our having the trouble of providing for them." You would be authorized to proceed immediately with its execution but for the anxiety which seems to exist respecting East Tennessee. If Longstreet were expelled from that country, you could star. for Mobile at once; I suppose General Halleck will communicate with you fully on this subject. I judge from my conversation with him that he does not understand clearly how an army, large enough to make Longstreet's dislodgment certain, can be supplied while operating against Rogersville and Bristol, and accordingly I presume that, first, as soon as it is settled that he must be left in that region, you will be allowed to proceed south with the main body of your forces, leaving, of course, a sufficient number of troops to observe Longstreet, and prevent his getting hold of Knoxville, Cumberland Gap, or any other controlling point now in our hands.

To my suggestion that the surest means of getting the rebels altogether out of East Tennessee is to be found in the Army of the Potomac; the reply is, that that is true, but from that army nothing is to be hoped under its present commander. This naturally led to your second proposition, namely, that either Sherman or W. F. Smith should be put in command of that army. To this the answer is such as to leave but little doubt in my mind that the second of these officers will be appointed to that post. Both the Secretary of War and General Halleck said to me that, as long as a fortnight before my arrival, they had come to the conclusion that when a change should be made,

General W. F. Smith would be the best person to try. Some doubts which they seemed to have respecting his disposition and personal character I think I was able to clear up. The Secretary of War has also directed me to inform him that he is to be promoted on the first vacancy. The President, the Secretary of War, and General Halleck, agree with you in thinking that it would be, on the whole, much better to select him than Sherman. As yet, however, nothing has been decided upon, and you will understand that I have somewhat exceeded my instructions from the Secretary of War in this communication, especially in the second branch of it, but it seems to me necessary that you should know all these particulars. C. A. DANA.

While all the records show that General Grant planned that Atlanta campaign which was finally executed, and that from its inception, it was in his mind a march to the sea, designed to divide the Confederacy; it is also true that this question of cutting through the territory of the rebels from the West, had been discussed at one or two prominent headquarters in the East, sometime before General Grant, in a different way from any suggested at these discussions, entered practically upon the work. Notes are in existence of a conversation at General McDowell's headquarters, on the day following the battle of Cedar Mountain in August, 1862, upon the policy of severing the Confederacy by an army operating from the West through Atlanta, a movement on Savannah and Charleston from the rear, and a march up the coast. These were General McDowell's ideas, though no definite combinations of troops were suggested for carrying them out.

Early in the following year, General Pope wrote Secretary Stanton presenting a very elaborate plan for an advance from Murfreesboro to Mobile, through Atlanta. It involved the immediate abandonment of Grant's move against Vicksburg, and the transfer of his army to Rosecrans' front, an advance by Burnside through Cumberland Gap, the occupation of Chattanooga with a permanent garrison of sixty thousand men, and a movement thence on Atlanta with a force at least one hundred and fifty thousand strong. At the same time he proposed that forty thousand men from the Eastern army should be thrown into Pensacola, and marched north on

Montgomery to meet an equal number to be sent from the one hundred and fifty thousand at Atlanta. The line thus taken was to be permanently held by sixty thousand at Chattanooga, one hundred thousand at Atlanta, sixty thousand at Montgomery, and ten thousand at Mobile and Pensacola. Such a division of the Confederacy, General Pope argued at length, would soon lead to its overthrow. This plan involved the abandonment of the attempt to open the Mississippi. It remained for General Grant, however, to achieve this most important river division of the Confederacy, and then turning eastward to divide it again by the move from Chattanooga. And this division, Sherman, under the direction of Grant, accomplished with his force of one hundred thousand, which furnished both his garrisons and his moving column.

So the records not only show that General Grant planned the March to the Sea which was finally executed, but also, that general plan of operations for the closing year of the war was his conception.

CHAPTER XII.

HARDEE'S ESCAPE FROM SAVANNAH.

GENERAL SHERMAN, having seen the enemy he had been fighting throughout the Spring and Summer well on his way toward the North, marched down to the sea at Savannah, and moved against a new enemy there.

Of the preparations, and the departure from Atlanta to the sea, General Sherman writes:

"It was surely a strange event—two hostile armies marching in opposite directions, each in the full belief that it was achieving a final and conclusive result in a great war." *   *   *   *

And again:

"Of course General Thomas saw that on him would likely fall the real blow, and was naturally anxious."

And the day of leaving Atlanta he thus records what he thought the general verdict would be:

"'There was a "devil-may-care" feeling pervading officers and men that made me feel the full load of responsibility, for success would be accepted as a matter of course, whereas, should we fail, this 'march' would be adjudged, the wild adventure of a crazy fool."

It will be well in the outset to look at the situation.

Sherman had marched off to the sea with over sixty-two thousand men. He had taken two of the strongest corps, the Fourteenth and the Twentieth, numbering over twenty-eight thousand men, from General Thomas' own army; had taken his efficient pontoon train, and dismounted General Wilson's cavalry to give Kilpatrick fresh horses. In short, every thing wanted in the shape of organized men, equipment, horses, and batteries, was taken from Thomas to fit out Sherman. Two small but organized and well-disciplined corps, numbering together twenty-two thousand men, were given Thomas. For the rest he had orders for two divisions of veteran troops to come from Missouri; he had bridge-guards distributed over four railroads, and small garrisons in a dozen towns. In Nashville he had quartermasters' employés to man the forts; and to meet Hood's twelve thousand well-equipped and enthusiastic cavalry he had seven thousand and General J. H. Wilson's dismounted men. To further strengthen him, some twenty new one-year regiments were arriving to replace veteran troops, whose terms had expired.

Hood's army, fully concentrated, confronted Thomas. The concentration of Thomas' army had only begun. A. J. Smith's veterans were still in Missouri. To meet Hood he had less than half Hood's force. To fall back slowly while he gathered his army from the immense territory over which the fragments which were finally to compose it were scattered, was, of course, his only chance of success. How well this object was accomplished, all the world knows. How Schofield gathered the troops in hand, reached Franklin and defeated Hood, will not be forgotten. The very day he fought there, Smith's veterans began to arrive at Nashville, and the next night Schofield and Smith had made the concentration complete at the latter place. Then came storms and sleet when Thomas would not risk his army, the threats to remove him, the order removing him, the clearing up of the storm, the melting of the ice which had prevented man or horse from moving, the great battle and his decisive victory. And Sherman, with the bulk of the organized army which Hood had so often checked upon the Atlanta campaign, had marched down to the sea, the roads before him, wherever he might choose, being, as he expressed it in a dispatch to Grant, "all open, with no serious enemy to oppose at present."

On the 10th of December Sherman, with sixty thousand men, had announced the investment of Savannah garrisoned by Hardee with a force supposed to be fifteen thousand. On the 17th he had demanded its surrender, and been refused on the ground that he had not invested the city, and that his guns could not even reach it.

On the 14th Thomas had successfully attacked Hood, and on the 15th had utterly defeated and routed him, and the War Department had telegraphed Thomas:

War Department, December 15, 1864.

Major-General Thomas, *Nashville.*

I rejoice in tendering to you and the gallant officers and soldiers of your command the thanks of this department for the brilliant achievements of this day, and hope that it is the harbinger of a decisive victory that will crown you and your army with honor, and do much toward closing the war. We shall give you a hundred guns to-morrow.

Edwin M. Stanton, Secretary of War.

On the 24th Mr. Stanton had notified Thomas of his nomination as a Major-General in the regular army for the "recent brilliant military operations" under his command, and expressed the opinion that "no one has more justly earned promotion by devoted, disinterested, and valuable services to his country."

On the 18th of December, in a letter to Sherman of warm congratulation over the success of the march to Savannah, General Grant added:

"My Dear General: * * * * If you capture the garrison of Savannah it certainly will compel Lee to detach from Richmond, or give us nearly the whole South. * * * * Congratulating you and the army again upon the splendid results of your campaign, the like of which is not read of in past history, I subscribe myself more than ever, if possible, your friend."

Eight days after, when the news arrived of the capture of Savannah and the escape of Hardee, it was guardedly acknowledged by Grant as follows, under date of December 26th:

"General: Your very interesting letter of the 22d inst., brought by Major Gray, of General Foster's staff, is just at hand. As the Major starts back at once, I can do no more at present than simply acknowledge its receipt. The capture of Savannah with all its immense stores must tell upon the people of the South. All well here."

Under the same date Secretary Stanton telegraphed Grant at City Point:

"I wish you a merry Christmas, if it is not too late, and thank you for the Savannah news.

"It is a sore disappointment that Hardee was able to get off his fifteen thousand from Sherman's sixty thousand. It looks like protracting the war while their armies continue to escape.

"I hope you will give immediate instructions to seize and hold the cotton. Thomas has been nominated for Major-General."

Of the approach to the coast, General Sherman writes:

"The weather was fine, the roads good, and every thing seemed to favor us Never do I recall a more agreeable sensation than the sight of our camps by night, lit up by the fires of fragrant pine knots. * * * * No enemy opposed us, and we could only occasionally hear the faint reverberation of a gun to our left rear, where we knew that General Kilpatrick was skirmishing with Wheeler's cavalry, which persistently followed him. But the infantry columns had met with no opposition whatever. * * *
* That night (December 8) we reached Pooler's Station, eight miles from Savannah, and during the next two days, December 9 and 10, the several corps reached the defenses of Savannah, * * * * thus completely investing the city."

This question of investing the city involves the one of responsibility for the escape of Hardee, and will bear a little attention.

On the 13th December General Sherman wrote Mr. Stanton, as quoted at page 201, Volume II:

"Before opening communication we had completely destroyed all railroads leading into Savannah and invested the city."

And on the 16th to General Grant, quoted on page 207:

"I had previously made you a hasty scrawl * * * * advising you that the army had reached the sea-coast * * * * investing closely the city of Savannah, and had made connection with the fleet. * * * * General Slocum occupies Argyle Island and the upper end of Hutchinson's Island and has a brigade on the South Carolina shore opposite, and is very urgent to pass one of his corps over to that shore. * * * * He [Hood] can draw nothing from South Carolina, save from a small corner down in the south-east, and that by a disused wagon road. I could easily get possession of this, but hardly deem it worth the risk of making a detachment, which would be in danger by its isolation from the main army." * * * *

In demanding the surrender of the city, on the 17th, he wrote Hardee:

"Also, I have for some days held and controlled every avenue by which the people and garrison of Savannah can be supplied, and I am, therefore, justified in demanding the surrender of the city of Savannah and its dependent forts; and shall wait a reasonable time for your answer before opening with heavy ordnance."

The same day Hardee, in refusing to surrender, thus gave him notice that he had not invested the city:

"Your statement that you have, for some days, held and controlled every avenue by which the people and garrison can be supplied, is incorrect. I am in free and constant communication with my department."

The effect of this last communication General Sherman thus relates (page 216):

"On the 18th of December, at my camp by the side of the plank road, eight miles back of Savannah, I received General Hardee's letter declining to surrender, when nothing remained but to assault. The ground was difficult, and as all former assaults had proved so bloody, I concluded to make one more effort to completely surround Savannah on all sides, so as further to excite Hardee's fears, and, in case of success, to capture the whole of his army. We had already completely invested the place on the north, west, and south; but there remained to the enemy, on the east, the use of the old dike or plank road leading into South Carolina, and I knew that Hardee would have a pontoon bridge across the river."

On the same day, December 18, he wrote General Grant in reference to this incredulousness of Hardee, as follows:

"In relation to Savannah, you will remark that General Hardee refers to his still being in communication with his department. This language he thought would deceive me, but I am confirmed in the belief that the route to which he refers (the Union plank road on the South Carolina shore) is inadequate to feed his army and the people of Savannah, and General Foster assures me that he has his force on that very road, near the head of Broad River, so that cars no longer run between Charleston and Savannah."

And yet, with this letter spread at length on the pages of his book, General Sherman goes on to say, following the last quotation preceding this letter to Grant:

"On examining my maps, I thought that the division of John P. Hatch, belonging to General Foster's command, might be moved from its then position at Broad River, by water, down to Bluffton, from which it could reach this plank road, fortify, and hold it—at some risk, of course, because Hardee could avail himself of his central position to fall on this detachment with his whole army."

That is to say, while writing to General Grant, after receiving Hardee's letter and before any further word from Foster, that the latter held this plank road, he thought, by looking at his maps, that one of Foster's divisions might be moved down to a point from which it could reach this road; but there would be risk, since Hardee with fifteen thousand men could leave Savannah in the face of Sherman's sixty thousand men, cross the river on pontoons, march ten miles inland over this one road leading through swamps or overflowed rice lands, and "fall on this detachment with his whole army."

General Sherman then continues (page 216, Vol. II):

* * * * "So, taking one or two of my personal staff, I rode back to King's Bridge, leaving with Generals Howard and Slocum orders to make all possible preparations, but not to attack, during my two or three days' absence; and there I took a boat for Warsaw Sound, whence Admiral Dahlgren conveyed me in his own boat (the Harvest Moon) to Hilton Head, where I represented the matter to General Foster, and he promptly agreed to give his personal attention to it. During the night of the 20th we started back, the wind blowing strong. Admiral Dahlgren ordered the pilot of the Harvest Moon to run into Tybee, and to work his way through to Warsaw Sound and the Ogeechee River by the Romney marshes. We were caught by a low tide and stuck in the mud. After laboring some time, the Admiral ordered out his barge. In it we pulled through this intricate and shallow channel, and toward evening of December 21 we discovered coming toward us a tug, called the Red Legs, belonging to the quartermaster's department, with a staff officer on board bearing letters from Colonel Dayton to myself and the Admiral, reporting that the city of Savannah had been found evacuated on the morning of December 21, and was then in our possession. General Hardee had crossed the Savannah River by a pontoon bridge, carrying off his men and light artillery, blowing up his iron-clads and navy-yard, but leaving for us all the heavy guns, stores, cotton, railway cars, steamboats, and an immense amount of public and private property." * * * *

Some light is thrown upon the question of the responsibility for Hardee's escape by the official records.

The aggregate strength of Sherman's army before Savannah on December 20, the day before its evacuation, was sixty thousand five hundred and ninety-eight men.

Hardee's field returns for the same day showed an aggregate for his garrison, of all arms and all sorts, of nine thousand and eighty-nine men.

On the 16th of December General Sherman, in a letter to General Grant, gave this opinion of the Confederate strength:

"I think Hardee, in Savannah, has good artillerists; some five or six thousand good infantry, and, it may be, a mongrel mass of eight to ten thousand militia."

General Sherman had "surrounded" the city, as he so fully explained—that is, he had not surrounded it. Hardee held the entire Savannah River front of the city. Hutchinson Island, opposite, reached from a point below the place to a point opposite the left of the Union line. Between Hutchinson Island and the South Carolina shore was Pennyworth Island. The only possible way of escape for Hardee, unless he cut through Sherman's sixty thousand, was by building pontoon bridges connecting these islands and the two shores. General Slocum, who occupied the Union left with the Twentieth Corps, had captured two small steamers, and collected a number of flats and small boats immediately after reaching the Savannah River, and was extremely anxious to cross a corps to the South Carolina side, which would have effectually invested the city. With an army of four corps, and either corps stronger than Hardee's entire army, his desire would appear to have been most judicious.

General Sherman thus explains why he did not accede to General Slocum's proposition to pass a sufficient force to the South Carolina shore, to close Hardee's only line of escape:

"General Slocum had already captured a couple of steamboats trying to pass down the Savannah River from Augusta, and had established some of his men on Argyle and Hutchinson Islands above the city, and wanted to transfer a whole corps to the South Carolina bank; but, as the enemy had iron-clad gun-boats in the river, I did not deem it prudent, because the same result would be better accomplished from General Foster's position at Broad River.

The following extracts from General Slocum's report of operations in the rear of Savannah will illustrate the vacillating course his orders obliged him to pursue:

"From the 13th to the 20th [December] several changes were made in the position of the troops. * * * * Two regiments from Geary occupied the upper end of Hutchinson's Island. Carman's brigade, First Division, was sent to Argyle Island, and subsequently across to the South Carolina shore, with one section of Battery I, First New York Artillery. * * * * During the 20th the report from Carman's brigade indicated that large columns were crossing to the Carolina shore, either to cover their own line of communication or preparatory to the final evacuation of the city.

"In the night General Geary reported to me that the movements across the river were still going on. The different commanders were instructed to keep on the alert and press their pickets close to the rebel works, but the enemy, intending to abandon his heavy guns, kept up a fire until the moment of quitting the works."

The following orders from General Slocum's headquarters to various officers under his command show the details of this movement threatening the rebel line of communication:

"*December* 11.—To General Geary: The General commanding directs that, if you can find any boats in the river, you send fifty or sixty men to Hutchinson's Island to ascertain what they can.

"*December* 13.—To General Geary: The General commanding directs that the forty-seven men of your command, under Major Hoyt, now on Hutchinson's Island, remain there until further orders.

"*December* 16.—To Colonel Hawley: The General commanding the corps directs that you have all the boats in your charge, or in that of Colonel Bloodgood, on your side of the river by 8 A. M. to-morrow, and in readiness to cross troops. The whole of Colonel Carman's brigade will cross.

"*December* 16.—To General Jackson: In accordance with directions from the General commanding the corps, the order for Colonel Carman to cross his brigade to the South Carolina side of the Savannah River to-morrow morning is hereby countermanded.

"The General commanding directs that you have him send over a force of ninety or one hundred men in small boats to effect a lodgment, if possible, and feel the enemy's position. He wishes him to take only such force as can be readily brought back in case the enemy be too strong for him.

"*December* 18.—To Colonel Carman: The Brigadier-General commanding the corps directs that you cross your command to the South Carolina side of the Savannah River to-morrow morning. You will commence the movement before daylight.

"*December* 21.—General Jackson: The General commanding directs that General Carman's brigade be moved to this side of the river, leaving one regiment on the island for the present. He wishes the brigade encamped on this side so that they will protect the two rice mills."

Colonel Charles C. Jones, Chief of Artillery on the staff of General Hardee during the siege of Savannah, in a work which he has published, thus describes the evacuation:

"*December* 14.—The evacuation of Savannah having been resolved upon, and it being impracticable by means of the few steamboats and river craft at command to cross the garrison, artillery, and requisite stores with convenience and safety to Screven's Ferry, orders were issued for the immediate construction of suitable pontoon bridges. The line of retreat selected by the engineers, and adopted upon the evacuation of the city, involved the location of a pontoon bridge extending from the foot of West Broad street to Hutchinson's Island, a distance of about a thousand feet, a roadway across that island in the direction of Pennyworth Island, a second pontoon bridge across the middle river, another roadway across Pennyworth Island, and a third pontoon bridge across Back River, the further end of which rested upon the rice field on the Carolina shore. The route then followed the most substantial and direct rice dam running north, a canal being on one side and an impracticable rice field on the other. This dam was just wide enough to permit the careful movement of field artillery and army wagons. The plantation bridges along the line of march were strengthened to bear the passage of these heavy conveyances. * * * *

"All available rice-field flats were collected. These being between seventy-five and eighty feet in length, and possessing sufficient width for the purpose, were swung into position with the tide, lashed end to end by means of ropes and stringers running from boat to boat continuously the entire length of the bridge, and were kept in their places by car wheels, the only anchors which could be procured. Above the stringers was a flooring of plank obtained from the city wharves.

"At eight o'clock on the evening of the 17th, the first pontoon bridge spanning the Savannah River from the foot of West Broad street to Hutchinson Island was completed, and by half-past eight o'clock P. M. on Monday, the 19th, the remaining bridges were finished, and the route in readiness for the retreat of the Confederate garrison. * * * * Two regiments of General Geary's division occupied the upper end of Hutchinson's Island, and Carman's brigade was pushed forward to Argyle Island. * * * *

"Heavy skirmishing occurred between General P. M. B. Young's command and the Federals on Argyle Island.

"In the effort to advance in the direction of the Confederate line of communication with the Carolina shore, the enemy was repulsed with considerable loss. The fighting along the rice dams was obstinate and bloody. As the retention of this route was essential to the safety of the troops engaged in the defense of Savannah, all General Wheeler's available forces, assisted by Young's troops, and such of the South Carolina light batteries as could be spared from points along the Charleston and Savannah Railroad, were concentrated for its protection. By these troops all attempts of the enemy to move upon our line were stubbornly and successfully resisted. * * * * The troops from the western lines were quietly withdrawn, in the order and at the hours indicated in the circulars issued by the Lieutenant-General for the evacuation of the city. No confusion prevailed, and the movement was executed silently and in good order.

"Guns were spiked, and ammunition destroyed as far as this could conveniently be done without attracting the notice of the enemy in our immediate front.

"To conceal the movement, occasional firing was kept up until the latest moment. Forty-nine pieces of artillery, with limbers, caissons, forges, battery wagons, and baggage wagons, were safely transported over the pontoon bridges. A single battery wagon was lost. Through some negligence of the driver, it got off the bridge. The horses attached to it were saved. No interruption was encountered at the hand of the enemy, and the Confederate army rendezvoused the next day at Hardeeville, South Carolina."

So much for what the records and this last account have to say in regard to Hardee's escape from General Sherman. The latter now contents himself with the following reflections (Vol. II, page 218):

"I was disappointed that Hardee had escaped with his army, but on the whole we had reason to be content with the substantial fruits of victory."

And at the time, in a letter to General Halleck, dated December 24th (not given in the Memoirs), he wrote:

"I felt somewhat disappointed at Hardee's escape from me, but really am not to blame. I moved as quick as possible to close up the "Union causeway," but intervening obstacles were such that before I could get my troops on the road Hardee had slipped out. Still, I know that the men that were in Savannah will be lost, in a measure, to Jeff. Davis, for the Georgia troops under G. W. Smith declared they would not fight in South Carolina, and they have gone north en route for Augusta; and I have reason to believe the North Carolina troops have gone to Wilmington; in other words, they are scattered."

But these reflections will scarcely break the force of Mr. Stanton's words, heretofore quoted, from a dispatch to General Grant:

"It is a sore disappointment that Hardee was able to get off his fifteen thousand from Sherman's sixty thousand. It looks like protracting the war while their armies continue to escape."

It might be supposed that in treating of the Savannah campaign after the lapse of so many years, General Sherman would not introduce matter reflecting upon Thomas, whose victory at Nashville furnished the only justification for the March to the Sea. How far he does violence to so charitable a supposition will appear in another chapter.

CHAPTER XIII.

AFFAIRS AT NASHVILLE CRITICISED FROM SAVANNAH.

No sooner had our army reached Savannah than a sickening anxiety set in about headquarters to hear from Nashville. An army of sixty thousand men had marched away from its enemy, leaving him moving toward the North, to be taken care of with what General Sherman calls the "somewhat broken forces" at the disposal of Thomas. Exultation over the "great march" was fast dying away at headquarters. The all-important question there was: Will Hood evade or defeat Thomas, and invade Kentucky and the North? Writing the day after he entered Savannah to General Webster, at Nashville, Sherman said in a letter, referred to in the Memoirs, but not given:

"I have also from the War Department a copy of General Thomas' dispatch, giving an account of the attack on Hood on the 15th, which was successful, but not complete. I await further accounts with anxiety, as Thomas' complete success is necessary to vindicate my plans for this campaign, and I have no doubt that my calculation that Thomas had in hand (including A. J. Smith's troops) a force large enough to whip Hood in a fair fight was correct."

There was no peace at headquarters till this doubt was fully resolved, and the painful suspense removed by the news of final and complete victory at Nashville. This victory was full deliverance for General Sherman from the verdict he had recorded as the march began, when he wrote: "Should we fail, this march would be adjudged the wild adventure of a crazy fool." Had Hood defeated Thomas, or reached the

Ohio River, this verdict would assuredly have passed into history.

And so, considering the bearings which the battle of Nashville had upon Sherman's campaign to the sea, his best friends may well be surprised to find his book stained by unjust reflections upon Thomas.

The following extracts from the Memoirs indicate the treatment which this branch of the subject receives:

"As soon as the army had reached Savannah, and had opened communication with the fleet, I endeavored to ascertain what had transpired in Tennessee since our departure. * * * *

"As before described, General Hood had three full corps of infantry—S. D. Lee's, A. P. Stewart's, and Cheatham's—at Florence, Alabama, with Forrest's corps of cavalry, numbering in the aggregate about forty-five thousand men. General Thomas was in Nashville, Tennessee, quietly engaged in reorganizing his army out of the somewhat broken forces at his disposal. He had posted his only two regular corps—the Fourth and Twenty-third—under the general command of Major-General J. M. Schofield, at Pulaski, directly in front of Florence, with the three brigades of cavalry (Hatch, Croxton, and Capron), commanded by Major-General Wilson, watching closely for Hood's initiative.

"This force aggregated about thirty thousand men, was therefore inferior to the enemy; and General Schofield was instructed, in case the enemy made a general advance, to fall back slowly toward Nashville, fighting till he should be reënforced by General Thomas in person. * * * *

"Meantime General Thomas had organized the employés of the quartermaster's department into a corps, commanded by the Chief-Quartermaster, General J. L. Donaldson, and placed them in the fortifications of Nashville, under the general direction of Major-General Z. B. Tower, now of the United States Engineers. He had also received the two veteran divisions of the Sixteenth Corps, under General A. J. Smith, long absent and long expected, and he had drawn from Chattanooga and Decatur (Alabama), the divisions of Steedman and of R. S. Granger.

"These, with General Schofield's army, and about ten thousand good cavalry, under General J. H. Wilson, constituted a strong army, capable, not only of defending Nashville, but of beating Hood in the open field. Yet Thomas remained inside of Nashville, seemingly passive, until General Hood had closed upon him and had intrenched his position. * * * * At that time the weather was cold and sleety, the ground was covered with ice and snow, and both parties for a time rested on the defensive. Thus matters stood at Nashville, while we were closing down on Savannah, in the early part of December, 1864; and the country, as well as General Grant, was alarmed at the seeming passive conduct of General Thomas; and General Grant at one time considered the situation so dangerous that he thought of going to Nashville in person, but General John A. Logan, happening to be at City Point, was sent out to supersede General Thomas. Luckily for the latter, he acted in time, gained a magnificent victory, and thus escaped so terrible a fate."

It seems never to have occurred to General Sherman that much of this trouble came to General Thomas through the misrepresentations he himself had made to General Grant of Thomas' force, in the dispatch of November 1st, and others of a similar purport.

After narrating the demand on Hardee to surrender Savannah, his refusal and subsequent escape, and the occupation of the city, General Sherman again recurs to Thomas before Nashville, and in more generous terms:

"Meantime, on the 15th and 16th of December, were fought, in front of Nashville, the great battles in which General Thomas so nobly fulfilled his promise to ruin Hood, the details of which are fully given in his own official reports, long since published. Rumors of these great victories reached us at Savannah by piecemeal, but his official report came on the 24th of December, with a letter from General Grant, giving in general terms the events up to the 18th, and I wrote at once through my Chief-of-Staff, General Webster, to General Thomas, complimenting him in the highest terms. His brilliant victory at Nashville was necessary to mine at Savannah to make a complete whole, and this fact was perfectly comprehended by Mr. Lincoln, who recognized it fully in his personal letter of December 26th, hereinbefore quoted at length, and which I also claimed at the time, in my Special Field Order No. 6, of January, 8, 1865, here given." * * * *

In comparing the above statements with the records, it is necessary to go back to the estimate General Sherman placed upon the forces of Hood, and those under the control of Thomas, when the object was to procure General Grant's permission to march for the sea without first destroying Hood.

From Resaca on November 1st, he telegraphed Grant as follows:

"As you foresaw, and as Jeff. Davis threatened, the enemy is now in the full tide of execution of his grand plan to destroy my communications and defeat this army. His infantry, about thirty thousand (30,000), with Wheeler and Roddy's cavalry, from seven to ten thousand (7,000 to 10,000), are now in the neighborhood of Tuscumbia and Florence, and the water being low, are able to cross at will. * * * *

"General Thomas has near Athens and Pulaski, Stanley's corps, about fifteen thousand strong, and Schofield's corps, ten thousand, *en route* by rail, and has at least twenty to twenty-five thousand men, with new regiments and conscripts arriving all the time, also. General Rosecrans promises the two divisions of Smith and Mower, belonging to me, but I doubt if they can reach Tennessee in less than ten days. * * * * I have retained about fifty thousand good troops and have sent back full twenty-five thousand, and have instructed General Thomas to hold defensively Nashville, Chattanooga, and Decatur, all strongly fortified and provisioned for a long siege." * * * *

The points to be noted in connection with this telegram are, that Hood's forces were then estimated by Sherman at from thirty-seven to forty thousand, while Thomas' troops were stated to be from forty-five to fifty thousand besides new regiments, conscripts arriving all the time, and the two divisions of A. J. Smith.

Instead of Smith's troops reaching Thomas in ten days, they did not reach him for thirty days.

General Sherman instead of retaining fifty thousand troops retained over sixty-two thousand.

Thomas was instructed to hold Nashville defensively.

To write at this late day of General Thomas being in Nashville "seemingly passive," and "quietly engaged in reorganizing his army," is, in view of the almost superhuman efforts which he with the "somewhat broken forces at his disposal" was making to prepare for the defeat of Hood, to perpetrate an injustice to the dead which the General of the army could easily have avoided.

And, as if to make this "passiveness and quiet" apparent to all and the more inexcusable, and the great risk which he saw in leaving Thomas to grapple Hood at every disadvantage less apparent, the Memoirs present the estimate given below of Thomas' strength, which agrees neither with the dispatch of November 1st, already quoted, nor with the fact as recorded in the official records. A summing up of the statement will show that it places Thomas' strength of all kinds at from eighty-two thousand seven hundred to eighty-eight thousand seven hundred, besides several garrisons, when in fact the official returns show that the effective force present at the battle of Nashville was fifty-five thousand four hundred and seventy-two, while the dispatch of November 1st fixed it at from sixty-three to seventy thousand.

Says General Sherman, Vol. II, page 162:

"He then had at Nashville about eight or ten thousand new troops, and as many more civil employés of the quartermaster's department, which were not suited for the field, but would be most useful in manning the excellent forts that already covered Nashville. At Chattanooga he had General Steedman's division, about five thousand men, besides garrisons for Chattanooga, Bridgeport, and Stevenson; at Murfreesboro he also had General Rousseau's division, which was full five thousand strong, independent of the necessary garrisons for the railroad. At Decatur and Huntsville, Alabama, was the infantry division of General R. S. Granger, estimated at four thousand, and near Florence, Alabama, watching the crossings of the Tennessee, were General Edward Hatch's division of cavalry, four thousand; General Croxton's brigade, twenty-five hundred, and Colonel Capron's brigade, twelve hundred. Besides which General J. H. Wilson had collected in Nashville about ten thousand dismounted cavalry, for which he was rapidly collecting the necessary horses for a remount. All these aggregated about forty-five thousand men.

"General A. J. Smith at that time was in Missouri with the two divisions of the Sixteenth Corps which had been diverted to that quarter to assist General Rosecrans in driving the rebel General Price out of Missouri. This object had been accomplished, and these troops, numbering from eight to ten thousand, had been ordered to Nashville. To these I proposed at first to add only the Fourth Corps (General Stanley), fifteen thousand, and that corps was ordered from Gaylesville to march to Chattanooga and thence to report for orders to General Thomas; but subsequently, on the 30th of October, at Rome, Georgia, learning from General Thomas that the new troops promised by General Grant were coming forward very slowly, I concluded to further reënforce him by General Schofield's corps (Twenty-third), twelve thousand, which corps accordingly marched for Resaca, and there took the cars for Chattanooga. I then knew that General Thomas would have an ample force with which to encounter General Hood any where in the open field, besides garrisons to secure the railroad to his rear, and as far forward as Chattanooga."

In the earlier quotations of this chapter will be found some generous words spoken of Thomas' success at Nashville, coupled with the statement that, upon learning the result, he wrote through General Webster, "complimenting him [Thomas] in the highest terms." Though not produced that letter exists in the records, and the part of it in any degree complimentary in its character is as follows:

> HEADQUARTERS MILITARY DIVISION OF THE MISSISSIPPI, }
> IN THE FIELD, SAVANNAH, GA., *December* 23, 1864. }

General J. D. WEBSTER, *Nashville, Tenn.*

DEAR GENERAL: Major Dixon arrived last night, bringing your letter of the 10th December, for which I am very much obliged, as it gives me a clear and distinct view of the situation of affairs at Nashville up to that date. I have also from the War Department a copy of General Thomas' dispatch, giving an account of the attack on Hood on the 15th, which was successful, but not complete. I await further accounts with anxiety, as Thomas' complete success is necessary to vindicate my plans for this campaign, and I have no doubt that my calculation that Thomas had in hand (including A. J. Smith's troops) a force large enough to whip Hood in a fair fight was correct. I approve of Thomas' allowing Hood to come north far enough to enable him to concentrate his own men, though I would have preferred that Hood should have been checked about Columbia. Still, if Thomas followed up his success of the 15th, and gave Hood a good whaling, and is at this moment following him closely, the whole campaign in my division will be even more perfect than the Atlanta campaign, for at this end of the line I have realized all I had reason to hope for, except in the release of our prisoners, which was simply an impossibility.

December 24.—I have just received a letter from General Grant, giving a detail of General Thomas' operations up to the 18th, and I am gratified beyond measure at the result.

Show this letter to General Thomas, and tell him to consider it addressed to him, as I have not time to write more now.   *   *   *   *

I am, very truly, yours,   W. T. SHERMAN, *Major-General.*

Perhaps the most glaring instance of injustice to General Thomas found in the book appears on page 209. It is contained in a general letter to Grant upon the situation before Savannah, and plans for a coming campaign, dated in front of the latter place December 16th. It has the following paragraph in regard to Thomas:

"I myself am somewhat astonished at the attitude of things in Tennessee. I purposely delayed at Kingston until General Thomas assured me that he was all ready, and my last dispatch from him of the 12th of November was full of confidence, in which he promised me that he would ruin Hood if he dared to advance from Florence, urging me to go ahead and give myself no concern about Hood's army in Tennessee.

"Why he did not turn on him at Franklin, after checking and discomfiting him, surpasses my understanding. Indeed, I do not approve of his evacuating Decatur, but think he should have assumed the offensive against Hood from Pulaski in the direction of Waynesburg. I know full well that General Thomas is slow in mind and in action, but he is judicious and brave, and the troops feel great confidence in him. I still hope he will outmaneuver and destroy Hood."

This letter, with the exception of the above extract, was printed in full by General Sherman in the report he placed before the Committee on the Conduct of the War, in May, 1865. The country was still ringing with the praise of Thomas. It would have been a serious thing to print it then; but now, when Thomas is dead, and Sherman is vindicating himself for history, this unjust paragraph is hunted up and given to the world, with the remark (page 207) that the letter now produced "is a little more full than the one printed in the report of the Committee on the Conduct of the War, because in that copy I omitted the matter concerning General Thomas which now need no longer be withheld."

Even if General Sherman believed the paragraph was just when he wrote it, he well knew it to be cruelly unjust when he printed it.

On the 23d of December, only a few days after the date of this letter, he had written General Webster in the one already quoted:

"I approve of Thomas' allowing Hood to come north far enough to enable him to concentrate his own men, though I would have preferred that Hood should have been checked about Columbia."

And in the text of his Memoirs, only a few pages in advance of where he reproduces this paragraph, after enumerating all the force available about Pulaski, he writes, as already quoted:

"This force aggregated about thirty thousand men, was therefore inferior to the enemy; and General Schofield was instructed, in case the enemy made a general advance, to fall back slowly toward Nashville, fighting till he should be reënforced by General Thomas in person."

General Sherman also knew well that only a portion of the veteran reënforcements ordered to General Thomas had succeeded in reaching Nashville the day of the battle of Franklin, and that the rest did not arrive till the day succeeding that battle.

Among the last dispatches he sent to General Thomas at Nashville, before starting on the March to the Sea, was this order, dated October 31st:

"You must unite all your men into one army and abandon all minor points if you expect to defeat Hood."

And the very last dispatch, before starting south, was one notifying Thomas of his belief that all information seemed to indicate that Beauregard (Hood) would attempt to work against Nashville:

"I can hardly believe that Beauregard would attempt to work against Nashville from Corinth as a base at this stage of the war, but all information seems to point that way."

Why General Thomas did not turn on Hood at Franklin appears from the following field dispatches from General Schofield, who was fighting a splendid battle at that place:

FRANKLIN, TENN., *November* 30, 1864, 12 M.
Major-General THOMAS, *Nashville.*

Your dispatch of 10:25 A. M. is received. I am satisfied that I have heretofore run too much risk in trying to hold Hood in check while so far inferior to him in both infantry and cavalry. The slightest mistake on my part, or failure of a subordinate, during the last three days, might have proved disastrous. I don't want to get into so tight a place again.

I will cheerfully act in accordance with your views if you think it expedient to hold Hood back as long as possible. When you get all your troops together, and in fighting condition, we can whip Hood easily, and I believe make the campaign a decisive one. Before that the most we can do is to husband our strength and increase it as much as possible. * * * *

J. M. SCHOFIELD, Major-General.

FRANKLIN, TENN., *November* 30, 3 P. M.
Major-General THOMAS, *Nashville.*

I have just received your dispatch, asking whether I can hold Hood here three days. I do not believe I can. I can doubtless hold him one day, but will hazard something in doing that. He now has a large force, probably two corps, in my front, and seems preparing to cross the river above and below. I think he can effect a crossing to-morrow in spite of all my efforts to prevent, or to-night if he attempts it. A worse place than this for an inferior force could hardly be found. I will refer your question to General Wilson this evening, yet fear he can do very little. I have no doubt Forrest will be in my rear to-morrow doing some greater mischief.

It appears to me that I ought to take position at Brentwood at once. If A. J. Smith's division and the Murfreesboro garrison join me there, I ought to be able to hold Hood in check for some time. I have just learned that the enemy's cavalry is already crossing three miles below. I will have lively times with my trains again. J. M. SCHOFIELD, *Major-General.*

And, if all thus far related is not enough to show that there was nothing in the situation at Nashville surpassing Sherman's understanding, the terms of the congratulatory order he prints in full a few pages beyond where he records the shock to his powers of comprehension, are conclusive, and a brief extract will suffice:

"Generals Thomas and Schofield, commanding the departments to our rear, returned to their posts and prepared to decoy General Hood into their meshes, while we came on to complete the original journey.

"Almost at the moment of our victorious entry into Savannah came the welcome and expected news that our comrades in Tennessee had also fulfilled nobly and well their part, had decoyed General Hood to Nashville and then turned on him, defeating his army thoroughly, capturing all his artillery, great numbers of prisoners, and were still pursuing the fragments down in Alabama."

There were several other paragraphs reflecting upon General Thomas, omitted from the letters furnished the Committee on the Conduct of the War, which are now reproduced by General Sherman, but the citation of one is sufficient.

There is a brief letter in the records, not quoted in the Memoirs, which contains a sentence fitted for the close of a chapter on the operations at Nashville and Savannah. Mr. Lincoln had written General Sherman, in a letter before quoted:

"Now, the undertaking being a success, the honor is all yours; for I believe none of us went further than to acquiesce. And taking the work of General Thomas into the count, as it should be taken, it is indeed a great success. Not only does it afford the obvious and immediate military advantages, but in showing to the world that your army could be divided, putting the stronger part to an important new service, and yet leaving enough to vanquish the old opposing force of the whole (Hood's army), it brings those who sat in darkness to see great light."

To which General Sherman replied:

"I am gratified at the receipt of your letter of December 26th, at the hands of General Logan, especially to observe that you appreciate the division I made of my army, and that each part was duly proportioned to its work."

Two pictures will rise here before the mind. In one appears General Thomas, struggling in the face of a veteran and concentrated enemy, then far outnumbering him at every point, to collect enough fragments to give battle, finally accomplishing the task, and achieving victory.

In the other picture, Sherman, with sixty-two thousand selected men, thoroughly armed and equipped, marches down to the sea unopposed, summons Hardee's ten thousand to surrender, who first refuse, and three days thereafter escape. And yet General Sherman was especially gratified with the conceit that each part of his army was duly proportioned to its work.

CHAPTER XIV.

THOMAS' TROUBLES AT NASHVILLE—THE HISTORY OF HIS CONTEMPLATED REMOVAL.

The causes which produced the dissatisfaction at City Point and Washington, over the apparent slowness of General Thomas at Nashville, can now be clearly traced. They sprung directly from the telegrams of General Sherman, overestimating the forces he had left to take care of Hood. General Grant and the authorities at the Capital looked upon Hood's northward advance with alarm. Sherman had been repeatedly notified that he must leave an ample force with Thomas to enable this officer to hold the line of the Tennessee. He as often replied that he had fully complied with these directions. General Grant naturally became solicitous lest Hood, if not attacked, should pass around Thomas, invade Kentucky, and possibly reach the North. As a result of this anxiety and unjust dissatisfaction, an order was given for the removal of Thomas, which order, however, was not executed in consequence of his battle and victory.

As has been seen, Sherman thus refers to this matter:

"Yet Thomas remained inside of Nashville, seemingly passive, until General Hood had closed upon him and had intrenched his position. * * * *

"At that time the weather was cold and sleety, the ground was covered with ice and snow, and both parties for a time rested on the defensive. Thus matters stood at Nashville while we were closing down on Savannah in the early part of December, 1864; and the country, as well as General Grant, was alarmed at the seeming passive conduct of General Thomas; and General Grant at one time considered the situation so dangerous that he thought of going to Nashville in person, but General John A. Logan, happening to be at City Point, was sent out to supersede General Thomas; luckily for the latter, he acted in time, gained a magnificent victory, and thus escaped so terrible a fate."

The full correspondence relating to this subject is not only interesting, but it throws much new light upon General Sherman's account of the movements connected with the March to the Sea.

General Thomas was in Nashville directing the concentration of his army. General Schofield was in command at the front. The great object was to hold Hood back until all available forces could be united to meet him, and the remount of the cavalry accomplished. Under these circumstances, and a week before the advance of A. J. Smith's troops arrived at Nashville, the enemy had reached Columbia, and his large force of cavalry under Forrest was becoming very active. At this time the correspondence between General Thomas and the authorities at the East began, and continued until the battle was fought.

Its opening dispatch was as follows:

CITY POINT, VA., November 21, 1864, 4 P. M.

Major-General GEORGE H. THOMAS, *Nashville, Tenn.*

* * * * Do not let Forrest get off without punishment.

U. S. GRANT, Lieutenant-General.

The answer gave strong reasons for not implicitly obeying this order, and, together with the telegrams which succeeded it, shows the real condition in which General Sherman left Thomas:

HEADQUARTERS DEPARTMENT OF THE CUMBERLAND,
NASHVILLE, TENN., November 25, 1864, 11 A. M.

Lieutenant General GRANT, *City Point, Va.*

Your dispatch of 4 P. M. yesterday just received. Hood's entire army is in front of Columbia, and so greatly outnumbers mine at this time that I am compelled to act on the defensive. None of General Smith's troops have arrived yet, although they embarked at St. Louis on Tuesday last. The transportation of Generals Hatch's and Grierson's cavalry was ordered by General Washburne I am told, to be turned in at Memphis, which has crippled the only cavalry I had at this time. All of my cavalry was dismounted to furnish horses to Kilpatrick's division, which went with General Sherman. My dismounted cavalry is now detained at Louisville, awaiting arms and horses. Horses are arriving slowly, and arms have been detained somewhere *en route* for more than a month. General Grierson has been delayed by conflicting orders in Kansas, and from Memphis, and it is impossible to say when he will reach here. Since being placed in charge of affairs in Tennessee, I have lost nearly fifteen thousand men discharged by expiration of service and permitted to go home to vote. My gain is probably twelve thousand perfectly raw troops. Therefore, as the enemy so greatly outnumbers me, both in infantry and cavalry, I am compelled for the present to act on the defensive. The moment I can get my cavalry, I will march against Hood, and if Forrest can be reached he shall be punished.

     GEO. H. THOMAS, *Major-General Volunteers commanding.*

     NASHVILLE, *December* 1, 1864, 9:30 P. M.
Major-General HALLECK, *Washington, D. C.*

After General Schofield's fight of yesterday, feeling convinced that the enemy very far outnumbered him both in infantry and cavalry, I determined to retire to the fortifications around Nashville until General Wilson can get his cavalry equipped. He has now but about one-fourth the number of the enemy, and consequently, is no match for him. I have two iron-clads here, with several gun-boats, and Commodore Fitch assures me that Hood can neither cross the Cumberland, nor blockade it. I, therefore, think it best to wait here until Wilson can equip all his cavalry. If Hood attacks me here he will be more seriously damaged than he was yesterday. If he remains until Wilson gets equipped, I can whip him, and will move against him at once. I have Murfreesboro strongly held, and therefore feel easy in regard to its safety. Chattanooga, Bridgeport, Stevenson, and Elk River bridges have strong garrisons.

     GEO. H. THOMAS, *Major-General U. S. Volunteers commanding.*

     WAR DEPARTMENT,
     WASHINGTON, *December* 2, 10:30 A. M.
Lieutenant-General GRANT, *City Point.*

The President feels solicitous about the disposition of Thomas to lay in fortifications for an indefinite period, "until Wilson gets equipments." This looks like the McClellan and Rosecrans strategy of do nothing, and let the enemy raid the country. The President wishes you to consider the matter.

     EDWIN M. STANTON, *Secretary of War.*

     CITY POINT, VA., *December* 2, 1864, 11 A. M.
Major-General GEO. H. THOMAS, *Nashville.*

If Hood is permitted to remain quietly about Nashville, we will lose all the roads back to Chattanooga, and possibly have to abandon the line of the Tennessee River. Should he attack you it is all well, but if he does not you should attack him before he fortifies. Arm and put in the trenches your quartermaster's employés, citizens, etc. U. S. GRANT, *Lieutenant-General.*

CITY POINT, VA., *December* 2, 1864, 1:30 P. M.

Major-General GEO. H. THOMAS, *Nashville.*

With your citizen employés armed you can move out of Nashville with all your army and force the enemy to retire or fight upon ground of your own choosing. After the repulse of Hood at Franklin it looks to me that instead of falling back to Nashville we should have taken the offensive against the enemy, but at this distance may err as to the method of dealing with the enemy. You will suffer incalculable injury upon your railroads if Hood is not speedily disposed of. Put forth, therefore, every possible exertion to attain this end. Should you get him to retreating give him no peace.

U. S. GRANT, *Lieutenant-General.*

HEADQUARTERS DEPARTMENT OF THE CUMBERLAND,
NASHVILLE, TENN., *December* 2, 1864, 10 P. M.

General U. S. GRANT, *City Point, Va.*

Your two telegrams of 11 A. M. and 1:30 P. M. to-day are received. At the time Hood was whipped at Franklin I had at this place but about five thousand (5,000) men of General Smith's command, which, added to the force under General Schofield, would not have given me more than twenty-five thousand (25,000) men. Besides, General Schofield felt convinced that he could not hold the enemy at Franklin until the five thousand could reach him. As General Wilson's cavalry force also numbered only about one-fourth that of Forrest, I thought it best to draw the troops back to Nashville and await the arrival of the remainder of General Smith's force, and also a force of about five thousand (5,000), commanded by General Steedman, which I had ordered up from Chattanooga. The division of General Smith arrived yesterday morning, and General Steedman's troops arrived last night. I now have infantry enough to assume the offensive if I had more cavalry, and will take the field anyhow as soon as the remainder of General McCook's division of cavalry reaches here, which I hope it will in two or three days.

We can neither get reënforcements nor equipments at this great distance from the North very easily, and it must be remembered that my command was made up of the two weakest corps of General Sherman's army, and all the dismounted cavalry except one brigade, and the task of reorganizing and equipping has met with many delays which have enabled Hood to take advantage of my crippled condition. I earnestly hope, however in a few more days I shall be able to give him a fight.

GEO. H. THOMAS, *Major-General U. S. Volunteers commanding.*

CITY POINT, VA., *December* 5, 1864, 6:30 P. M.

Major-General GEO. H. THOMAS, *Nashville, Tenn.*

Is there not danger of Forrest's moving down the Tennessee River where he can cross it? It seems to me, while you should be getting up your cavalry

as rapidly as possible to look after Forrest, Hood should be attacked where he is.
Time strengthens him, in all probability, as much as it does you.
U. S. GRANT, *Lieutenant-General.*

NASHVILLE, *December* 6, 1864.
Lieutenant-General U. S. GRANT, *City Point.*
Your telegram of 6:30 P. M., December 5, is just received. As soon as I get up a respectable force of cavalry I will march against Hood. General Wilson has parties out now pressing horses, and I hope to have some six or eight thousand cavalry mounted in three days from this time. General Wilson has just left me, having received instructions to hurry the cavalry remount as rapidly as possible. I do not think it prudent to attack Hood with less than six thousand (6,000) cavalry to cover my flanks, because he has under Forrest at least twelve thousand (12,000). I have no doubt Forrest will attempt to cross the river, but I am in hopes the gun-boats will be able to prevent him. The enemy has made no new developments to-day. Breckinridge is reported at Lebanon with six thousand (6,000) men, but I can not believe it possible.
GEO. H. THOMAS, *Major-General U. S. Volunteers commanding.*

This statement did not give satisfaction, and the following order for an attack was telegraphed:

CITY POINT, VA., *December* 6, 1864, 4 P. M.
Major-General GEO. H. THOMAS, *Nashville.*
Attack Hood at once and wait no longer for a remount for your cavalry. There is great danger in delay resulting in a campaign back to the Ohio.
U. S. GRANT, *Lieutenant-General.*

This was acted upon, but General Thomas protested against the wisdom of the order:

NASHVILLE, *December* 6, 1864, 9 P. M.
Lieutenant-General U. S. GRANT, *City Point.*
Your dispatch of 4 P. M. this day received. I will make the necessary disposition and attack Hood at once, agreeably to your orders, though I believe it will be hazardous with the small force of cavalry now at my service.
GEO. H. THOMAS, *Major-General U. S. Volunteers commanding.*

WAR DEPARTMENT,
WASHINGTON, *December* 7, 1864, 10:20 A. M.
Lieutenant-General GRANT.
You remember that when Steele was relieved by Canby he was ordered to Cairo to report to this department. What shall be done with him? The order superseding Rosecrans by Dodge has been issued. Thomas seems

unwilling to attack because it is hazardous, as if all war was any but hazardous. If he waits for Wilson to get ready, Gabriel will be blowing his last horn.
EDWIN M. STANTON.

CITY POINT, VA., December 8, 1864.
Major-General HALLECK, *Washington.*

Please direct General Dodge to send all the troops he can spare to General Thomas. With such an order he can be relied on to send all that can properly go. They had probably better be sent to Louisville, for I fear either Hood or Breckinridge will go to the Ohio River. I will submit whether it is not advisable to call on Ohio, Indiana, and Illinois for sixty thousand men for thirty days. If Thomas has not struck yet he ought to be ordered to hand over his command to Schofield. There is no better man to repel an attack than Thomas, but I fear he is too cautious to take the initiative.
U. S. GRANT, *Lieutenant-General.*

WAR DEPARTMENT,
WASHINGTON, D. C., December 8, 1864.
Lieutenant-General GRANT, *City Point.*

If you wish General Thomas relieved give the order. No one here will, I think, interfere. The responsibility, however, will be yours, as no one here, so far as I am informed, wishes General Thomas removed.
H. W. HALLECK, *Major-General, Chief of Staff.*

NASHVILLE, TENN., December 7, 1864, 9 P. M.
Major-General H. W. HALLECK, *Washington, D. C.*

The enemy has not increased his force on our front. Have sent gun-boats up the river above Carthage. One returned to-day and reported no signs of the enemy on the river bank from forty miles above Carthage to this place. Captain Fitch, United States Navy, started down the river yesterday with a convoy of transport steamers, but was unable to get them down, the enemy having planted three batteries on a bend of the river between this and Clarksville. Captain Fitch was unable to silence all three of the batteries yesterday, and will return again to-morrow morning, and with the assistance of the Cincinnati, now at Clarksville, I am in hopes will now be able to clear them out. So far the enemy has not materially injured the Nashville and Chattanooga Railroad.
GEO. H. THOMAS, *Major-General U. S. Volunteers commanding.*

CITY POINT, VA., December 8, 7:30 P. M.
Major-General GEO. H. THOMAS, *Nashville.*

Your dispatch of yesterday received. It looks to me evident the enemy are trying to cross the Cumberland, and are scattered. Why not attack at once? By all means avoid the contingency of a foot race to see which, you or Hood, can beat to the Ohio. If you think necessary call on the Governors of States to send a force into Louisville to meet the enemy if he should cross the river. You clearly never should cross, except in rear of the enemy. Now is one of

THOMAS' TROUBLES AT NASHVILLE.

the fairest opportunities ever presented of destroying one of the three armies of the enemy. If destroyed he can never replace it Use the means at your command, and you can do this and cause a rejoicing from one end of the land to the other. U. S. GRANT, *Lieutenant-General.*

CITY POINT, VA., *December 8, 1864, 10 P. M.*
Major-General HALLECK, *Washington.*

Your dispatch of 9 P. M. just received. I want General Thomas reminded of the importance of immediate action. I sent him a dispatch this evening, which will probably urge him on. I would not say relieve him until I hear further from him. U. S. GRANT, *Lieutenant-General.*

NASHVILLE, TENN., *December 8, 1864, 11:30 P. M.*
Lieutenant-General U. S. GRANT, *City Point, Va.*

Your dispatch of 7:30 P. M. is just received. I can only say, in further extenuation why I have not attacked Hood, that I could not concentrate my troops, and get their transportation in order, in shorter time than it has been done, and am satisfied I have made every effort that was possible to complete the task. GEO. H. THOMAS, *Major-General commanding.*

WASHINGTON, *December 9, 1864, 10:30 A. M.*
Major-General GEO. H. THOMAS, *Nashville, Tenn.*

Lieutenant-General Grant expresses much dissatisfaction at your delay in attacking the enemy. If you wait till General Wilson mounts all his cavalry you will wait till doomsday, for the waste equals the supply. Moreover, you will be in the same condition that Rosecrans was last year—with so many animals that you can not feed them. Reports already come in of a scarcity of forage. H. W. HALLECK, *Major-General and Chief of Staff.*

NASHVILLE, *December 9, 1864, 2 P. M.*
Major-General H. W. HALLECK, *Washington, D. C.*

Your dispatch of 10:30 A. M., this date, is received. I regret that General Grant should feel dissatisfaction at my delay in attacking the enemy. I feel conscious that I have done everything in my power to prepare, and that the troops could not have been gotten ready before this. And if he should order me to be relieved I will submit without a murmur.

A terrible storm of freezing rain has come on since daylight, which will render an attack impossible till it breaks.
GEO. H. THOMAS, *Major-General U. S. Vols. commanding.*

The next step was a dispatch from General Grant, ordering that General Thomas should be relieved:

CITY POINT, VA., *December 9, 1864, 11 A. M.*
Major-General HALLECK, *Washington, D. C.*

Dispatch of 8 P. M. last evening, from Nashville, shows the enemy scattered for more than seventy miles down the river, and no attack yet made by Thomas. Please telegraph orders relieving him at once, and placing Schofield in command. Thomas should be ordered to turn over all orders and dispatches, received since the battle of Franklin, to Schofield.

U. S. GRANT, *Lieutenant-General.*

In obedience to this dispatch, according to Halleck, the following order was drawn up in the War Department, but never issued, and no trace of it can now be found there:

WAR DEPARTMENT, ADJUTANT-GENERAL'S OFFICE,
WASHINGTON, *December* 9, 1864.

[General Orders No. —.]

The following dispatch having been received from Lieutenant-General Grant, viz.: "Please telegraph orders relieving him (General Thomas) at once, and placing (General) Schofield in command," the President orders:

1. That Major-General J. M. Schofield relieve, at once, Major-General G. H. Thomas, in command of the Department and Army of the Cumberland.

2. General Thomas will turn over to General Schofield all orders and instructions received by him since the battle of Franklin.

E. D. TOWNSEND, *A. A. G.*

NASHVILLE, TENN., *December* 9, 1864, 1 P. M.

Lieutenant-General U. S. GRANT, *City Point.*

Your dispatch of 8:30 P. M. of the 8th is just received. I have nearly completed my preparations to attack the enemy to-morrow morning, but a terrible storm of freezing rain has come on to-day, which will make it impossible for our men to fight to any advantage. I am, therefore, compelled to wait for the storm to break and make the attack immediately after. Admiral Lee is patrolling the river above and below the city, and I believe will be able to prevent the enemy from crossing. There is no doubt but Hood's forces are considerably scattered along the river, with the view of attempting a crossing, but it has been impossible for me to organize and equip the troops for an attack at an earlier time. Major-General Halleck informs me that you are very much dissatisfied with my delay in attacking. I can only say I have done all in my power to prepare, and if you should deem it necessary to relieve me, I shall submit without a murmur.

GEO. H. THOMAS, *Major-General U. S. Vols. commanding.*

WAR DEPARTMENT,
WASHINGTON, *December* 9, 1864, 4 P. M.

Lieutenant-General GRANT, *City Point.*

Orders relieving General Thomas had been made out when his telegram of this P. M. was received. If you still wish these orders telegraphed to Nashville they will be forwarded. H. W. HALLECK, *Chief of Staff.*

CITY POINT, VA., *December* 9, 1864, 5:30 P. M.

Major-General HALLECK, *Washington.*

General Thomas has been urged in every possible way to attack the enemy; even to giving the positive order. He did say he thought he should be able to attack on the 7th, but he did not do so, nor has he given a reason for not doing it. I am very unwilling to do injustice to an officer who has done so much good service as General Thomas has, however, and will, therefore, suspend the order relieving him until it is seen whether he will do anything.

U. S. GRANT, *Lieutenant-General.*

CITY POINT, VA., *December* 9, 1864, 7:30 P. M.

Major-General THOMAS, *Nashville.*

Your dispatch of 1 P. M. to-day is received. I have as much confidence in your conducting the battle rightly as I have in any other officer, but it has seemed to me you have been slow, and I have had no explanation of affairs to convince me otherwise. Receiving your dispatch to Major-General Halleck of 2 P. M. before I did the first to me, I telegraphed to suspend the order relieving you until we should hear further. I hope most sincerely that there will be no necessity of repeating the order, and that the facts will show that you have been right all the time. U. S. GRANT, *Lieutenant-General.*

CITY POINT, VA., *December* 11, 1864, 4 P. M.

Major-General GEO. H. THOMAS, *Nashville.*

If you delay attacking longer, the mortifying spectacle will be witnessed of a rebel army moving for the Ohio, and you will be forced to act, accepting such weather as you find. Let there be no further delay. Hood can not stand even a drawn battle so far from his supplies of ordnance stores. If he retreats and you follow, he must lose his material and most of his army. I am in hopes of receiving a dispatch from you to-day announcing that you have moved. Delay no longer for weather or reënforcements.

U. S. GRANT, *Lieutenant-General.*

NASHVILLE, TENN., *December* 11, 1864, 10:30 P. M

Lieutenant-General U. S. GRANT, *City Point, Va.*

Your dispatch of 4 P. M. this day is just received. I will obey the order as promptly as possible, however much I may regret it, as the attack will have to be made under every disadvantage. The whole country is covered with a perfect sheet of ice and sleet, and it is with difficulty the troops are able to move about on level ground. It was my intention to attack Hood as soon as the ice melted, and would have done so yesterday had it not been for the storm.

GEO. H. THOMAS, *Major-General U. S. Vols. commanding.*

The following telegram shows that an attempt was made by

General Thomas to obey implicitly the order for attack, and the reason why the movement was not made:

NASHVILLE, TENN., *December* 12, 1864, 10:30 P. M.
Major-General HALLECK, *Washington, D. C.*

I have the troops ready to make the attack on the enemy as soon as the sleet, which now covers the ground, has melted sufficiently to enable the men to march. The whole country is now covered with a sheet of ice so hard and slippery it is utterly impossible for troops to ascend the slopes, or even move over level ground in anything like order. It has taken the entire day to place my cavalry in position, and it has only been finally effected with imminent risk and many serious accidents, resulting from the numbers of horses falling with their riders on the road. Under these circumstances, I believe that an attack at this time would only result in a useless sacrifice of life.

GEO. H. THOMAS, *Major-General U. S. Vols. commanding.*

On the 13th of December General Logan, then at City Point, was ordered to proceed to Nashville, and informed by General Grant that he was to take command of the Army of the Cumberland, relieving General Thomas, provided no movement had taken place upon his arrival at Nashville; and, further, that he (Grant) would leave in a few days to assume command of the forces around Nashville and fight a battle.

The order to General Logan was as follows:

HEADQUARTERS ARMIES OF THE UNITED STATES, }
CITY POINT, VA., *December* 13, 1864. }

[Special Orders No. 149.]

I. Major-General John A. Logan, United States Volunteers, will proceed immediately to Nashville, Tennessee, reporting by telegraph to the Lieutenant-General his arrival at Louisville, Kentucky, and also his arrival at Nashville, Tennessee. * * * *

By command of *Lieutenant-General* GRANT.

T. S. BOWERS, *Assistant Adjutant-General.*

WASHINGTON, *December* 14, 1864, 12:30 M.
Major-General GEO. H. THOMAS, *Nashville.*

It has been seriously apprehended that while Hood, with a part of his forces, held you in check near Nashville, he would have time to coöperate against other important points, left only partially protected. Hence, Lieutenant-General Grant was anxious that you should attack the rebel forces in your front, and expresses great dissatisfaction that his order has not been carried out. Moreover, so long as Hood occupies a threatening position in Tennes-

THOMAS' TROUBLES AT NASHVILLE. 193

see, General Canby is obliged to keep large forces on the Mississippi River to protect its navigation, and to hold Memphis, Vicksburg, etc., although General Grant had directed a part of these forces to coöperate with Sherman.

Every day's delay on your part, therefore, seriously interferes with General Grant's plans.   H. W. HALLECK, *Major-General and Chief of Staff.*

On the 14th General Grant himself left City Point for Nashville to assume command, but was met at Washington by the news of Thomas' victory.

NASHVILLE, *December* 14, 1864, 8 P. M.

Major-General H. W. HALLECK, *Washington, D. C.*

Your telegram of 12:30 M. to-day is received. The ice having melted away to-day, the enemy will be attacked to-morrow morning. Much as I regret the apparent delay in attacking the enemy, it could not have been done before with any reasonable prospect of success.

GEO. H. THOMAS, *Major-General U. S. Vols. commanding.*

NASHVILLE, TENN., 9 P. M., *December* 15, 1864.

Major-General HALLECK, *Chief of Staff.*

Attacked enemy's left this morning, drove it from the river, below city, very nearly to Franklin pike, distance about eight miles.   *   *   *   *

GEO. H. THOMAS, *Major-General.*

The body of the above dispatch contains a lengthy account of the movements.

WASHINGTON, *December* 15, 1864, 11:30 P. M.

Major-General GEO. H. THOMAS, *Nashville.*

I was just on my way to Nashville, but receiving a dispatch from Van Duzen, detailing your splendid success of to-day, I shall go no further. Push the enemy now, and give him no rest until he is entirely destroyed. Your army will cheerfully suffer many privations to break up Hood's army, and make it useless for future operations. Do not stop for trains or supplies, but take them from the country, as the enemy has done. Much is now expected.

U. S. GRANT, *Lieutenant-General.*

WASHINGTON, *December* 15, 1864, 12 Midnight.

Major-General GEO. H. THOMAS, *Nashville.*

Your dispatch of this evening just received. I congratulate you and the army under your command for to-day's operations, and feel a conviction that to-morrow will add more fruits to your victory.

U. S. GRANT, *Lieutenant-General.*

13

THOMAS' TROUBLES AT NASHVILLE.

HEADQUARTERS DEPARTMENT OF THE CUMBERLAND, EIGHT MILES FROM NASHVILLE,
6 P. M., *December* 16, 1864.

To the President of the United States, Hon. E. M. STANTON *and General* U. S. GRANT.

This army thanks you for your approbation of its conduct yesterday, and begs to assure you that it is not misplaced.

I have the honor to report, etc. [Here follows a second report in detail.]

GEO. H. THOMAS, *Major-General.*

On reaching Louisville, General Logan learned that Thomas had made a successful move, and in reporting to General Grant, requested that he might be ordered back to his command:

LOUISVILLE, KY., 10 A. M., *December* 17, 1864.

Lieutenant-General U. S. GRANT, *Burlington, N. J.*

Have just arrived. Weather bad; raining since yesterday morning. People here jubilant over Thomas' success. Confidence seems to be restored. I will remain here to hear from you. All things going right. It would seem best that I return to join my command with Sherman.

JOHN A. LOGAN, *Major-General.*

In reply to this, General Grant telegraphed an order directing Logan to report to General Sherman.

Immediately after the congratulatory dispatches, and while every effort was being made to press Hood's retreat, General Thomas was appealed to by Halleck to "capture or destroy Hood's army in order that General Sherman can entirely crush out the rebel military power in all the Southern States."

WASHINGTON, *December* 21, 1864, 12 M.

Major-General GEO. H. THOMAS.

Permit me, General, to urge the vast importance of a hot pursuit of Hood's army. Every possible sacrifice should be made, and your men for a few days will submit to any hardships and privations to accomplish the great result. If you can capture or destroy Hood's army General Sherman can entirely crush out the rebel military force in all the Southern States. He begins a new campaign about the first of January, which will have the most important results if Hood's army can now be used up. A most vigorous pursuit on your part is, therefore, of vital importance to General Sherman's plans. No sacrifice must be spared to obtain so important a result.

H. W. HALLECK, *Major-General and Chief of Staff.*

To this General Thomas replied at length and with spirit:

IN THE FIELD, *December* 21, 1864.

Major-General HALLECK, *Washington, D. C.*

Your dispatch of 12 M., this day, is received. General Hood's army is being pursued as rapidly and as vigorously as it is possible for one army to pursue another. We can not control the elements, and you must remember that, to resist Hood's advance into Tennessee, I had to reorganize and almost thoroughly equip the force now under my command. I fought the battle of the 15th and 16th instants with the troops but partially equipped; and, notwithstanding the inclemency of the weather and the partial equipment, have been enabled to drive the enemy beyond Duck River, crossing two streams with my troops, and driving the enemy from position to position, without the aid of pontoons, and with but little transportation to bring up supplies of provisions and ammunition. I am doing all in my power to crush Hood's army, and, if it be possible, will destroy it. But pursuing an enemy through an exhausted country, over mud roads completely sogged with heavy rains, is no child's play, and can not be accomplished as quickly as thought of. I hope, in urging me to push the enemy, the department remembers that General Sherman took with him the complete organization of the Military Division of the Mississippi, well equipped in every respect, as regards ammunition, supplies, and trasportation, leaving me only two corps, partially stripped of their transportation to accommodate the force taken with him, to oppose the advance into Tennessee of that army which had resisted the advance of the army of the Military Division of the Mississippi on Atlanta, from the commencement of the campaign till its close, and which is now, in addition, aided by Forrest's cavalry. Although my progress may appear slow, I feel assured that Hood's army can be driven from Tennessee, and eventually driven to the wall by the force under my command. But too much must not be expected of troops which have to be reorganized, especially when they have the task of destroying a force, in a Winter's campaign, which was able to make an obstinate resistance to twice its numbers in Spring and Summer. In conclusion, I can safely state that this army is willing to submit to any sacrifice to oust Hood's army, or to strike any other blow which may contribute to the destruction of the rebellion.

GEO. H. THOMAS, *Major-General.*

WASHINGTON, *December* 22, 1864, 9 P. M.

Major-General GEO. H. THOMAS.

I have seen to-day General Halleck's dispatch of yesterday, and your reply. It is proper for me to assure you that this department has the most unbounded confidence in your skill, vigor, and determination to employ to the best advantage all the means in your power to pursue and destroy the enemy. No department could be inspired with more profound admiration

and thankfulness for the great deeds which you have already performed, or more confiding faith that human effort could do no more, and no more than will be done by you and the accomplished and gallant officers and soldiers of your command.   E. M. STANTON, *Secretary of War.*

On the same day General Grant telegraphed:

CITY POINT, *December* 22, 1864.
Major-General GEO. H. THOMAS.

You have the congratulations of the public for the energy with which you are pushing Hood. I hope you will succeed in reaching his pontoon bridge at Tuscumbia before he gets there. Should you do so, it looks to me that Hood is cut off. If you succeed in destroying Hood's army, there will be but one army left to the so-called Confederacy, capable of doing us harm. I will take care of that, and try to draw the sting from it, so that in the Spring we shall have easy sailing. You have now a big opportunity, which I know you are availing yourself of. Let us push and do all we can before the enemy can derive benefit, either from the raising of negro troops on the plantations or white troops now in the field.   U. S. GRANT, *Lieutenant-General.*

Two dispatches properly close this correspondence:

WAR DEPARTMENT, *December* 24, 1864.
Major-General THOMAS, *Nashville.*

With great pleasure I inform you that for your skill, courage, and conduct in the recent brilliant military operations under your command, the President has directed your nomination to be sent to the Senate as a Major-General in the United States Army, to fill the only vacancy existing in that grade. No official duty has been performed by me with more satisfaction, and no commander has more justly earned promotion by devoted, disinterested, and valuable services to his country.   EDWIN M. STANTON, *Secretary of War.*

To which General Thomas, then in the field directing the pursuit of Hood, replied:

HEADQUARTERS DEPARTMENT OF THE CUMBERLAND,
McKANES' CHURCH, TENN.

Hon. E. M. STANTON, *Secretary of War.*

I am profoundly sensible of the kind expressions of your telegram of December 24th, informing me that the President had directed my name to be sent to the Senate for confirmation as Major-General United States Army, and beg to assure the President and yourself, that your approval of my services is of more value to me than the commission itself.

GEO. H. THOMAS, *Major-General commanding.*

In the succeeding July, General Grant in that portion of his final report which related to the campaign about Nashville, made the following manly acknowledgment that the result had vindicated General Thomas' judgment:

"Before the battle of Nashville I grew very impatient over, as it appeared to me, the unnecessary delay. This impatience was increased upon learning that the enemy had sent a force of cavalry across the Cumberland into Kentucky. I feared Hood would cross his whole army and give us great trouble there. After urging upon General Thomas the necessity of immediately assuming the offensive, I started West to superintend matters there in person. Reaching Washington City, I received General Thomas' dispatch announcing his attack upon the enemy, and the result as far as the battle had progressed. I was delighted. All fears and apprehensions were dispelled. I am not yet satisfied but that General Thomas, immediately upon the appearance of Hood before Nashville, and before he had time to fortify should have moved out with his whole force and given him battle, instead of waiting to remount his cavalry, which delayed him until the inclemency of the weather made it impracticable to attack earlier than he did. But his final defeat of Hood was so complete, that it will be accepted as a vindication of that distinguished officer's judgment."

General Sherman himself, after introducing into his book several passages that he has for years suppressed, and which severely reflected upon General Thomas' action before Nashville, closes his consideration of the subject with these more generous words:

"Meantime, on the 15th and 16th of December, were fought in front of Nashville, the great battles in which General Thomas so nobly fulfilled his promise to ruin Hood, the details of which are fully given in his own official reports, long since published."

CHAPTER XV.

THE CAPTURED COTTON AT SAVANNAH—CHARACTER OF THE ATTACK ON SECRETARY STANTON—THE JEFF. DAVIS GOLD.

ATTACKS upon dead men may fairly be called one of the features of General Sherman's Memoirs. Thomas, McPherson, and Stanton, with others less prominent, are in turn rudely and unjustly assailed in their graves. In writing history it would have been not only allowable for an honorable author to set down exact truth in regard to these noted actors in the war, even though it were unpalatable to their friends, but his bounden duty to do so. But when an author of General Sherman's position writes of his famous associates, having close at hand and conveniently arranged for reference all means of ascertaining the exact facts about every question which could arise, he stands without excuse before his countrymen if he wrongfully writes disgrace over graves where he should strew laurel.

On page 243, Vol. II, of his Memoirs, General Sherman relates that he was instructed by Mr. Stanton to transfer the cotton captured in Savannah to an agent of the Treasury. This General Sherman did by an order dated January 12, 1865. He then continues as follows, charging that Mr. Stanton's action in this matter caused great loss to the Government:

"Up to this time all the cotton had been carefully guarded, with orders to General Easton to ship it by the return vessels to New York for the adjudication of the nearest prize court, accompanied with invoices and all evidence of title to ownership. Marks, numbers, and other figures were carefully preserved on the bales, so that the court might know the history of each bale. But Mr. Stanton, who surely was an able lawyer, changed all this, and ordered the obliteration of all the marks, so that no man, friend or foe, could trace his identical cotton. I thought it strange at the time, and think it more so now, for I am assured that claims real and fictitious have been proved up against this identical cotton of three times the quantity actually captured, and that reclamations on the Treasury have been *allowed* for more than the actual quantity captured, viz., thirty-one thousand bales."

Here General Sherman, once a practicing attorney, forgot both his law and the facts, for cotton thus captured would not fall within the jurisdiction of a prize court, and the records show that what he charges upon Mr. Stanton never occurred.

As there were nearly forty thousand bales of this cotton, in view of the high price then prevailing and the necessities of the Treasury, the proper care and handling of this most valuable capture were matters of the greatest importance to the Government. That Mr. Stanton was fully aware of all this, that he caused the business to be promptly and properly attended to, and that every reflection made upon him by General Sherman in the above extract is utterly unfounded, will now be made to appear.

Secretary Stanton's first dispatch, upon learning of the capture of Savannah, related to the care of this cotton, and a copy of it was immediately sent to General Sherman and its receipt acknowledged by him. It was as follows:

WAR DEPARTMENT,
WASHINGTON, *December* 26, 1864.

Lieutenant-General GRANT, *City Point.*

I wish you a merry Christmas if not too late, and thank you for the Savannah news. It is a sore disappointment that Hardee was able to get off his fifteen thousand from Sherman's sixty thousand. It looks like protracting the war while their armies continue to escape. I hope you will give immediate instructions to seize and hold the cotton. All sorts of schemes will be got up to hold it under sham titles of British and other private claimants. They should all be disregarded; and it ought not to be turned over to any Treasury agent, but held by the military authorities until a special order of the department is given for the transfer. Thomas has been nominated for Major-General. EDWIN M. STANTON, *Secretary of War.*

THE CAPTURED COTTON AT SAVANNAH.

The part relating to cotton was sent by General Grant to General Sherman, and was thus answered by the latter:

HEADQUARTERS MILITARY DIVISION OF THE MISSISSIPPI, }
IN THE FIELD, SAVANNAH, GA., *January* 2, 1865. }

Hon. E. M. STANTON, *Secretary of War, Washington, D. C.*

I have just received from Lieutenant-General Grant a copy of that part of your telegram to him of December 26th relating to cotton, a copy of which has been immediately furnished to General Easton, Chief Quartermaster, who will be strictly governed by it.

I had already been approached by all the consuls and half the people of Savannah on this cotton question, and my invariable answer was that all the cotton in Savannah was prize of war, belonged to the United States, and nobody should recover a bale of it with my consent; that, as cotton had been one of the chief causes of this war, it should have to pay its expenses; that all cotton became tainted with treason from the hour the first act of hostility was committed against the United States some time in December, 1860, and that no bill of sale subsequent to that date could convey title.

My orders were that an officer of the Quartermaster's Department, United States Army, might furnish the holder, agent, or attorney a mere certificate of the fact of seizure, with description of the bales, marks, etc., the cotton then to be turned over to the agent of the Treasury Department to be shipped to New York for sale. But since the receipt of your dispatch I have ordered General Easton to make the shipment himself to the quartermaster at New York, where you can dispose of it at pleasure. I do not think the Treasury Department ought to bother itself with the prizes as captures of war.

W. T. SHERMAN, *Major-General.*

Soon after Mr. Stanton reached Savannah, and his first order there in regard to the cotton was this:

WAR DEPARTMENT, }
SAVANNAH, GA., *January* 12, 1865. }

Brevet Major-General MEIGS, *Quartermaster-General U. S. A., Savannah, Ga.*

SIR: The Secretary of War directs that you assume the charge of the captured cotton in this city, and provide for its proper care and preservation until further orders.

You will consider yourself charged with the duty of having sufficient guards and precautions for its security, and will apply to the commanding general for any force required.

You will also detail a competent quartermaster for the special duty of seeing to its being turned over and receipted for by the agents of the Treasury Department.

I am, sir, very respectfully, your obedient servant,

E. D. TOWNSEND, *Assistant Adjutant-General.*

In pursuance of this order General Meigs, then in Savannah, issued the following:

[Special Orders, No. 1.]

SAVANNAH, GA., *January* 12, 1865.

The Secretary of War having directed the Quartermaster-General to assume the charge of the captured cotton in this city and provide for its proper care and preservation, and to detail a competent quartermaster for the special duty of seeing to its being turned over and receipted for by the agents of the Treasury Department, Lieutenant Colonel H. C. Ransom is hereby detailed for this duty.

Brevet Brigadier-General L. C. Easton will place Lieutenant-Colonel Ransom in charge of all the cotton in his possession.

Lieutenant-Colonel Ransom will immediately make a careful inspection of the stores containing the captured cotton, and will make requisition for guards sufficient to prevent all danger of unauthorized persons entering the storehouses or meddling with the cotton.

No person not in the employment of the United States will be permitted to enter into or to loiter about the neighborhood of the buildings.

He will afford every facility for the operations of the Treasury agent, Simeon Draper, collector of the port of New York, who is charged by the Treasury Department with the care and disposition of this captured property.

He will employ competent clerks to attend to the weighing of each bale, who will keep an accurate register of the number and weight of each bale, and will take duplicate receipts in detail from the special agent of the Treasury Department before allowing any of it to leave the harbor. He will forward one copy of these receipts to the Quartermaster-General's office in Washington by the first mail after their execution.

The other copy and the books and all papers containing the records of this business he will himself carry in person to Washington, and will deliver them to the Quartermaster-General.

For the cotton already stored on board vessels, he will take receipts in detail from the special agent, based upon the accounts and invoices of this property prepared by Captain George B. Cadwallader, heretofore in charge of this duty.

In default of such receipts he will order the vessels to proceed to New York, invoicing the cotton to Brevet Brigadier-General Van Vliet, Chief Quartermaster, forwarding with the bills of lading an official copy of this order.

General Van Vliet will transfer the cotton in this case to the special agent of the Treasury in New York, upon receiving such receipts as are herein prescribed.

Lieutenant-Colonel Ransom will collect and register all the information offered to him of claims to the former ownership of this cotton. He will take this information with him to Washington, but will give copies or extracts from it to no one in Savannah but the Quartermaster-General.

The utmost vigilance will be exercised by Colonel Ransom in the execution of this important trust committed to him. He will himself visit the guards, and the presses and storehouses continually. He will see that no fires are lighted near the storehouses, or in the open streets or squares surrounding them. He will report to the officer commanding the guards all neglect or inattention on the part of the guards, and if this does not immediately produce a reform he will report the facts to the commanding officer of the post of Savannah. * * * *

Lieutenant-Colonel Ransom will confer freely with the special agent of the Treasury Department, and will call for such military assistance as may be necessary to discover and place him in possession of all the cotton in the city of Savannah, or within the lines occupied by its garrison. It is all prize of war. * * * *

M. C. MEIGS, *Quartermaster-General, Brevet Major-General.*

Next, in order that there might be no mistake in regard to the responsibility of the various parties charged with these duties, the following memorandum was drawn up, signed, and put on record:

OFFICE OF THE GENERAL AGENCY FOR CAPTURED AND ABANDONED PROPERTY, SAVANNAH, GA.

1. Cotton captured in Savannah, that is, all the cotton within the military post of Savannah and its defenses, has been taken possession of and is now held by the Quartermaster-General, under the order of the Secretary of War.

2. The Quartermaster-General has also, under the order of the Secretary of War, detailed Lieutenant-Colonel Ransom, of the Quartermaster Department, to take charge of the cotton personally, to cause it to be weighed and a careful and accurate account to be taken and recorded.

To exclude all persons not employed by the United States and needed in this operation from the warehouses and docks and their vicinity.

To transfer the cotton to the special agent of the Treasury Department, taking duplicate receipts therefor in detail, said receipts specifying the number and weight of every bale thus transferred to the special agent of the Treasury Department.

To allow none of the cotton to leave the harbor until said receipts are given to him by the agent aforesaid. * * * *

4. The original instructions of the Secretary of the Treasury of 28th December, 1864, designated Simeon Draper, Esq., as the special agent to take charge of the captured cotton, and to give receipts therefor as provided by law.

The instructions of the 7th January to Albert G. Browne, special agent, communicated also to Simeon Draper, Esq., direct that Mr. Browne shall receive from the military authorities who are in possession of the cotton, and give receipts therefor in the form prescribed by the Treasury regulations. * * * *

M. C. MEIGS, *Q. M. Gen., Brevet Major-Gen. U. S. A.*
ALBERT G. BROWNE, *Supervising Special Ag't Treas. Dep't.*
S. DRAPER, *Treasury Agent.*
S. H. KAUFFMAN.

In addition to the above, Mr. Draper carried special instructions from Secretary Fessenden, and approved by the President, for his " government in the examination of marks and numbers, former ownership, as near as it can be ascertained, and its shipment."

Among many other details these instructions provided that:

"The marks and numbers must be carefully recorded, not only such as are complete, but also such as have been in part obliterated, as nearly as can be ascertained.

"These directions you will cause to be carefully observed, that the records may be complete in regard to any bales, or package, or number of packages, belonging to the same lot, so that any package or lot, or the proceeds thereof, may be clearly identified should any question in relation thereto hereafter be brought before the Court of Claims."

These various extracts from the open records are quite sufficient to show that, so far from ordering any marks obliterated, directions were given to have the greatest care exercised to obtain a full record of them. The single paragraph in the order given by Mr. Stanton, directing all receipts to be given in the form prescribed by the Treasury regulations, insured the preservation of every mark.

As a matter of fact, the records in Washington which relate to this cotton are very complete. Every bale captured was fully and carefully registered, and the military officers in charge received and filed a receipt from the Treasury agents for every pound of it. These receipts are on file in the War Department and in the Treasury, and accessible to all who desire information, and they have been constantly consulted by counsel of the United States and of claimants in all cases yet tried or prepared for trial. In a few instances, in re-pressing and repairing torn covering, some of the marks were unavoidably defaced.

The officers charged with preserving all means of identification, employed a force of citizen clerks, who had long been engaged in the cotton warehouses of Savannah, to superintend the re-pressing and shipping of the cotton, and they selected the books and blanks in common use for this purpose, and copied into and upon these all marks by which the merchants of Savannah and the shippers from that port had been accustomed to insure the perfect identification of cotton.

Aside from the records thus made, and forwarded afterward to Washington, there existed in each of the great cotton warehouses of Savannah a full record and description of each bale on hand when General Sherman's army took possession of the city, and these have been accessible to all interested.

Of the existence and completeness of the records here, General Sherman could have satisfied himself in a very few moments on any occasion. He could have ascertained all the above facts any day, and in less time than it must have taken him to compile the page of errors concerning the matter which his book contains.

If these records had been filed away among the musty documents pertaining to the war, there would have been a slight show of excuse for General Sherman; but what shall be said for him in view of the fact that he wrote thus recklessly about Secretary Stanton, with these records open to all men, in the War Department, with duplicates of them in the Treasury, in the Court of Claims, and in the printed files of Congress. They are records of the most public character. They have been consulted by the parties to every suit in which this cotton was involved. The War Department had furnished transcripts of the marks for seventy-seven cases to the Court of Claims, and the Government had printed them. Congress had called on the War Department for the entire record, embracing all the orders and directions which were given, and the receipts in full taken by Colonel Ransom, setting forth all the marks collected by the officers detailed for the duty by Mr. Stanton's order, and had printed the whole of it, and furnished copies to the War Department, and the completed history of the matter was at Sherman's elbow in the very building where he wrote.

The statement of the Memoirs that the Treasury Department has allowed claims for more than the total amount of cotton captured, and that claims have been proved up amounting to three times the whole capture, is without the least foundation.

The following is a statement prepared at the Treasury Department in regard to this Savannah cotton:

"The Treasury Department has not passed upon a single claim for cotton captured at Savannah, nor has it paid out a dollar on such claims, except upon judgments of the Court of Claims, under the act of March 12th, 1863.

"The following is a statement of the proceeds of said cotton and the claims therefor:

No. bales sold at New York	39,358	
No. bales allowed by Court of Claims	31,657	
	7,701	
No. bales claimed in cases pending in Court of Claims	4,901	
	2,800	
Net proceeds paid into Treasury	$7,259,499	73
Amount allowed by the Court of Claims	5,873,159	90
	$1,386,339	88
Proceeds claimed in pending cases	865,678	26
	$520,661	62

"If all pending claims are allowed there will remain two thousand eight hundred bales which are unclaimed, and a balance of $520,661 62 in the Treasury."

And now it will be interesting, in view of the severe though unjust strictures in which General Sherman indulges upon Mr. Stanton, to see what kind of orders Sherman gave looking to the preservation of the marks upon this cotton, when it was passing from his possession into the hands of the Treasury Department. He had previously preserved the marks, but on transferring it, directed the receipt to be taken in gross. This is the order:

[Special Field Orders No. 10.]
HEADQUARTERS MILITARY DIVISION OF THE MISSISSIPPI,
IN THE FIELD, SAVANNAH, GA., *January* 12, 1865.

1. Brevet Brigadier-General Easton, Chief Quartermaster, will turn over

to Simeon Draper, Esq., agent of the United States Treasury Department, all cotton now in the city of Savannah, prize of war, taking his receipt for the same in gross, and returning for it to the Quartermaster-General. * * *
By order of *General W. T. Sherman.*

L. M. Dayton, *Aide-de-Camp.*

And so it appears that General Sherman's transfer called only for a receipt in gross, and that Mr. Stanton's orders alone secured the full record with which the Government has protected itself against fictitious claims.

There is another instance in which General Sherman attempts, with as little reason and success, to be severe upon Mr. Stanton, which may properly be presented in this connection.

In the second bulletin which the Secretary of War published on April 27th, concerning General Sherman's arrangements with General Johnston, the following paragraphs appeared from a dispatch of General Halleck's, dated Richmond, April 26th, 9:30 P. M.:

"The bankers here have information to-day that Jeff. Davis' specie is moving south from Goldsboro, in wagons, as fast as possible. * * * *
"The specie taken with them is estimated here at from six to thirteen million dollars."

Commenting upon these paragraphs, General Sherman says:

"The assertion that Jeff. Davis' specie train, of six to thirteen million dollars was reported to be moving south from Goldsboro in wagons as fast as possible, found plenty of willing ears, though my army of eighty thousand men had been at Goldsboro from March 22d to the date of his dispatch, April 26th; and such a train would have been composed of from fifteen to thirty-two six-mule teams to have hauled this specie, even if it all were in gold. I suppose the exact amount of treasure which Davis had with him is now known to a cent; some of it was paid to his escort when it disbanded at and near Washington, Georgia, and at the time of his capture he had a small parcel of gold and silver coin, not to exceed ten thousand dollars, which is now retained in the United States Treasury vault at Washington, and shown to the curious.

"The thirteen millions of treasure with which Jeff. Davis was to corrupt our armies and buy his escape, dwindled down to the contents of a hand valise! To say that I was merely angry at the tone and substance of these published bulletins of the War Department, would hardly express the state of my feelings. I was outraged beyond measure, and was resolved to resent the insult, cost what it might."

This ridicule of Halleck is based upon a perfectly evident misprint of "Goldsboro" for "Greensboro" in transmitting Halleck's dispatch of the 26th April, as it was through the latter place the rebel Cabinet passed.

How little reason he had for this outburst upon the question of Jeff. Davis' gold, will appear from the fact that the day before this telegram of Halleck's was written, General Sherman had himself telegraphed substantially the same thing to Admiral Dahlgren, and also to General Gillmore. The following is Sherman's gold dispatch:

RALEIGH, N. C., *April* 25, 1865.

Major-General G. A. GILLMORE, Commanding Department of the South,
and
Real-Admiral JOHN A. DAHLGREN, *Commanding S. A. B. Squadron.*

I expect Johnston will surrender his army. We have had much negotiation, and things are settling down to the terms of Lee's army. Jeff. Davis and his Cabinet, with considerable specie, is making his way toward Cuba. He passed Charlotte, going south, on the 23d, and I think he will try to reach the Florida coast either at Cedar Keys or lower down. It would be well to catch him. Can't you watch the East coast, and send word round to the West coast? W. T. SHERMAN, *Major-General.*

The facts presented from the records in this chapter, are quite sufficient to show the totally unreliable character of what the General of the army has written reflecting upon the great War Secretary.

CHAPTER XVI.

THE BATTLE OF BENTONVILLE—THE CARELESS ADVANCE OF AN ARMY.

THE battle of Bentonville affords one of the most marked examples of carelessness in the management of a great army which can be found in the history of the war.

Unlike the march from Atlanta to the sea, that from Savannah northward through the Carolinas originated with General Sherman. And in all respects it was a wonderful movement.

The first instructions of General Grant contemplated an entrenched camp near Savannah, and the transportation of the bulk of Sherman's force by sea to City Point. General Sherman was very anxious, however, to capture Savannah, and then march northward by land. The reasons he gave Grant were such as to induce the latter to accept Sherman's plan as better than his own.

The campaign from Savannah was in every way more difficult and hazardous than the march from Atlanta. In coming down to the sea there had been no veteran enemy in front, nor indeed, any force worthy of mention, nor had there been important garrisons on either flank to threaten or annoy. The roads were in the general direction of the larger streams, and the country was well adapted to the march of an army.

But from the moment of leaving Savannah grave difficulties were to be expected at every step. The country was low and exceedingly swampy, the rains had swollen the streams and flooded the low lands, and the direction of the march was across them all. In front was Hardee with a force which might be formidable in contending the passage of the larger rivers. On the right were the garrisons of Charleston, Georgetown, and Wilmington. There was reason to expect that a portion of Hood's army would arrive on the left and strike from the direction of Augusta. Lastly, Wade Hampton, then popular in South Carolina, had been sent down from Lee's army to rally an opposing force. And, as the result proved, before serious battle was delivered, an army estimated at thirty-seven thousand veteran Confederate troops concentrated at Bentonville, under Sherman's old antagonist Johnston. The Union force at the time was fifty-seven thousand.

In free conversation between General Schofield's officers and the prominent commanders in the Confederate forces, when they were paroled a few weeks later, all expressed great admiration for the campaign northward from Savannah and astonishment at its success. They had confidently expected, when the Union army began to push through the great swamps, that it would lose its artillery and its trains, and never emerge in an organized condition. But the roads, constructed of logs and brush, which sunk to the axles of the artillery under the march of each successive division, were rebuilt by the division which followed, and the resistless columns moved steadily and surely against natural difficulties such as no other army breasted during the war.

Sherman had left smoking South Carolina, with its ruined railroads, behind him; his four corps had converged at Fayetteville, and there crossed the Cape Fear River. Here the right and left wings again separated, but marched in the general direction of Goldsboro. All the Confederate garrisons of points below were piled up in his front, the provisions were running low in his trains, and there was need of unusual care and prudence. How great was the neglect instead, and how narrow the escape of Sherman from serious disaster, **the history of the battle of Bentonville will show.**

14

Little became known at the time, of the real character of this battle. The surrender of Lee, which occurred before the facts connected with Bentonville could be disclosed, and the appalling death of Mr. Lincoln, occupied the full attention of the country. By the time it so recovered as to turn its mind toward North Carolina, Johnston had offered to surrender, and so Bentonville passed almost unnoticed.

It is just to General Sherman to say, that in his Memoirs he brings the real facts connected with this action into bolder relief than any other of his mistakes of which he treats. But the official record supplies some important omissions.

Concerning the start from Savannah northward, General Sherman writes:

"I knew full well at the time that the broken fragments of Hood's army (which had escaped from Tennessee) were being hurried rapidly across Georgia, by Augusta, to make junction in my front, estimating them at the maximum, twenty-five thousand men, and Hardee's, Wheeler's, and Hampton's forces at fifteen thousand, made forty thousand, which, if handled with spirit and energy, would constitute a formidable force, and might make the passage of such rivers as the Santee and Cape Fear a difficult undertaking."

His whole army reached Fayetteville, North Carolina, and crossed the Cape Fear to move on Goldsboro, where he expected to make a junction with General Schofield, then advancing from Newbern. From this point, in a letter to General Grant, dated March 12, 1865, he said:

"Jos. Johnston may try to interpose between me here and Schofield about Newbern, but I think he will not try that, but concentrate his scattered armies at Raleigh, and I will go straight at him as soon as I get our men reclothed and our wagons reloaded."

And in another letter of the same date to General Terry, he wrote:

"I can whip Jos. Johnston provided he does not catch one of my corps in flank, and I will see that the army marches hence to Goldsboro in compact form."

But, in spite of this good resolution, the right and left wings were marched on roads from ten to fifteen miles apart, and each wing was strung out at great length.

Of the start from Fayetteville, General Sherman writes:

"I then knew that my special antagonist, General Jos. Johnston, was back, with part of his old army; that he would not be misled by feints and false reports, and would, somehow, compel me to exercise more caution than I had hitherto done. I then overestimated his force at thirty-seven thousand infantry, supposed to be made up of S. D. Lee's corps, four thousand; Cheatham's, five thousand; Hope's, eight thousand; Hardee's, ten thousand; and other detachments, ten thousand; with Hampton's, Wheeler's, and Butler's cavalry, about eight thousand. Of these, only Hardee and the cavalry were immediately in our front, while the bulk of Johnston's army was supposed to be collecting at or near Raleigh. * * * *

"On the 15th of March the whole army was across Cape Fear River, and at once began its march for Goldsboro—the Seventeenth Corps still on the right, the Fifteenth next in order, then the Fourteenth and Twentieth on the extreme left, the cavalry acting in close concert with the left flank. With almost a certainty of being attacked on this flank, I had instructed General Slocum to send his corps trains, under strong escort, by an interior road, holding four divisions ready for immediate battle. General Howard was in like manner ordered to keep his trains well to his right, and to have four divisions, unencumbered, about six miles ahead of General Slocum, within easy support." * * * *

On the 16th, about Averysboro, "the opposition continued stubborn," and General Slocum had quite a brisk fight, losing twelve officers and sixty-five men killed, and four hundred and seventy-seven wounded.

The succeeding events are thus described in the Memoirs:

"From Averysboro the left wing turned east toward Goldsboro, the Fourteenth Corps leading. I remained with this wing until the night of the 18th, when we were within twenty-seven miles of Goldsboro, and five from Bentonville; and, supposing that all danger was over, I crossed over to join Howard's column, to the right, so as to be nearer to Generals Schofield and Terry, known to be approaching Goldsboro. I overtook General Howard at Falling Creek Church, and found his column well drawn out, by reason of the bad roads. I had heard some cannonading over about Slocum's head of column, and supposed it to indicate about the same measure of opposition by Hardee's troops and Hampton's cavalry, before experienced. But, during the day, a messenger overtook me, and notified me, that, near Bentonville, General

Slocum had run up against *Johnston's whole army*. I sent back orders for him to fight defensively, to save time, and that I would come up, with reënforcements, from the direction of Cox's Bridge, by the road which we had reached near Falling Creek Church. The country was very obscure, and the maps extremely defective.

"By this movement I hoped General Slocum would hold Johnston's army facing west, while I would come on his rear from the east. The Fifteenth Corps, less one division (Hazen's), still well to the rear, was turned at once toward Bentonville; Hazen's division was ordered to Slocum's flank; and orders were also sent for General Blair, with the Seventeenth Corps, to come to the same destination. Meantime the sound of cannon came from the direction of Bentonville.

"The night of the 19th caught us near Falling Creek Church; but early the next morning the Fifteenth Corps, General C. R. Wood's division leading, closed down on Bentonville, near which it was brought up by encountering a line of fresh parapet, crossing the road and extending north toward Mill Creek.

"After deploying, I ordered General Howard to proceed with due caution, using skirmishers alone, till he had made junction with General Slocum, on his left. These deployments occupied all day, during which two divisions of the Seventeenth Corps also got up. At that time General Johnston's army occupied the form of a V, the angle reaching the road leading from Averysboro to Goldsboro, and the flanks resting on Mill Creek, his lines embracing the village of Bentonville.

"General Slocum's wing faced one of these lines, and General Howard's the other; and, in the uncertainty of General Johnston's strength, I did not feel disposed to invite a general battle, for we had been out from Savannah since the latter part of January, and our wagon trains contained but little food. I had also received messages during the day from General Schofield, at Kinston, and General Terry, at Faison's Depot, approaching Goldsboro; both expected to reach it by March 21. During the 20th we simply held our ground, and started our trains back to Kinston for provisions, which would be needed in the event of being forced to fight a general battle at Bentonville. The next day (21st) it began to rain again, and we remained quiet till about noon, when General Mower, ever rash, broke through the rebel line on his extreme left flank, and was pushing straight for Bentonville and the bridge across Mill Creek. I ordered him back to connect with his own corps, and, lest the enemy should concentrate on him, ordered the whole rebel line to be engaged with a strong skirmish fire.

"I think I made a mistake there, and should rapidly have followed Mowers' lead with the whole of the right wing, which would have brought on a general battle, and it could not have resulted otherwise than successfully to us, by reason of our vastly superior numbers; but at the moment, for the reasons given, I preferred to make junction with Generals Terry and Schofield, before engaging Johnston's army, the strength of which was utterly unknown.

The next day he was gone, and had retreated on Smithfield; and, the roads all being clear, our army moved to Goldsboro. The heaviest fighting at Bentonville was on the first day, viz.: the 19th, when Johnston's army struck the head of Slocum's column, knocking back Carlin's division. But as soon as General Slocum had brought up the rest of the Fourteenth Corps into line, and afterward the Twentieth on his left, he received and repulsed all attacks, and held his ground, as ordered, to await the coming back of the right wing."

General Sherman's formal report of this battle, dated Goldsboro, April 4, 1865, contains the following very contradictory statements concerning the attack:

"All the signs induced me to believe that the enemy would make no further opposition to our progress, and would not attempt to strike us in flank while in motion."

A few paragraphs below, in the same report, he again refers to the matter, as follows:

"Johnston had moved, by night, from Smithfield, with great rapidity, and without unnecessary wheels, intending to overwhelm my left flank before it could be relieved by its coöperating columns. But he reckoned without his host. I had expected just such a movement all the way from Fayetteville, and was prepared for it."

From the above extracts it is quite evident that Johnston attempted to concentrate his forces, fall upon the left wing of Sherman's army, crush it before the others could arrive, and then, in turn, attack the right, and that he came much nearer success than it is pleasant to contemplate. The warnings of such a concentration, as will be seen, were abundant. That they were not heeded seems marvelous and the extreme of carelessness. Some of the telegrams accompanying a former printed report of General Sherman make the situation still clearer.

The advance of the left wing began at seven o'clock on the 19th of March, and was stubbornly contested from the first. About ten o'clock General Slocum became convinced that he had encountered the enemy in force. He therefore concluded to assume the offensive, and communicate with General Sherman. The two wings were so far separated that it was six or seven hours before the commanding general, who was with the right wing, could be reached.

At five P. M., of the 19th, he sent the following dispatch to General Schofield, then approaching Goldsboro:

"Since making my dispatch to-day (2 P. M.) General Slocum reports the enemy in force between him and Cox's Bridge; thinks it is the main army of the enemy. I can hardly suppose the enemy will attempt to fight us this side of the Neuse, but will direct all my columns on Cox's Bridge to-morrow. You must secure Goldsboro, and fortify."

At the same hour he dispatched General Kilpatrick:

"Your report of to-day is received. General Slocum thinks the whole rebel army is in his front. I can not think Johnston would fight us with the Neuse to his rear."

On the morning of the 20th, at 4 A. M., General Sherman wrote as follows to General Terry:

"Johnston, with his concentrated force, made an unsuccessful attack on my left wing yesterday, near Bentonville. I am just starting with my right wing to attack him."

And again to General Terry at 6 A. M.:

"Yesterday Johnston, with his force concentrated, struck my left wing, near Bentonville, and they had a severe battle, lasting until night. General Slocum beat them off, but was uneasy. I am now turning the right wing on Bentonville. * * * * By to-night I will know if Jos. Johnston intends to fight me in force, when I will communicate further."

To General Schofield, at 2 P. M., of the 20th, he wrote:

"I am now within two miles of Slocum, but Johnston is between us. We are now skirmishing."

As will be observed, this was twenty-eight hours after the attack in force began on Slocum.

At 8 P. M., of the 20th, he wrote General Slocum:

"We struck the enemy on his left rear about noon and have pressed him very hard, and have dislodged him from all his barricades except the line constructed as against you, which may be double or inclosed, for our men find parapets from the road well down to Mill Creek. Johnston hoped to overcome your wing before I could come to your relief; having failed in that I can not see why he remains, and still think he will avail himself of night to get back to Smithfield. I would rather avoid a general battle if possible, but if he insists on it we must accommodate him. In that event, if he be in position to-morrow, I want you to make a good road around his flank into this, and to-morrow night pass your trains and dispose your troops so that we have our back toward Faison's and Goldsboro. General Schofield was to leave Kinston for Goldsboro to-day, and General Terry has arrived with nine thousand infantry at Faison's, and I have ordered him to Cox's Bridge to be drawn up here if we need him. I can also draw on General Schofield in a few days for ten thousand men, but I think we have enough."

At 9 P. M. of the same day the following dispatch was sent General Terry:

"We struck Johnston on his left rear to-day, and have been skirmishing pretty hard all day. We have opened communication with General Slocum, who had a hard fight yesterday. We are now ready for battle, if Johnston desires it, to-morrow; but as he has failed to overcome one wing he will hardly invite battle with both. I don't want to fight now or here, and therefore won't object to his drawing off to-night toward Smithfield, as he should."

To General Schofield he wrote, March 21, from Bentonville:

"Captain Twining is here, and I send by him an order that you will perceive looks to staying here some days.

"I thought Johnston, having failed as he attempted to crush one of my wings, finding he had not succeeded, but that I was present with my whole force, would withdraw; but he has not, and I must fight him here. He is twenty (20) miles from Smithfield, and with a bad road to his rear, but his position is in the swamps, difficult of approach, and I don't like to assail his parapets, which are of the old kind."

In a letter to General Grant dated March 22, quoted in the Memoirs, reviewing the affair of Bentonville at length, the following passage occurs:

"I wrote you from Fayetteville, North Carolina, on Tuesday, the 14th instant, that I was all ready to start for Goldsboro, to which point I had also ordered General Schofield from Newbern and General Terry from Wilmington. I knew that General Jos. Johnston was in supreme command against me, and that he would have tried to concentrate a respectable army to oppose the last stage of this march * * * * On Tuesday, the 15th [probably a misprint for Thursday the 16th], General Slocum found Hardee's army from Charleston, which had retreated before us from Cheraw, in position across the narrow swampy neck between Cape Fear and North Rivers where the road branches off to Goldsboro. There a pretty severe fight occurred, in which General Slocum's troops carried handsomely the advanced line, held by a South Carolina brigade commanded by a Colonel Butler. * * * *

"We resumed the march toward Goldsboro. I was with the left wing until I supposed all danger had passed, but when General Slocum's head of column was within four miles of Bentonville, after skirmishing as usual with cavalry, he became aware that there was infantry at his front. He deployed a couple of brigades, which, on advancing, sustained a partial repulse, but soon rallied, and he formed a line of the two leading divisions, Morgan's and Carlin's, of Jeff. C. Davis' corps. The enemy attacked these with violence, but was repulsed. This was in the forenoon of Sunday, the 19th. General Slocum brought forward the two divisions of the Twentieth Corps, hastily disposed of them for defense, and General Kilpatrick massed his cavalry on the left.

"General Jos. Johnston had the night before marched his whole army (Bragg, Cheatham, S. D. Lee, Hardee, and all the troops he had drawn from every quarter), determined, as he told his men, to crush one of our corps and then defeat us in detail He attacked General Slocum in position from 3 P. M. on the 19th till dark, but was every where repulsed and lost heavily. At the time I was with the Fifteenth Corps marching on a road more to the right, but on hearing of General Slocum's danger directed that corps toward Cox's Bridge, in the night brought Blair's corps over, and on the 20th marched rapidly on Johnston's flank and rear. We struck him about noon and forced him to assume the defensive and to fortify. Yesterday we pushed him hard and came very near crushing him, the right division of the Seventeenth Corps, however, having broken in to within a hundred yards of where Johnston himself was, at the bridge across Mill Creek. Last night he retreated, leaving us in possession of the field, dead, and wounded." * * * *

The report of General Hazen, commanding the First Division of the right wing which started to the relief of the left, gives a clear idea of the distance of the left wing from the nearest support. Writing of his march to the relief of General Slocum, he says:

"On the 15th the march was resumed in the direction of Goldsboro, which was continued at slow stages till midnight of the 19th, when I received orders to turn back to the assistance of General Slocum, and reported to him with the division near Bentonville at daylight, having marched since sunset twenty miles.

"At 12 M. of the 20th the division was moved to the rear of the Fourteenth Corps, and two regiments were deployed and connected with the First Division of the Fifteenth Corps on the right and the Fourteenth Corps on the left, engaged the enemy on their lines." * * * *

The extent to which the left wing was stretched out on the road is shown by a paragraph in General Slocum's report:

"On the following morning (20th) Generals Baird and Geary, each with two brigades of their respective divisions, and General Hazen, of the Fifteenth Corps, with his entire division, arrived on the field."

The first-named generals belonged to the left wing and Hazen to the right. As to the arrival of the left wing in force General Slocum says:

"On the morning of the 21st the right wing came up and connected with General Hazen."

The battle began about ten o'clock on the 19th. One division of the right wing, by a long night march, came up the next morning, but the main body of that wing was not ready to strike the enemy until the morning of the 21st.

The situation of affairs around Bentonville, then, was about this: With a full knowledge that Johnston was rapidly concentrating all available forces in his front, the two wings of the Union army, each inferior to Johnston's supposed numbers, were allowed to march in extremely open order, and so far apart that, when an attack in force began on the left wing at ten o'clock on the 19th, it was not until noon of the next day that part of the other wing came within striking distance, and even then it was not able to communicate directly with the left wing because the enemy was interposed in force.

The total strength of the left wing was less than twenty-six thousand, and only a portion of this could be brought up for the first day's fight. General Johnston's force was then estimated at thirty-seven thousand, though he afterward stated that he had only fourteen thousand infantry engaged.

The Union officers and men fought splendidly, and thus

neutralized the effect of General Sherman's carelessness and saved their wing of the army. Still, in spite of their gallant fighting against superior numbers, it was probably owing to a mistake on the Confederate side that the left wing was not wholly overpowered.

A general assault had been contemplated by the Confederate generals about an hour before sundown. But by some error in conveying commands, or in obeying them, night came on before their lines were ready for the movement, and so the opportunity for crushing Sherman's left wing passed. Thus narrowly did this magnificent army escape serious disaster in its last battle.

General Sherman speaks repeatedly of Generals Schofield and Terry as if they were independent commanders, and says: "Wilmington was captured by General Terry on the 22d of February."

Accurately, General Terry's forces formed a portion of the command of General Schofield, and advanced on Wilmington upon the left bank of the Cape Fear River, while the Twenty-Third Corps formed the other part of Schofield's army, and advanced on the right bank of the river. General J. D. Cox's troops of this latter corps, with one division of Terry's troops, assisted by the fleet, drove the enemy out of Fort Anderson, and then by secretly passing Casement's brigade in flats over Town Creek near its mouth, General Cox secured the main crossing over that strongly guarded stream, and opened the way to the rear of Wilmington, which, as a consequence, was immediately evacuated. As General Schofield directed all the movements, a careful writer would have said Wilmington was captured by General Schofield.

CHAPTER XVII.

THE TERMS WITH JOHNSTON—THE FIRST DRAFT MADE BY A CONFEDERATE CABINET OFFICER.

GENERAL SHERMAN sneers at political generals, and then devotes thirty pages of his Memoirs to an inaccurate history of his own political surrender to General Jos. E. Johnston near Raleigh.

The country will never forget its joy over the news from Appomattox, or the chill which shortly after fell upon it when the true character of Sherman's terms became known. If the country at large ever does forget the circumstances attending the latter event, those who were at Raleigh at the time never will.

The real character of these terms was carefully concealed there, even from very prominent officers, and was known first at the North. It was given out at Sherman's headquarters that the terms granted Johnston were virtually the same as those extended by Grant to Lee, and special stress was laid upon the statement that in no sense had General Sherman recognized the political existence of the Confederacy.

When General Grant arrived and announced the prompt rejection of these terms, their real nature first became known. There was much indignation in consequence at Sherman's course, and many comparisons of views among officers of rank as to his motives. The speedy and successful correction of his great error, and the immediate close of the war, over which the Nation was so busy with its rejoicing, alone saved him from damaging criticism. If it had been made known then that the first draft of Sherman's terms was written by the rebel Postmaster-General at a consultation had between this member of Davis' Cabinet, his Secretary of War, Generals Johnston, and Wade Hampton, it would have made General Sherman's position most uncomfortable before the people. But in view of the services he had rendered, this, and other unpleasant facts did not find their way to the public then. Now that he has so recklessly invited criticism, and published an inaccurate version of these very negotiations, he can not complain if the beliefs which were entertained among prominent officers at Raleigh, find expression, and documents captured soon after the surrender are made public.

The theory of General Sherman's negotiation with General Johnston, as held by many prominent officers, whose opportunities for obtaining knowledge were excellent, was about this:

General Sherman was elated almost beyond measure at his March to the Sea, and northward through the Carolinas. He had rested and refurnished his army at Goldsboro, and had just issued an order for it to march for the purpose of joining the Army of the Potomac, when down came the news, first, of the evacuation of Richmond, and, following close, of the surrender of Lee. General Grant had captured the great army of the Confederacy; all the rest must follow, as a matter of course; Sherman was not in at the death; the war was to close with General Grant its greatest military hero. Then came the proposal for a conference from Johnston. While first writing to Johnston that he would extend the same terms given by Grant to Lee, and immediately writing General Grant that he would "be careful not to complicate any points of civil policy;" yet, doubtless influenced by his own reflections upon the secondary position in which events were leaving him, and by the cunning manipulations of the rebel Cabinet, he conceived the idea, not only of receiving the surrender of the remaining military forces of the rebellion, and declaring "peace from the Potomac to the Rio Grande," but of becoming the political reconstructor of the Nation, and thus the most prominent character emerging from the war.

Before any pronounce this theory chimerical, let them read the narratives, extracts, and records which follow.

The material points of General Sherman's account of his negotiations with General Johnston are these:

On April 14, 1865, a note was received from Johnston, dated the day before, asking whether, since "the results of the recent campaign in Virginia have changed the relative military character of the belligerents," General Sherman was willing, in order "to stop the further effusion of blood and devastation of property," to ask from General Grant a suspension of hostilities for the purpose of permitting "the civil authorities to enter into the needful arrangements to terminate the existing war."

General Sherman wrote Johnston the same day that he had authority to suspend hostilities, that he would meet Johnston to confer upon the subject, and added: "that a basis of action may be had, I undertake to abide by the same terms and conditions as were made by Generals Grant and Lee at Appomattox Court House on the 9th inst., relative to our two armies."

The same evening he wrote General Grant as follows, though this letter is not given in the Memoirs:

"I send copies of a correspondence begun with General Johnston, which I think will be followed by terms of capitulation. I will grant the same terms as General Grant gave General Lee, and be careful not to complicate any points of civil policy."

On the 17th the opposing commanders met alone in a farmhouse near Durham Station, when, after some conversation over the assassination of Mr. Lincoln, Sherman says:

"I then told Johnston that he must be convinced that he could not oppose my army, and that since Lee had surrendered he could do the same with honor and propriety. He plainly and repeatedly admitted this, and added that any further fighting would be '*murder*,' but he thought that instead of surrendering piecemeal we might arrange terms that would embrace *all* the Confederate armies. I asked him if he could control other armies than his own. He said not then, but intimated that he could procure authority from Mr. Davis. I then told him that I had recently had an interview with General Grant and President Lincoln, and that I was possessed of their views. * * * * That the terms that General Grant had given to General Lee's army were certainly most generous and liberal. All this he admitted, but always recurred to the idea of a universal surrender, embracing his own army, that of Dick Taylor in Louisiana and Texas, and of Maury, Forrest, and others in Alabama and Georgia. * * * *

"Our conversation was very general and extremely cordial, satisfying me that it could have but one result, and that which we all desired, viz.: to end the war as quickly as possible; and, being anxious to return to Raleigh before the news of Mr. Lincoln's assassination could be divulged, on General Johnston's saying that he thought that, during the night, he could procure authority to act in the name of all the Confederate armies in existence, we agreed to meet again the next day at noon, at the same place, and parted, he for Hillsboro and I for Raleigh."

On the 18th the two Generals met again near Durham. The Memoirs give the following account of the interview:

* * * * "We again entered Bennett's house and I closed the door. General Johnston then assured me that he had authority over all the Confederate armies, so that they would obey his orders to surrender on the same terms with his own, but he argued that, to obtain so cheaply this desirable result, I ought to give his men and officers some assurance of their political rights after their surrender. I explained to him that Mr. Lincoln's proclamation of amnesty of December 8, 1863, still in force, enabled every Confederate soldier and officer below the rank of colonel to obtain an absolute pardon by simply laying down his arms and taking the common oath of allegiance, and that General Grant, in accepting the surrender of General Lee's army, had extended the same principle to *all* the officers, General Lee included. Such a pardon, I understood, would restore to them all their rights of citizenship. But he insisted that the officers and men of the Confederate army were unnecessarily alarmed about this matter as a sort of bugbear. He then said that Mr. Breckinridge was near at hand, and he thought that it would be well for him to be present. I objected on the score that he was then in Davis' Cabinet, and our negotiations should be confined strictly to belligerents. He then said Breckinridge was a Major-General in the Confederate army, and might sink his character of Secretary of War. I consented, and he sent one of his staff officers back, who soon returned with Breckinridge, and he entered the room. General Johnston and I then again went over the whole ground, and Breckinridge confirmed what he had said as to the uneasiness of the Southern officers and soldiers about their political rights in case of surrender. While we were in consultation, a messenger came with a parcel of papers, which General Johnston said were from Mr. Reagan, Postmaster-General. He and Breckinridge looked over them, and, after some side conversation, he handed one of the papers to me. It was in Reagan's handwriting, and began with a long preamble and terms, so general and verbose that I said they were inadmissible. Then recalling the conversation of Mr. Lincoln at City Point, I sat down at the table and wrote off the terms, which, I thought, concisely expressed his views and wishes, and explained that I was willing to submit these terms to the new President, Mr. Johnson, provided that both armies should remain in *statu quo* until the truce therein declared should expire. I had full faith that General Johnston would religiously respect the truce, which he did; and that I would be the gainer, for, in the few days it would take to send the papers to Washington and receive an answer, I could finish the railroad up to Raleigh, and be the better prepared for a long chase.

"Neither Mr. Breckinridge nor General Johnston wrote one word of that paper. I wrote it myself, and announced it as the best I could do, and they readily assented."

General Johnston, in his Narrative, gives the following account of the consultation held at President Davis' quarters at Charlotte, after the news of Lee's surrender was received:

"In a telegram dated Greensboro, 4:30 P. M., the President directed me to leave the troops under Lieutenant-General Hardee's command, and report to him there.

"Taking the first train, about midnight, I reached Greensboro about eight o'clock in the morning on the 12th, and was General Beauregard's guest. His quarters were a burden car, near, and in sight of those of the President. The General and myself were summoned to the President's office in an hour or two, and found Messrs. Benjamin, Mallory, and Reagan with him. We had supposed that we were to be questioned concerning the military resources of our department, in connection with the question of continuing or terminating the war.

"But the President's object seemed to be to give, not to obtain information; for, addressing the party, he said that in two or three weeks he would have a large army in the field by bringing back into the ranks those who had abandoned them in less desperate circumstances, and by calling out the enrolled men whom the conscript bureau, with its forces, had been unable to bring into the army. It was remarked, by the military officers, that men who had left the army when our cause was not desperate, and those who, under the same circumstances, could not be forced into it, would scarcely, in the present desperate condition of our affairs, enter the service upon mere invitation. Neither opinions nor information was asked, and the conference terminated. Before leaving the room, we learned that Major-General Breckinridge's arrival was expected in the course of the afternoon, and it was not doubted that he would bring certain intelligence of the state of affairs in Virginia.

"General Breckinridge came as expected, and confirmed the report of the surrender of the army in Virginia. General Beauregard and myself, conversing together after the intelligence of the great disaster, reviewed the condition of our affairs, and carefully compared the resources of the belligerents, and agreed in the opinion that the Southern Confederacy was overthrown. In conversation with General Breckinridge afterward, I repeated this, and said that the only power of government left in the President's hands was that of terminating the war, and that this power should be exercised without more delay. I also expressed my readiness to suggest to the President the absolute necessity of such action, should an opportunity to do so be given me. General Breckinridge promised to make me this opportunity.

"Mr. Mallory came to converse with me on the subject, and showed great anxiety that negotiations to end the war should be commenced, and urged that I was the person who should suggest the measure to the President. I, on the contrary, thought that such a suggestion would come more properly from one of his 'constitutional advisers,' but told Mr. Mallory of my conversation with General Breckinridge.

"That gentleman fulfilled his engagement promptly; and General Beauregard and myself were summoned to the President's office an hour or two after the meeting of his Cabinet there next morning. Being desired by the President to do it, we compared the military forces of the two parties to the war: ours, an army of about twenty thousand infantry and artillery, and five thousand mounted troops; those of the United States, three armies that could be combined against ours, which was insignificant compared with either—Grant's, of a hundred and eighty thousand men; Sherman's, of a hundred and ten thousand at least; and Canby's, of sixty thousand—odds of seventeen or eighteen to one, which in a few weeks could be more than doubled.

"I represented that, under such circumstances, it would be the greatest of human crimes for us to attempt to continue the war; for, having neither money nor credit, nor arms but those in the hands of our soldiers, nor ammunition but that in their cartridge boxes, nor shops for repairing arms or fixing ammunition, the effect of our keeping the field would be not to harm the enemy, but to complete the devastation of our country and ruin of its people. I, therefore, urged that the President should exercise at once the only function of government still in his possession, and open negotiations for peace.

"The members of the Cabinet present were then desired by the President to express their opinions on the important question. General Breckinridge, Mr. Mallory, and Mr. Reagan, thought that the war was decided against us; and that it was absolutely necessary to make peace. Mr. Benjamin expressed the contrary opinion. The latter made a speech for war, much like that of Sempronius in Addison's play. The President replied to our suggestion as if somewhat annoyed by it. He said that it was idle to suggest that he should attempt to negotiate, when it was certain, from the attempt previously made, that his authority to treat would not be recognized, nor any terms that he might offer considered by the Government of the United States. I reminded him that it had not been unusual, in such cases, for military commanders to initiate negotiations upon which treaties of peace were founded; and proposed that he should allow me to address General Sherman on the subject. After a few words in opposition to that idea, Mr. Davis reverted to the first suggestion, that he should offer terms to the Government of the United States—which he had put aside; and sketched a letter appropriate to be sent by me to General Sherman, proposing a meeting to arrange the terms of an armistice to enable the civil authorities to agree upon terms of peace. That this course might be adopted at once, I proposed that he should dictate the letter then to Mr. Mallory, who was a good penman, and that I should sign and send it to the Federal commander immediately. The letter, prepared in that way, was sent by me with all dispatch to Lieutenant-General Hampton, near Hillsboro, to be forwarded by him to General Sherman. It was delivered to the latter next day, the 14th, and was in these terms:

"'The results of the recent campaign in Virginia have changed the relative military condition of the belligerents. I am, therefore, induced to address you, in this form, the inquiry whether, in order to stop the further effusion of blood and devastation of property, you are willing to make a temporary suspension of active operations, and to communicate to Lieutenant General Grant, commanding the armies of the United States, the request that he will take like action in regard to other armies—the object being to permit the civil authorities to enter into the needful arrangements to terminate the existing war.'"

After mentioning the means taken to secure a meeting, the Narrative continues with an account of the interview, which General Sherman thus indorses:

"General Johnston's account of our interview, in his Narrative (page 402, *et seq.*), is quite accurate and correct, only I do not recall his naming the capitulation of Loeben to which he refers."

Johnston's statement, thus referred to and indorsed, is as follows:

"When General Sherman understood what seemed to have escaped him in reading my letter, that my object was to make such an armistice as would give opportunity for negotiation between the 'civil authorities' of the two countries, he said that such negotiations were impossible, because the Government of the United States did not acknowledge the existence of a Southern

Confederacy; nor, consequently, its civil authorities as such. Therefore, he could not receive, for transmission, any proposition addressed to the Government of the United States by those claiming to be the civil authorities of a Southern Confederacy. He added, in a manner that carried conviction of sincerity, expressions of a wish to divert from the South such devastation as the continuance of the war would make inevitable; and, as a means of accomplishing that object, so far as the armies we commanded were concerned, he offered me such terms as those given to General Lee.

"I replied that our relative positions were too different from those of the armies in Virginia to justify me in such a capitulation, but suggested that we might do more than he proposed; that, instead of a partial suspension of hostilities, we might, as other generals had done, arrange the terms of a permanent peace, and among other precedents reminded him of the preliminaries of Loeben, and the terms in which Napoleon, then victorious, proposed negotiation to the Archduke Charles, and the sentiment he expressed, that the civic crown earned by preserving the life of one citizen, confers truer glory than the highest achievement merely military. General Sherman replied, with heightened color, that he appreciated such a sentiment, and that to put an end to further devastation and bloodshed, and restore the Union, and with it the prosperity of the country, were to him objects of ambition.

"We then entered into a discussion of the terms that might be given to the Southern States, on their submission to the authority of the United States. General Sherman seemed to regard the resolutions of Congress and the declarations of the President of the United States as conclusive that the restoration of the Union was the object of the war, and to believe that the soldiers of the United States had been fighting for that object. A long official conversation with Mr. Lincoln, on Southern affairs, a very short time before, had convinced him that the President then adhered to that view.

"In the course of the afternoon we agreed upon the terms expressed in the memorandum drawn up on the 18th, except that General Sherman did not consent to include Mr. Davis and the officers of his Cabinet in an otherwise general amnesty. This consideration was mine of course. General Sherman did not desire the arrest of these gentlemen. He was too acute not to foresee the embarrassment their capture would cause; therefore, he wished them to escape. Much of the afternoon was consumed in endeavors to dispose of this part of the question in a manner that would be satisfactory both to the Government of the United States and the Southern people, as well as to the Confederate President; but at sunset no conclusion had been reached, and the conference was suspended, to be resumed at 10 o'clock next morning. Thinking it probable that the confidential relations of the Secretary of War with Mr. Davis might enable him to remove the only obstacle to an adjustment, I requested him by telegraph to join me as soon as possible.

"General Breckinridge and Mr. Reagan came to General Hampton's quarters together an hour or two before daybreak. After they had received from me as full an account of the discussion of the day before as my memory enabled me to give, and had learned the terms agreed upon, and the difficulty in the way of full agreement, Mr. Reagan proposed to reduce them to writing to facilitate reconsideration. In doing so, he included the article for amnesty without exceptions, the only one not fully agreed to. This paper being unfinished when General Breckinridge and myself set out to the place of meeting, was to be sent to me there.

When we met, I proposed to General Sherman that General Breckinridge should be admitted to our discussion, as his personal relations with the President of the Confederacy might enable him to remove the obstacle to agreement that we had encountered the day before. He assented, and that gentleman joined us.

"We had conversed on the subject discussed the day before, perhaps a half hour, when the memorandum written by Mr. Reagan was brought. I read this paper to General Sherman, as a basis for terms of peace, pointing out to him that it contained nothing which he had not already accepted, but the language that included the President and Cabinet in the terms of amnesty. After listening to General Breckinridge, who addressed him six or eight minutes in advocacy of these conditions of peace, General Sherman wrote very rapidly the memorandum that follows, with the paper presented by me before him. He wrote so rapidly that I thought at the time that he must have come to the place prepared to agree to amnesty, with no exceptions. His paper differed from mine only in being fuller."

General Sherman gives the following account of his consultations with his principal officers after his first interview with Johnston in regard to the character of terms that should be offered:

"During the evening of the 17th and morning of the 18th, I saw nearly all the general officers of the army (Schofield, Slocum, Howard, Logan, Blair), and we talked over the matter of the conference at Bennett's house of the day before, and without exception, all advised me to agree to some terms, for they all dreaded the long and harassing march in pursuit of a dissolving and fleeing army; a march that might carry us back again over the thousand miles that we had just accomplished. We all knew that if we could bring Johnston's army to bay, we could destroy it in an hour, but that was simply impossible in the country in which we found ourselves. We discussed all the probabilities, among which was, whether, if Johnston made a point of it, I should assent to the escape from the country of Jeff. Davis and his fugitive Cabinet; and some one of my general officers, either Logan or Blair, insisted that if asked for, we should even provide a vessel to carry them to Nassau from Charleston."

In Craven's Prison Life of Jeff. Davis, the author gives this version of the circumstances attending the surrender of Johnston, which contains also an allusion to the proposition for Davis' escape, mentioned in the Memoirs. Mr. Craven says:

"At Lexington he (Davis) received a dispatch from Johnston requesting that the Secretary of War, (General Breckinridge) should repair to his headquarters near Raleigh—General Sherman having submitted a proposition for laying down arms which was too comprehensive in its scope for any mere military commander to decide upon. Breckinridge and Postmaster-General Reagan immediately started for Johnston's camp, where Sherman submitted the terms of surrender on which an armistice was declared; the same terms subsequently disapproved by the authorities at Washington.

"One of the features of the proposition submitted by General Sherman was a declaration of amnesty to all persons, both civil and military. Notice being called to the fact particularly, General Sherman said: 'I mean just that,' and gave as his reason that it was the only way to have perfect peace. He had previously offered to furnish a vessel to take away such persons as Mr. Davis might select, to be freighted with whatever personal property they might want to take with them, and to go wherever it pleased.

"General Johnston told Sherman that it was more than useless to carry such a proposition as the last to him (Davis). Breckinridge also informed General Sherman that his proposition contemplated the adjustment of certain matters which even Mr. Davis was not empowered to control. The terms were accepted, however, with the understanding that they should be liberally construed on both sides, and fulfilled in good faith; General Breckinridge adding that certain parts of the terms would require to be submitted to the various State Governments of the Confederacy for ratification."

These statements of General Sherman and Mr. Davis correspond with those made by General Johnston.

By comparing the accounts of Generals Sherman and Johnston, it will appear that the former officer says he read the draft of terms drawn up by Mr. Reagan, the Confederate Postmaster-General, but found them so general and verbose as not to be admissible. Johnston's account (indorsed as accurate by Sherman) states that the latter wrote his memorandum with Reagan's paper before him, and that it differed from Reagan's only in being fuller.

A copy of this draft was afterward sent to the War Department by General Sherman, indorsed in his own hand as follows: "Copy of a project sent by General Johnston, being the production of Mr. Reagan, P. M. General of the Confederates."

The original of this draft was soon after captured by a Union officer, and below is an exact copy of it and of the attached note transmitting it to General Johnston during the interview:

"As the avowed motive of the Government of the United States for the prosecution of the existing war with the Confederate States is to secure a reunion of all the States under one common government, and as wisdom and sound policy alike require that a common government should rest on the consent and be supported by the affections of all the people who compose it, now, in order to ascertain whether it be practicable to put an end to the existing war and to the consequent destruction of life and property, having in view the correspondence and conversation which has recently taken place between Major-General W. T. Sherman and myself, I propose the following points as a basis of pacification:

"1. The disbanding of the military forces of the Confederacy; and

"2. The recognition of the Constitution and authority of the Government of the United States, on the following conditions:

"3. The preservation and continuance of the existing State Governments.

"4. The preservation to the people of all the political rights, and rights of person and property, secured to them by the Constitution of the United States and of their several States.

"5. Freedom from future persecutions or penalties for their participation in the present war.

"6. Agreement to a general suspension of hostilities pending these negotiations."

The above draft of terms was accompanied by the following note:

General Johnston will see that the accompanying memorandum omits all reference to details, and to the necessary action of the States, and the preliminary reference of the proposition to General Grant for his consent to the suspension of hostilities, and to the Government of the United States for its action. He will also see that I have modified the first article, according to his suggestion, by omitting the reference to the consent of the President of the Confederate States, and to his employing his good offices to secure the acquiescence of the several States to this scheme of adjustment and pacification. This may be done at a proper subsequent time.

April 17, 1865. JOHN H. REAGAN.

By comparing the above draft with the one written by General Sherman with Reagan's before him, it will be seen that Johnston is correct in asserting that Sherman's paper differed from his only in being fuller, and that Sherman's principal additions were the provisions restoring the courts, and the submission of questions pertaining to divided States to the Supreme Court:

Memorandum, or basis of agreement, made this 18*th day of April, A. D.* 1865, *near Durham's Station, in the State of North Carolina, by and between General Joseph E. Johnston, Commanding the Confederate Army, and Major-General W. T. Sherman, Commanding the Army of the United States in North Carolina, both present.*

I. (See 6, Reagan's draft.) The contending armies now in the field to maintain the *status quo* until notice is given by the Commanding General of any one to his opponent, and reasonable time, say forty-eight hours, allowed.

II. (See 1, Reagan.) The Confederate armies now in existence to be disbanded and conducted to their several State capitals, there to deposit their arms and public property in the State arsenal, and each officer and man to execute and file an agreement to cease from acts of war, and to abide the action of the State and Federal authorities. The number of arms and munitions of war to be reported to the Chief of Ordnance at Washington City, subject to the future action of the Congress of the United States, and in the meantime to be used solely to maintain peace and order within the borders of the States respectively.

III. (See 3, Reagan.) The recognition by the Executive of the United States of the several State Governments on their officers and Legislatures taking the oaths prescribed by the Constitution of the United States, and where conflicting State Governments have resulted from the war, the legitimacy of all shall be submitted to the Supreme Court of the United States.

IV. The reëstablishment of all Federal courts in the several States, with powers as defined by the Constitution and laws of Congress.

V. (See 4, Reagan.) The people and inhabitants of all States to be guaranteed, so far as the Executive can, their political rights and franchises, as well as their rights of person and property, as defined by the Constitution of the United States and of the States respectively.

VI. (See 5, Reagan.) The Executive authority of the Government of the United States not to disturb any of the people by reason of the late war, so long as they live in peace and quiet, abstain from acts of armed hostility, and obey the laws in existence at the place of their residence.

FAC-SIMILE
[Reduced]

OF THE

ORIGINAL DRAFT

OF

SHERMAN'S TERMS WITH JOHNSTON,

AS DRAWN BY THE

REBEL POST-MASTER GENERAL

JOHN H. REAGAN.

As the avowed motive of the government of the United States, for the prosecution of the existing war with the Confederate States, is to secure a re-union of all the States under one common ~~government~~, and as ~~both~~ wisdom and sound policy alike require that a common government should rest on the consent and be supported by the affections, of all the people who compose it, now in order to ascertain whether it be practicable to put an end to the existing war, and to the consequent distruction of life and property, having in view the correspondence and conversation which has recently taken place between Major General W. S. Hancock and myself, I propose the following points as a basis of pacification.

1st The disbanding of the Military forces of the Konfederacy; and

2nd The recognition of the constitution and authority of the government of the United States, on the following conditions

3rd The preservation and continuance of the existing State governments.

4th The preservation to the people of all the political rights and rights of person and property secured to them by the constitution of the United States and of their several States.

5th Freedom from future prosecution or penalties for their participation in the present war.

6th Agreement to a general suspension of hostilities pending these negotiations.

General Johnston will see that the accompanying memorandum omits all reference to details, and to the necessary action of the States & the preliminary reference of the proposition to General Grant for his consent to the suspension of hostilities, and to the Government of the United States for its action. He will also see that I have modified the 1st article, according to his suggestion, by omitting the reference to the consent of the President of the Confederate States, and to his employing his good offices to secure the acquiescence of the several States to this scheme of adjustment and pacification. This may be done at a proper subsequent time.

John H. Reagan

April 17th /65.

VII. In general terms the war to cease, a general amnesty, so far as the Executive of the United States can command, on condition of the disbandment of the Confederate armies, the distribution of the arms, and the resumption of peaceful pursuits by the officers and men hitherto composing said armies.

Not being fully empowered by our respective principals to fulfill these terms, we individually and officially pledge ourselves to promptly obtain the necessary authority, and to carry out the above programme.

W. T. SHERMAN,
Major-General Commanding Army of the United States in North Carolina.

J. E. JOHNSTON,
General Commanding Confederate States Army in North Carolina.

Both the Confederate and National Cabinets held a consultation over Sherman's terms on the same day, the former at Charlotte, North Carolina, and the latter at Washington. All the members of President Davis' Cabinet advised him to accept the terms; all the Cabinet officers at Washington advised that they be rejected.

General Johnston thus relates what occurred at his headquarters upon the receipt of information that the terms had been rejected at Washington:

"In the afternoon of the 24th, the President of the Confederacy, then in Charlotte, communicated to me, by telegraph, his approval of the terms of the Convention of the 17th and 18th, and, within an hour, a special messenger from General Hampton brought me two dispatches from General Sherman. In one of them he informed me that the Government of the United States rejected the terms of peace agreed upon by us; and in the other he gave notice of the termination of the armistice in forty-eight hours from noon that day.

"The substance of these dispatches was immediately communicated to the Administration by telegraph (at 6 P. M.), instructions asked for, and the disbanding of the army suggested, to prevent further invasion and devastation of the country by the armies of the United States. The reply, dated eleven o'clock P.M., was received early in the morning of the 25th; it suggested that the infantry might be disbanded, with instructions to meet at some appointed place, and directed me to bring off the cavalry, and all other soldiers who could be mounted by taking serviceable beasts from the trains, and a few light field pieces. I objected, immediately, that this order provided for the performance of but one of the three great duties then devolving upon us—that of securing the safety of the high civil officers of the Confederate Government; but neglected the other two—the safety of the people and that of the army. I also advised the immediate flight of the high civil functionaries under proper escort.

"The belief that impelled me to urge the civil authorities of the Confederacy to make peace, that it would be a great crime to prolong the war, prompted me to disobey these instructions—the last that I received from the Confederate Government.

"They would have given the President an escort too heavy for flight, and not strong enough to force a way for him; and would have spread ruin over all the South, by leading the three great invading armies in pursuit. In that belief, I determined to do all in my power to bring about a termination of hostilities. I therefore proposed to General Sherman another armistice and conference for that purpose, suggesting as a basis, the clause of the recent convention relating to the army. This was reported to the Confederate Government at once. General Sherman's dispatch, expressing his agreement to a conference, was received soon after sunrise on the 26th; and I set out for the former place of meeting, as soon as practicable, after announcing to the Administration that I was about to do so.

"We met at noon in Mr. Bennett's house as before. I found General Sherman, as he appeared in our previous conversation, anxious to prevent further bloodshed, so we agreed without difficulty upon terms putting an end to the war within the limits of our commands which happened to be co-extensive—terms which we expected to produce a general pacification."

As will be remembered, Mr. Stanton caused to be made public the following "among others," as the grounds upon which the original terms were rejected:

"First—It was an exercise of authority not vested in General Sherman, and on its face shows that both he and Johnston knew that General Sherman had no authority to enter into any such arrangement.

"Second—It was an acknowledgment of the rebel Government.

"Third—It is understood to reëstablish rebel State Governments that had been overthrown at the sacrifice of many thousands of loyal lives and immense treasure, and placed arms and munitions of war in the hands of rebels at their respective capitals, which might be used as soon as the armies of the United States were disbanded, and used to conquer and subdue loyal States.

"Fourth—By the restoration of the rebel authority in their respective States, they would be enabled to reëstablish slavery.

"Fifth—It might furnish a ground of responsibility by the Federal Government to pay the rebel debt, and certainly subjects loyal citizens of the rebel States to debts contracted by rebels in the name of the States.

"Sixth—It put in dispute the existence of loyal State Governments, and the new State of West Virginia, which had been recognized by every department of the United States Government.

"Seventh—It practically abolished the confiscation laws, and relieved rebels of every degree who had slaughtered our people, from all pains and penalties for their crimes.

"Eighth—It gave terms that had been deliberately, repeatedly, and solemnly rejected by President Lincoln, and better terms than the rebels had ever asked in their most prosperous condition.

"Ninth—It formed no basis of true and lasting peace, but relieved the rebels from the pressure of our victories, and left them in condition to renew their effort to overthrow the United States Government, and subdue the loyal States, whenever their strength was recruited, and any opportunity should offer."

While waiting to hear from Washington in regard to the fate of his terms, General Sherman, in the course of a letter transmitting some orders to General J. H. Wilson, then operating with cavalry in Georgia, thus expressed his ideas concerning slavery to General Johnston:

> HEADQUARTERS MILITARY DIVISION OF THE MISSISSIPPI,
> IN THE FIELD, RALEIGH, N. C., *April 21.*

General J. E. JOHNSTON, *Commanding Confederate Army.*

GENERAL: * * * * I shall look for Major Hitchcock back from Washington on Wednesday, and shall promptly notify you of the result. By the action of General Weitzel in relation to the Virginia Legislature, I feel certain we will have no trouble on the score of recognizing existing State Governments. It may be the lawyers will want us to define more minutely what is meant by the guarantee of rights of person and property. It may be construed into a compact for us to undo the past as to the rights of slaves, and "leases of plantations" on the Mississippi, of "vacant and abandoned" plantations. I wish you would talk to the best men you have on these points, and, if possible, let us in our final convention make these points so clear as to leave no room for angry controversy.

I believe, if the South would simply and publicly declare what we all feel, that slavery is dead, that you would inaugurate an era of peace and prosperity that would soon efface the ravages of the past four years of war. Negroes would remain in the South, and afford you abundance of cheap labor, which otherwise will be driven away; and it will save the country the senseless discussions which have kept us all in hot water for fifty years.

Although, strictly speaking, this is no subject of a military convention, yet I am honestly convinced that our simple declaration of a result will be accepted as good as law every where. Of course, I have not a single word from Washington on this or any other point of our agreement, but I know the effect of such a step by us will be universally accepted.

I am, with great respect, your obedient servant,

W. T. SHERMAN, *Major-General U. S. A.*

Through the unheralded arrival of General Grant at Raleigh, General Sherman was made acquainted with the primary disapproval of his terms by the former, and their subsequent rejection by the Cabinet. He was also instructed to give immediate notice of the termination of the truce at the close of the forty-eight hours required by its provision. Such notice was sent forward early on the 24th of April, and on the same day General Sherman notified General Johnston that he was instructed not to attempt civil negotiations, and further, that he demanded the surrender of the Confederate army simply upon the terms extended to Lee.

To these notes General Johnston sent the following replies:

HEADQUARTERS ARMY OF THE TENNESSEE,
IN THE FIELD, *April* 25, 1865.

Major-General SHERMAN, *United States Army.*

Your dispatch of yesterday is received. I propose a modification of the terms you offer, such terms for the army as you wrote on the 18th, they also modified according to changes of circumstances, and a further armistice to arrange details, and a meeting for that purpose.

J. E. JOHNSTON, *General.*

IN THE FIELD, *April* 26, 1865.

Major-General W. T. SHERMAN, *Commanding United States Forces.*

GENERAL: I have had the honor to receive your dispatch summoning this army to surrender on the terms accepted by General Lee at Appomattox Court House. I propose, instead of such a surrender, terms based on those drawn up by you on the 18th for the disbandment of this army, and a further armistice and conference to arrange these terms.

The disbandment of General Lee's army has afflicted this country with bands having no means of subsistence but robbery, a knowledge of which would, I am sure, induce you to agree to other terms.

Most respectfully your obedient servant,

J. E. JOHNSTON, *General.*

At a subsequent meeting, and after a protracted discussion, final terms of surrender, drawn up by General Schofield, not by General Sherman, were agreed upon, approved by General Grant, and forwarded to Washington.

Then arrived the Northern papers containing Mr. Stanton's bulletins in regard to the character of the first terms, the action thereon by the Cabinet, and the orders given by General

Halleck, who had been placed in command of the Army of the James, to push on, cut off Johnston's retreat, and pay no attention to orders from Sherman. These awoke that storm of abuse which the latter poured out upon Mr. Stanton and General Halleck.

For his criticisms upon the latter, General Grant so far reprimanded him, as to formally suggest the modification of the report in which he reflected upon that officer. The letter upon this subject was as follows:

HEADQUARTERS ARMIES OF THE UNITED STATES,
WASHINGTON, D. C., May 25, 1865.

Major-General W. T. SHERMAN, *Comd'g Military Division of the Mississippi.*

GENERAL: General Grant directs me to call your attention to the part of your report in which the necessity of maintaining your truce, even at the expense of many lives, is spoken of. The General thinks that, in making a truce, the commander of an army can control only his own army, and that the hostile general must make his own arrangements with other armies acting against him.

Whilst independent generals, acting against a common foe, would naturally act in concert, the General deems that each must be the judge of his own duty, and responsible for its execution.

If you should wish, the report will be returned for any change you deem best. Very respectfully your obedient servant,

T. S. BOWERS, *Assistant Adjutant-General.*

The part of the report thus alluded to was as follows:

HEADQUARTERS MILITARY DIVISION OF THE MISSISSIPPI,
IN THE FIELD, CITY POINT, VA., May 9, 1865.

GENERAL: * * * * It now becomes my duty to paint, in justly severe characters, the still more offensive and dangerous matter of General Halleck's dispatch of April 26th, to the Secretary of War, embodied in his to General Dix of April 27th.

General Halleck had been chief of staff of the army at Washington, in which capacity he must have received my official letter of April 18th, wherein I wrote clearly that if Johnston's army about Greensboro were "pushed" it would "disperse," an event I wished to prevent. About that time he seems to have been sent from Washington to Richmond to command the new Military Division of the James, in assuming charge of which, on the 22d, he defines the limits of his authority to be the "Department of Virginia, the Army of the Potomac, and such part of North Carolina as may not be occupied by the command of Major-General Sherman." (See his General Orders No. 1.)

Four days later, April 26th, he reports to the Secretary that he has ordered Generals Mead, Sheridan, and Wright to invade that part of North Carolina which was occupied by my command, and pay "no regard to any truce or orders of" mine. They were ordered to "push forward, regardless of any orders save those of Lieutenant-General Grant, and cut off Johnston's retreat." He knew at the time he penned that dispatch and made those orders that Johnston was not retreating, but was halted under a forty-eight hours' truce with me, and was laboring to surrender his command and prevent its dispersion into guerrilla bands, and that I had on the spot a magnificent army at my command, amply sufficient for all purposes required by the occasion.

The plan of cutting off a retreat from the direction of Burksville and Danville is hardly worthy one of his military education and genius. When he contemplated an act so questionable as the violation of a "truce" made by competent authority within his sphere of command, he should have gone himself, and not have sent subordinates, for he knew I was bound in honor to defend and maintain my own truce and pledge of faith, even at the cost of many lives.

When an officer pledges the faith of his Government, he is bound to defend it, and he is no soldier who would violate it knowingly.

As to Davis and his stolen treasure, did General Halleck, as chief of staff or commanding officer of the neighboring military division, notify me of the facts contained in his dispatch to the Secretary? No he did not. If the Secretary of War wanted Davis caught, why not order it, instead of, by publishing in the newspapers, putting him on his guard to hide away and escape? No orders or instructions to catch Davis or his stolen treasure ever came to me; but, on the contrary, I was led to believe that the Secretary of War rather preferred he should effect an escape from the country, if made "unknown" to him. But even on this point, I inclose a copy of my letter to Admiral Dahlgren, at Charleston, sent him by a fleet steamer from Wilmington on the 25th of April, two days before the bankers of Richmond had imparted to General Halleck the important secret as to Davis' movements, designed, doubtless, to stimulate his troops to march their legs off to catch their treasure for their own use.

I know, now, that Admiral Dahlgren did receive my letter on the 26th, and had acted on it before General Halleck had even thought of the matter; but I don't believe a word of the treasure story; it is absurd on its face, and General Halleck or anybody has my full permission to chase Jeff. Davis and Cabinet, with their stolen treasure, through any part of the country occupied by my command.

The last and most obnoxious feature of General Halleck's dispatch is wherein he goes out of his way, and advises that my subordinates, Generals Thomas, Stoneman, and Wilson, should be instructed not to obey "Sherman's" commands.

This is too much, and I turn from the subject with feelings too strong for words, and merely record my belief that so much mischief was never before embraced in so small a space as in the newspaper paragraph headed "Sherman's Truce Disregarded," authenticated as "official," by Mr. Secretary Stanton, and published in the New York papers of April 28th. * * *

W. T. SHERMAN, *Major-General commanding.*

General Sherman, however, declined to make the change suggested by General Grant, and gave his reasons at length:

HEADQUARTERS MILITARY DIVISION OF THE MISSISSIPPI,
WASHINGTON, D. C., *May* 26, 1865.

Colonel T. S. BOWERS, *Assistant Adjutant-General, Washington, D. C.*

COLONEL: I had the honor to receive your letter of May 25th last evening, and hasten to answer. I wish to precede it by renewed assurance of my confidence and respect for the President and Lieutenant-General Grant, and that in all matters I will be most willing to shape my official and private conduct to suit their wishes. The past is beyond my control, and the matters embraced in the operations to which you refer are finished. It is but just the reasons that actuated me, right or wrong, should stand of record, but in all future cases, should any arise, I will respect the decision of General Grant, though I think it wrong. * * * *

In discussing this matter, I would like to refer to many writers on military law, but am willing to take Halleck as the text (see his Chapter No. 27). In the very first article he prefaces that "Good Faith" should always be observed between enemies in war, because when our faith has been pledged to him, as far as the promise extends he ceases to be an enemy. He then defines the meaning of compacts and conventions, and says they are made sometimes for a general or a partial suspension of hostilities, for the surrender of an army, etc. They may be special, limited to particular places, or to particular forces, but of course can only bind the armies subject to the general who makes the truce, and co-extensive only with the extent of his command.

This is all I ever claimed, and clearly covers the whole case. All of North Carolina was in my immediate command, with General Schofield its department commander, and his army present with me. I never asked the truce to have effect beyond my own territorial command. General Halleck himself, in his Orders No. 1, defines his own limits clearly enough, viz.: "Such part of North Carolina as was not occupied by the command of Major-General Schofield." He could not pursue and cut off Johnston's retreat toward Saulsbury and Charlotte without invading my command, and so patent was his purpose to *defy* and *violate* my truce that Mr. Stanton's publication of the fact, not even yet recalled, modified, or explained, was headed: "Sherman's Truce Disregarded," that the whole world drew but one inference. It admits of no other. I never claimed that the truce bound Generals Halleck and Canby within the sphere of their respective commands as defined by themselves. It was a *partial* truce of very short duration, clearly within my limits and rights, justified by events, and, as in the case of prisoners in my custody, or the violation of a safeguard given by me in my own territorial limits, I was bound to maintain "Good Faith."

I prefer not to change my report; but again repeat that in all future cases I am willing to be governed by the interpretation of General Grant, although I again invite his attention to the limits of my command and those of General Halleck at the time, and the pointed phraseology of General Halleck's dispatch to Mr. Stanton, wherein he reports that he had ordered his generals to pay no heed to my orders within the clearly defined area of my own command. I am, etc.,

W. T. SHERMAN, *Major-General commanding.*

The movements of General Halleck, of which General Sherman thus pointedly complained, were made in pursuance of the following order from General Grant:

FORTRESS MONROE, *April* 22, 1865.

Major-General HALLECK, *Richmond, Va.*

The truce entered into by Sherman will be ended as soon as I can reach Raleigh. Move Sheridan with his cavalry toward Greensboro, North Carolina, as soon as possible. I think it will be well to send one corps of infantry also, the whole under Sheridan. The infantry need not go further than Danville, unless they receive orders hereafter to do so.

U. S. GRANT, *Lieutenant-General.*

General Sherman's report and the subsequent correspondence in relation to it between himself and General Grant, having been brought to the attention of General Halleck, the latter thus reviewed the whole subject:

HEADQUARTERS MILITARY DIVISION OF THE JAMES,
RICHMOND, VA., *June* 7, 1865.

Hon. E. M. STANTON, *Secretary of War.*

SIR: I have just received the Army and Navy Gazette of May 30th, containing an official publication of Major-General Sherman's letters of May 9th and 26th, with other papers on the same subject, parts of which had been previously published in the newspapers. In these letters and papers General Sherman has made statements and reflections on my official conduct, which are incorrect and entirely unjustified by the facts of the case.

1st. He charges that I encroached upon his military command, by directing a portion of my troops to march upon Greensboro in North Carolina.

By direction of the President, I was, on the 19th of April last, assigned to the command of the Military Division of the James, which included "such parts of North Carolina as were not occupied by the command of Major-General Sherman." At the time my troops were ordered to Greensboro, General Sherman's troops did not occupy that part of North Carolina; it was occupied by the enemy, and consequently within my command, as defined by General Orders, No. 71, of the War Department.

But whether or not Greensboro, or any part of North Carolina, was in my command, General Sherman's remarks are equally without justification. On the 22d of April Lieutenant-General Grant notified me that Sherman's arrangements had been disapproved and orders given to resume hostilities, and directed me to move my troops on Danville and Greensboro, precisely as I did move them, there to await his further orders. My instructions to Generals Meade, Sheridan, and Wright were just such instructions as General Grant had directed me to give. The offense, or whatever he may please to call it, if any there was, of marching my troops within territory claimed by General Sherman, was not mine, but General Grant's, and all the abuse which he has directed upon me for that act must fall upon the General-in-Chief.

2d. General Sherman charges that by marching my troops into North Carolina I violated his truce, which he was bound to enforce even at the cost of many lives by a collision of our respective armies.

General Sherman had never sent me his truce; I had never seen it and did not know its terms or conditions. I only knew that his truce or "arrangement," whatever it was, had been disapproved and set aside by the President, and General Grant in ordering the movement of my troops simply notified me of this fact and of the renewal of hostilities. Even if Sherman's truce had been binding on me, which it was not, I had no knowledge of the clause relating to forty-eight hours' notice.

It is strange that he should seek to bind me by conditions of the existence of which I was ignorant, and he had taken no measures to inform me. But even had I known them I could not have acted otherwise than I did. I simply carried out the orders of my superior officer, who had seen the truce and knew its terms. If General Sherman was, under the circumstances, justified in stopping the movements of my troops, even by destroying the commands of General Sheridan and General Wright, the responsbility of this sacrifice of human life must have rested either upon General Sherman or upon General Grant, for I simply obeyed the orders of the latter in regard to these movements.

General Sherman reflects on me for not going in person to violate, as he is pleased to call it, a truce which he "was bound in honor to defend and maintain," "even at the cost of many lives," and upon the marching powers of the troops which I sent into North Carolina. In reply to this I can only say that I was not ordered to go with these troops, but to *send* them under their commanders to certain points, there to await further orders from Lieutenant-General Grant, precisely as I directed. The troops were mostly selected by General Grant, not by me, and as he had commanded them for a year he probably knew something of their capacity for marching, and whether or not they would march their legs off "to catch the treasure for their own use."

3. Again, General Sherman complains that my orders of April 26th to push forward against Johnston's army were given at the very time I knew that that army was surrendering to him.

In making this statement he forgets time and circumstances. He must have known that I did not have, and could not possibly have had at that time, any official information of any new arrangements between him and Johnston for the surrender of the latter's army. Neither General Sherman nor any one else could have sent me such official information otherwise than by sea, which would have required several days. I only knew from General Grant that Sherman's "arrangements" had been disapproved, that orders had been given to resume hostilities, and that I was directed by him to push forward my troops to Greensboro, where they would receive further orders. All other information from North Carolina came from rebel sources.

4th. The burthen of General Sherman's complaint on this subject is, that I ordered Generals Sheridan and Wright to push forward their troops as directed by General Grant, "regardless of any orders from any one except General Grant."

This was simply carrying out the spirit of my instructions from General Grant. He had notified me that orders had been given to resume hostilities, and had directed me to send certain troops to Greensboro to await his further orders. As these troops approached the boundaries of North Carolina, Johnston, Beauregard, and other rebel officers tried, on the alleged grounds of arrangements with Sherman, to stop the movement ordered by General Grant When informed of this, I directed my officers to execute the commands which General Grant had given to me, regardless of orders from any one except Grant himself. I respectfully submit that I could not have done less without neglecting my duty.

5th. General Sherman sneers at my sending troops from the direction of Burkesville and Danville against Davis in North Carolina as "hardly worthy of" my "military education and genius." However ridiculous General Sherman may consider these movements, they were made precisely as General Grant had directed them.

6th. He complains that I did not notify him in regard to Davis and his stolen treasure. For the reason that I had no communication open to him. My most direct way of communicating with him was through the Department at Washington, and I sent all information to the Department as soon as it was received.

However "absurd" General Sherman may have considered the information, it was given by some of the most respectable and reliable business men in Richmond, through a gentleman whose character and position would prevent me from pronouncing his statements "absurd," and of saying, without examination, "I don't believe a word of the treasure story."

7th. In order to sustain his position that the movements of my troops ordered by General Grant were in violation of his truce, which I was bound to observe, even without knowing its terms, and that he would have been justified to resent, "even at the the cost of many lives," General Sherman refers to a chapter of International Law. His reference is most pointedly against his positions and doctrines, and the case given in illustration in paragraph 4 was one of which General Sherman was personally cognizant. In that case a subordinate commander refused to be bound by a truce of his superior commanding another department. General Sherman was not even my superior. I contend that all my orders were justified by the laws of war and military usage, even if they had not been directed by superior authority.

8th. General Sherman says that General Grant "reached the Chesapeake in time to *countermand* General Halleck's orders and prevent his violating my truce." This is not true. General Grant neither disapproved nor countermanded any orders of mine, nor was there at that time any truce. It had ceased by General Grant's orders to resume hostilities and the subsequent surrender of Johnston's army of which he then notified me, and recalled a part of the troops which he had directed me to send to Danville and Greensboro.

9th. There is but one other point in General Sherman's official complaint that I deem it necessary to notice. I refer to the suggestion made to you in regard to orders to Generals Thomas and Wilson for preventing the escape of Davis and his Cabinet. Although these officers were under the nominal command of General Sherman, yet after he left Atlanta, they received their instructions and orders from yourself and General Grant *direct*, not through General *Sherman*.

This is recognized and provided for by the regulations of the War Department and has been practised for years. I have transmitted hundreds of orders in this way, and General Sherman was cognizant of the fact. The movements of Generals Thomas, Stoneman, Wilson, A. J. Smith, etc., while within General Sherman's general command, have been directed in this way for more than six months. In suggesting that orders be sent to these officers *directly* and not through General Sherman, I suggested no departure from well established official channels. But even if I had, the responsibility of adopting that course must rest upon the authority who sent the orders.

If his complaint is directed against the *form* of the suggestions, I can only say that I was innocent of any *intended* offense. My telegram was hurriedly written, intended for yourself, not the public, and had reference to the state of facts as reported to me. It was reported that orders purporting to come from General Sherman had been received through rebel lines for General Wilson to withdraw from Macon, release his prisoners, and that all hostilities should cease. These orders threw open the doors for the escape of Davis and his party. This I knew was contrary to the wishes and orders of the Government; but I had no means of knowing whether or not Sherman had been so informed. I at the time had no communication with him or with General Grant, and I was not aware that either could communicate with our officers in the West, except through rebel authorities, who, of course, could not be relied on. I repeat that my suggestions had reference only to the facts and wishes of the Government as known to me at the time, and was intended in no respect to reflect upon, or be disrespectful to General Sherman. If I had been able to communicate with General Sherman, or had known at the time the condition of affairs in North Carolina, there would have been no necessity or occasion for any suggestion to you, and most probably none would have been made.

With these remarks, I respectfully submit that General Sherman's report, so far as he refers to me, is unjust, unkind, and contrary to military usage, and that his statements are contrary to the real facts of the case. I beg leave further to remark that I have, in no way, shape, or manner, criticised or reflected upon General Sherman's course in North Carolina, or upon his truce, or as General Grant styles it "arrangement" with Johnston and Breckinridge, but have simply acted upon the orders, instructions, and expressed wishes of my superiors as communicated to me, and as I understand them.

Very respectfully, your obedient servant,

H. W. HALLECK, *Major-General.*

The same officer who captured the original of Mr. Reagan's draft of the rejected terms, also secured the written opinions of the different members of Mr. Davis' Cabinet, rendered in accordance with his request, made at the session of his Cabinet held on the 21st of April, at Charlotte, N. C. All reviewed the situation at length.

A few extracts from these opinions will serve to show that the rebel Cabinet held substantially the same views of the scope of Sherman's terms as, according to Mr. Stanton, were entertained at Washington.

Mr. Reagan wrote:

* * * * "The agreement under consideration secures to our people, if ratified by both parties, the uninterrupted continuance of the existing State Governments; the guarantees of the Federal Constitution, and of the Constitutions of their respective States; the guarantee of their political rights, and of their rights of person, and property, and immunity from future prosecutions, and penalties for their participation in the existing war, on the condition that we accept the Constitution and Government of the United States, and disband our armies by marching the troops to their respective States, and depositing their arms in the State arsenals, subject to the future control of that Government, but with a verbal understanding that they are only to be used for the preservation of peace and order in the respective

States. It is also to be observed that the agreement contains no direct reference to the question of slavery; requires no concessions from us in regard to it, and leaves it subject to the Constitution and Laws of the United States and of the several States just as it was before the war."

Mr. Benjamin, Secretary of State, summed up the terms as follows:

"The Military Convention made between General Johnston and General Sherman is, in substance, an agreement that if the Confederate States will cease to wage war for the purpose of establishing a separate government, the United States will receive the several States back into the Union, with their State Governments unimpaired, with all their Constitutional rights recognized, with protection for the persons and property of the people, and with a general amnesty."

Mr. George Davis, Attorney-General, wrote:

"Taken as a whole, the convention amounts to this, that the States of the Confederacy shall reënter the old Union upon the same footing on which they stood before seceding from it."

In the light of these opinions, how unjust does General Sherman's attack upon the memory of Secretary Stanton appear!

General Sherman relates that at the first meeting with Johnston, after the rejection of these terms, the latter, "without hesitation agreed to, and we executed" the final terms. But even these were drawn up by General Schofield, and this officer, during the subsequent absence of General Sherman, also made supplementary terms with Johnston, which were found to be necessary to complete the details of the surrender.

From all of which it appears that the records tell a very different story of the negotiations with General Johnston from that contained in the Memoirs.

CHAPTER XVIII.

OPINIONS OF JEFF. DAVIS' CABINET OFFICERS ON SHERMAN'S TERMS.

General Sherman, in his Memoirs, returns with increased violence to his old attack upon Secretary Stanton, and attempts to hold him chiefly responsible for a course in regard to the Sherman-Johnston terms, which at the time was approved by the President, General Grant, General Halleck, every member of the Cabinet, and by the loyal North.

He attempts to convey the impression that Mr. Stanton exceeded his authority in the matter, by the statement that President Johnson, and nearly all the members of the Cabinet assured him, after his arrival in Washington, that they knew nothing of Mr. Stanton's publications setting forth the nature of his terms and the reasons of the Cabinet for rejecting them. This is an attempt to escape upon a technicality. The President, and every member of the Cabinet, had united in rejecting the terms on the grounds which Mr. Stanton made known. It is doubtless true that none of them, except Mr. Stanton, knew that these reasons were to be made public in the shape they were till they saw them in the newspapers. And, as the Secretary of War "offered no word of explanation or apology," General Sherman concluded to insult him in public, which he seems to think he afterward did, by refusing to take Mr. Stanton's hand, or as he expresses it, speaking of his own behavior on the stand at the great review, "I shook hands with the President, General Grant, and each member of the Cabinet. As I approached Mr. Stanton, he offered me his hand, but I declined it publicly, and the fact was universally noticed"—but how decidedly to the discredit of General Sherman he does not relate in his new capacity of historian.

His main complaint is directed at the reasons assigned by Mr. Stanton for the rejection of his terms. He contends that personally he "cared very little whether they were approved, modified, or disapproved *in toto*," only he "wanted instructions;" and yet in a letter to Halleck, quoted in the Memoirs, and written the day these terms were agreed upon, is this appeal:

"Please give all orders necessary according to the views the Executive may take, and influence him, if possible, not to vary the terms at all, for I have considered every thing, and believe that the Confederate armies once dispersed, we can adjust all else fairly and well."

It is now known, from documents which might have slept but for General Sherman's revival of this matter, that the members of Jeff. Davis' Cabinet construed the Sherman-Johnston terms exactly as Mr. Stanton and the other members of Lincoln's Cabinet did.

It has already been made to appear that Mr. Reagan, the Confederate Postmaster-General; Mr. Breckinridge, Secretary of War; Wade Hampton, and General Johnston held a consultation at the headquarters of the latter, late at night, after the first conference with General Sherman. Up to that time no draft of "terms" had been prepared by either side, and Mr. Reagan thereupon drew up outlines, based upon Johnston's conversations with Sherman, and this paper was the next day handed to the latter, and, with it before him, he wrote the memorandum, which was afterward signed. This was agreed to, and did not differ in its most important points from the draft prepared by Mr. Reagan.

The latter, therefore, was well qualified to inform Mr. Davis of the character of these terms; and a few days later, when they had been under consideration in the rebel Cabinet, he, in common with his associate members, at the request of Mr.

Davis, gave a written opinion upon the terms and the question of accepting them.

This paper, which is now both interesting and pertinent to the questions General Sherman has raised, is as follows:

Views of Postmaster-General Reagan:

To the President. CHARLOTTE, N. C., *April* 22, 1865.

SIR—In obedience to your request for the opinions in writing of the members of the Cabinet on the questions: first, as to whether you should assent to the preliminary agreement of the 18th inst., between General Joseph E. Johnston, of the Confederate army, and Major-General W. T. Sherman, of the army of the United States, for the suspension of hostilities and the adjustment of the difficulties between the two countries; and, if so, second, the proper mode of executing this agreement on our part, I have to say that, painful as the necessity is, in view of the relative condition of the armies and resources of the belligerents, I must advise the acceptance of the terms of the agreement.

General Lee, the General-in-Chief of our armies, has been compelled to surrender our principal army, heretofore employed in the defense of our capital, with the loss of a very large part of our ordnance, arms, munitions of war, and military stores of all kinds, with what remained of our naval establishment. The officers of the civil government have been compelled to abandon the capital, carrying with them the archives, and thus to close, for the time being at least, the regular operations of its several departments, with no place now open to us at which we can reëstablish and put these departments in operation, with any prospect of permanency or security for the transaction of the public business and the carrying on of the Government. The army under the command of General Johnston has been reduced to fourteen or fifteen —— infantry and artillery and —— cavalry, and this force is, from demoralization and despondency, melting away rapidly by the troops abandoning the army and returning to their homes singly and in numbers large and small; it being the opinion of Generals Johnston and Beauregard that with the men and means at their command they can oppose no serious obstacle to the advance of General Sherman's army. General Johnston is of opinion that the enemy's forces now in the field exceed ours in numbers by probably ten to one. Our forces in the South, though still holding the fortifications at Mobile, have been unable to prevent the fall of Selma and Montgomery in Alabama, and of Columbus and Macon in Georgia, with their magazines, workshops, and stores of supplies.

The army west of the Mississippi is unavailable for the arrest of the victorious career of the enemy east of that river, and is inadequate for the defense of the country west of it. The country is worn down by a brilliant and heroic, but exhausting and bloody struggle of four years. Our ports are closed so as to exclude the hope of procuring arms and supplies from abroad; and we are unable to arm our people if they were willing to continue the struggle. The supplies of quartermaster and commissary stores in the country are very limited in amount, and our railroads are so broken and destroyed as to prevent, to a great extent, the transportation and accumulation of those remaining. Our currency has lost its purchasing power, and there is no other means of supplying the treasury; and the people are hostile to impressments and endeavor to conceal such supplies as are needed for the army from the officers charged with their collection. Our armies, in case of a prolongation of the struggle, will continue to melt away as they retreat through the country. There is danger, and I think I might say certainty, based on the information we have, that a portion, and probably all of the States will make separate terms with the enemy as they are overrun, with the chance that the terms so obtained will be less favorable to them than those contained in the agreement under consideration. And the despair of our people will prevent a much longer continuance of serious resistance, unless they shall be hereafter urged to it by unendurable oppressions.

The agreement under consideration secures to our people, if ratified by both parties, the uninterrupted continuance of the existing State Governments; the guarantees of the Federal Constitution, and of the Constitutions of their respective States; the guarantee of their political rights and of their rights of person and property, and immunity from future prosecutions and penalties for their participation in the existing war, on the condition that we accept the Constitution and Government of the United States, and disband our armies by marching the troops to their respective States, and depositing their arms in the State arsenals, subject to the future control of that Government, but with a verbal understanding that they are only to be used for the preservation of peace and order in the respective States. It is also to be observed that the agreement contains no direct reference to the question of slavery, requires no concessions from us in regard to it, and leaves it subject to the Constitution and Laws of the United States and of the several States just as it was before the war.

With these facts before us, and under the belief that we can not now reasonably hope for the achievement of our independence, which should be dearer than life if it were possibly attainable, and under the belief that a continuance of the struggle, with its sacrifices of life and property, and its accumulation of sufferings, without a reasonable prospect of success, would be both unwise and criminal, I advise that you assent to the agreement as the best you can now do for the people who have clothed you with the high trust of your position.

In advising this course I do not conceal from myself, nor would I withhold from your Excellency, the danger of trusting the people who drove us to war by their unconstitutional and unjust aggressions, and who will now add the consciousness of power to their love of dominion and greed of gain.

It is right also for me to say that much as we have been exhausted in men and resources, I am of opinion that if our people could be induced to continue the contest with the spirit which animated them during the first years of the war, our independence might yet be within our reach. But I see no reason to hope for that now.

On the second question, as to the proper mode of executing the agreement, I have to say that whatever you may do looking to the termination of the contest by an amicable arrangement which may embrace the extinction of the Government of the Confederate States, must be done without special authority to be found in the Constitution. And yet, I am of opinion that, charged as you are with the duty of looking to the general welfare of the people, and without time or opportunity, under the peculiarity and necessities of the case, to submit the whole question to the States for their deliberation and action without danger of losing material advantages provided for in the agreement; and, as I believe that you, representing the military power and authority of all the States, can obtain better terms for them than it is probable they could obtain each for itself; and, as it is in your power, if the Federal authorities accept this agreement, to terminate the ravages of war sooner than it can be done by the several States, while the enemy is still unconscious of the full extent of our weakness, you should, in case of the acceptance of the terms of this agreement by the authorities of the United States, accept them on the part of the Confederate States, and take steps for the disbanding of the Confederate armies on the terms agreed on. As you have no power to change the government of the country, or to transfer the allegiance of the people, I would advise that you submit to the several States, through their governors, the question as to whether they will, in the exercise of their own sovereignty, accept, each for itself, the terms proposed.

To this it may be said, that after the disbanding of our armies and the abandonment of the contest by the Confederate Government, they would have no alternative but to accept the terms proposed or an unequal and hopeless war, and that it would be needless for them to go through the forms and incur the trouble and expense of assembling a convention for the purpose. To such an objection, if urged, it may be answered that we entered into the contest to maintain and vindicate the doctrine of State rights and State sovereignty, and the right of self-government, and that we can only be faithful to the Constitution of the United States, and true to the principles in support of which we have expended so much blood and treasure, by the employment of the same agencies to return into the old Union which we employed in separating from it and in forming our present Government; and that if this should be an unwelcome and enforced action by the States, it would not be more so on the part of the States than on the part of the President, if he were to undertake to execute the whole agreement, and while they would have authority for acting he would have none.

This plan would at least conform to the theory of the Constitution of the United States, and would, in future, be an additional precedent, to which the friends of State rights could point in opposing the doctrine of the consolidation of powers in the central government. And if the future shall disclose a disposition (of which I fear the chance is remote) on the part of the people of the United States to return to the spirit and meaning of the Constitution, then this action on the part of the States might prove to be of great value to the friends of constitutional liberty and good government.

In addition to the terms of agreement, an additional provision should be asked for, which will probably be allowed without objection, stipulating for the withdrawal of the Federal forces from the several States of the Confederacy, except a sufficient number to garrison the permanent fortifications and take care of the public property until the States can call their conventions and take action on the proposed terms.

In addition to the necessity for this course, in order to make their action as free and voluntary as other circumstances will allow, it would aid in softening the bitter memories which must necessarily follow such a contest as that in which we are engaged.

Nothing is said in the agreement about the public debt and the disposition of our public property beyond the turning over of the arms to the State arsenals.

In the final adjustment we should endeavor to secure provisions for the auditing of the debt of the Confederacy, and for its payment in common with the war debt of the United States.

We may ask this on the ground that we did not seek this war, but only sought peaceful separation to secure our people and States from the effects of unconstitutional encroachments by the other States, and because, on the principles of equity, allowing that both parties had acted in good faith, and gone to war on a misunderstanding which admitted of no other solution, and now agree to a reconciliation, and to a burial of the past, it would be unjust to compel our people to assist in the payment of the war debt of the United States, and for them to refuse to allow such of the revenues as we might contribute to be applied to the payment of our creditors. If it should be said that this is a liberality never extended by the conqueror to the conquered, the answer is that if the object of the pacification is to restore the Union in good faith and to reconcile the people to each other, to restore confidence and faith, and prosperity, and homogenity, then it is of the first importance that the terms of reconciliation should be based on entire equity, and that no just ground of grief or complaint should be left to either party. And to both parties, looking not only to the present but to the interest of future generations, the amount of money which would be involved, though large, would be as nothing when compared with a reconciliation entirely equitable, which should leave no sting to honor, and no sense of wrong to rankle in the memories of the people, and lay the foundation for new difficulties and for future wars. It is to this feature, it seems to me, the greatest attention should be given by both sides. It will be of the highest importance to all, for the present as well as for the future, that the frankness, sincerity, and justice of both parties shall be as conspicuous in the adjustment of past difficulties, as their courage and endurance have been during the war, if we would make peace on a basis which would be satisfactory and might be rendered perpetual.

In any event provisions should be made which will authorize the Confederate authorities to sell the public property remaining on hand, and to apply the proceeds, as far as they will go, to the payment of our public liabilities, or for such other disposition as may be found advisable.

But if the terms of this agreement should be rejected, or so modified by the Government of the United States as to refuse a recognition of the right of local self-government and our political rights, and rights of persons and property, or as to refuse amnesty for past participation in this war, then it will be our duty to continue the struggle as best we can, however unequal it may be; as it would be better and more honorable to waste our lives and substance in such a contest than to yield both to the mercy of a remorseless conqueror.

I am, with great respect, your Excellency's obedient servant,

JOHN H. REAGAN, *Postmaster-General.*

It will be seen that Mr. Reagan, whose opportunities for being well informed were excellent, looked upon the Sherman terms as "preliminary," and held, as Mr. Stanton said our Cabinet did, that subsequently a claim might be made that the North should help pay the rebel war debt.

The views of the other members of the Davis Cabinet, submitted in writing at the same time, were as follows:

Views of Mr. Benjamin, Secretary of State:

CHARLOTTE, N. C., 22d *April,* 1865.

To the President.

SIR: I have the honor to submit this paper as the advice in writing which you requested from the heads of the departments of the Government.

The military convention made between General Johnston and General Sherman is, in substance, an agreement that if the Confederate States will cease to wage war for the purpose of establishing a separate government, the United States will receive the several States back into the Union with their State Governments unimpaired, with all their constitutional rights recognized, with protection for the persons and property of the people, and with a general amnesty.

The question is whether, in view of the military condition of the belligerents, the Confederate States can hope for any better result by continuing the war; whether there is any reason to believe that they can establish their independence and final separation from the United States.

To reach a conclusion it is requisite to consider our present condition and the prospect of a change for the better.

The General-in-Chief of the armies of the Confederacy has capitulated, and his army, the largest and finest within our country, is irretrievably lost.

The soldiers have been dispersed and remain at home as paroled prisoners.

The artillery, arms, and munitions of war are lost, and no help can be expected from Virginia, which is at the mercy of the conqueror.

The army next in numbers and efficiency is known as the Army of Tennessee, and is commanded by Generals Johnston and Beauregard.

Its rolls call for more than seventy thousand men. Its last returns show a total present for duty, of all arms, of less than twenty thousand men. This number is daily diminishing by desertions and casualties. In a recent conference with the Cabinet at Greensboro Generals Johnston and Beauregard expressed the unqualified opinion that it was not in their power to resist Sherman's advance, and that as fast as their army retreated, the soldiers of the several States on the line of retreat would abandon the army and go home.

We also hear on all sides, and from citizens well acquainted with public opinion, that the State of North Carolina will not consent to continue the struggle after our armies shall have withdrawn further south, and this withdrawal is inevitable if hostilities are resumed.

This action of North Carolina would render it impossible for Virginia to maintain her position in the Confederacy, even if her people were unanimous in their desire to continue the contest.

In the more southern States we have no army except the forces now defending Mobile and the cavalry under General Forrest. The enemy are so far superior in numbers that they have occupied within the last few weeks Selma, Montgomery, Columbus, and Macon, and could continue their career of devastation through Georgia and Alabama without our being able to prevent it by any forces now at our disposal.

It is believed that we could not at the present moment gather together an army of thirty thousand men by a concentration of all our forces east of the Mississippi River.

Our sea-coast is in possession of the enemy, and we can not obtain arms and munitions from abroad except in very small quantities and by precarious and uncertain means of transportation.

We have lost possession in Virginia and North Carolina of our chief resources for the supply of powder and lead.

We can obtain no aid from the Trans-Mississippi Department, from which we are cut off by the fleets of gun-boats that patrol the river.

We have not a supply of arms sufficient for putting into the field even ten thousand additional men, if the men themselves were forthcoming.

The Confederacy is, in a word, unable to continue the war by armies in the field, and the struggle can no longer be maintained in any other manner than by a guerrilla or partisan warfare. Such a warfare is not, in my opinion, desirable, nor does it promise any useful result. It would entail far more suffering on our own people than it would cause damage to the enemy; and the people have been such heavy sufferers by the calamities of the war for the last four years that it is at least questionable whether they would be willing to engage in such a contest, unless forced to endure its horrors in preference to dishonor and degradation.

The terms of the convention imply no dishonor, impose no degradation, exact only what the victor always requires—the relinquishment by his foe of the object for which the struggle was commenced.

Seeing no reasonable hope of our ability to conquer our independence, admitting the undeniable fact that we have been vanquished in the war, it is my opinion that these terms should be accepted, being as favorable as any that we, as the defeated belligerents, have reason to expect or can hope to secure.

It is further my opinion that the President owes it to the States and to the people to obtain for them, by a general pacification, rights and advantages which they would, in all probability, be unable to secure by the separate action of the different States. It is natural that the enemy should be willing to accord more liberal conditions for the purpose of closing the war at once than would be granted if each State should continue the contest till separate terms could be made for itself.

The President is the chief political executive of the Confederacy, as well as the Commander-in-Chief of its armies. In the former capacity he is powerless to act in making peace on any other basis than that of independence. In the latter capacity he can ratify the military convention under consideration, and execute its provisions relative to the disbandment of the army and the distribution of the arms. He can end hostilities.

The States alone can act in dissolving the Confederacy and returning to the Union, according to the terms of the convention.

I think that if this convention be ratified by the United States, the President should, by proclamation, inform the States and the people of the Confederacy of the facts above recited; should ratify the convention so far as he has authority to act as Commander-in-Chief, and should execute the military provisions; should declare his inability, with the means remaining at his disposal, to defend the Confederacy or maintain its independence, and should resign a trust which it is no longer possible to fulfill.

He should further invite the several States to take into immediate consideration the terms of this convention, with a view to their adoption and execution as being the best and most favorable that they could hope to obtain by a continuance of the struggle.

Very respectfully, your obedient servant,

J. P. BENJAMIN, *Secretary of State.*

Views of Mr. Mallory, Secretary of the Navy:

CHARLOTTE, N. C., 24th *April*, 1865.

MR. PRESIDENT: In compliance with your suggestion I have the honor briefly to present the following views upon the propositions discussed in Cabinet council yesterday.

These propositions, agreed upon and signed by General Joseph E. Johnston and W. T. Sherman, may fairly be regarded as providing for the immediate cessation of hostilities, the disbandment of our armies, and the return of our soldiers to the peaceful walks of life; the restoration of the several States of our Confederacy to the old Union, with the integrity of their State Governments preserved; the security of their "people and inhabitants" in their rights of person and property under the Constitution and the Laws of the United States, equally with the people of any other State, guaranteed, and a general amnesty for and on account of any participation in the present war.

The very grave responsibility devolved upon you by these propositions is at once apparent. To enter at all upon their discussion is to admit that independence, the great object of our struggle, is hopeless. I believe and admit this to be the case, and therefore do I advise you to accept these propositions so far as you have the power to do so; and my conviction is that nine-tenths of the people of every State of the Confederacy would so advise if opportunity were presented them. They are weary of the war and desire peace. If they could be rallied and brought to the field, a united and determined people might even yet achieve independence; but many circumstances admonish us that we can not count upon their cordial and united action.

The vast army of deserters and absentees from our military service during the past twelve months, the unwillingness of the people to enter the armies, the impracticability of recruiting them, the present utter demoralization of our troops consequent upon the destruction of the Army of Virginia, the rapid decrease by desertion of General Johnston's army, which as it retreats south, if retreat it can, will retain in its ranks but few soldiers beyond the by-paths and cross-roads which lead to their homes, together with the recent successes of the enemy, the fall of Selma, Montgomery, Columbus, and Macon, his forces in the field and his vast resources, all dictate the admission I have made.

I do not believe that by any possibility we could organize, arm, and equip, and bring into the field this side of the Mississippi fifteen thousand men within the next sixty days, and I am convinced that both General Beauregard and General Johnston are utterly hopeless of continuing the contest. A guerrilla warfare might be carried on in certain portions of our country for a time, perhaps for years, but while such a warfare would be more disastrous to our own people than it could possibly be to the enemy, it would exercise little or no influence upon his military operations, or upon his hold upon the country. Conducted upon our own soil our own people would chiefly feel its evils, and would afford it neither countenance nor support. Guerrilla warfare never has been and never can be carried on by and between peoples of a common origin, language, and institutions.

Our sea-board and our ports being in the enemy's hands we can not rely upon supplies of arms and other munitions of war from abroad, and our means of producing them at home, already limited, are daily decreasing. The loss of Selma and of Columbus, where much valuable machinery for the construction of ordnance and ordnance stores was collected, must materially circumscribe our ability in this respect.

Our currency is nearly worthless, and will become utterly so with further military disasters, and there is no hope that we can improve it.

The arms of the United States have rendered the great object of our struggle hopeless, have conquered a reconstruction of the Union, and it becomes your duty to secure to the people, as far as practicable, life, liberty, and property.

The propositions signed by the opposing generals are more favorable to these great objects than could justly have been anticipated.

Upon you, with a more thorough knowledge of the condition of our country, the character and sentiments of our people, and of our means and resources, than is possessed by others, is devolved the responsibility of promptly accepting or of promptly rejecting them. I advise their acceptance; and that, having notified General Johnston of your having done so, you promptly issue, so soon as you shall learn the acceptance thereof by the authorities of the United States, a proclamation to the people of the Confederate States, setting forth clearly the condition of the country, your inability to resist the enemy's overwhelming numbers, or to protect the country from his devastating and desolating march, the propositions submitted to you, and the reasons which, in your judgment, render their acceptance by the States and the people wise and expedient. You can not, under the Constitution, dissolve the Confederacy and remit the States composing it to the Government of the United States.

But the Confederacy is conquered. Its days are numbered. Virginia is lost to it, and North Carolina must soon follow, and State after State, under the hostile tread of the enemy, must reënter the old Union. The occasion, the emergency, the dire necessities and misfortunes of the country, the vast interests at stake, were never contemplated by those who framed the Constitution. They are all outside of it, and in the dissolution of the Confederacy and the wreck of all their hopes, the States and the people will turn to you, whose antecedents and whose present position and powers constitute you, more than any other living man, the guardian of their honor and their interests, and will expect you not to stand upon constitutional limitations, but to assume and exercise all powers which to you may seem necessary and proper to shield them from useless war, and to save from the wreck of the country all that may be practicable of honor, life, and property.

If time were allowed for the observance of constitutional forms I would advise the submission of these propositions to the executives of the several States to the end that, through the usual legislative and conventional action, the wills of the people of the States respectively might be known. But in the present condition of the country such delay as this course would involve would be the death-blow to all hopes founded upon them.

The pacification of the country should be as speedy as practicable, to the end that the authorities of the States may enter upon the establishment and maintenance of law and order. Negotiations for this purpose can more appropriately follow upon the overwhelming disaster of General Lee than at a future time. The wreck of our hopes results immediately from it.

I omit all reference to the details which must be provided for by the contending parties to this agreement for future consideration.

Very respectfully, your obedient servant,

S. R. MALLORY, *Secretary of the Navy.*

Views of Attorney-General Davis:

CHARLOTTE, N. C., 22d *April*, 1865.

To the President.

SIR: The questions submitted by you to the members of your Cabinet for their opinions are:

1. Whether the convention agreed upon on the 18th inst., by and between General Johnston, commanding the Confederate forces, and Major-General Sherman, commanding the forces of the United States, in North Carolina, should be ratified by you.

2. If so, in what way should it be done.

The terms of that convention are substantially as follows:

That the armies of the Confederate States shall be disbanded and their arms surrendered.

That the several State Governments shall be recognized by the Executive of the United States, upon their officers and legislatures taking the oaths prescribed by the Constitution of the United States; and where there are conflicting State Governments the question to be referred to the decision of the Supreme Court.

That all political rights and franchises, and all rights of person and property, shall be respected and guaranteed.

That a general amnesty be granted, and no citizen be molested in person or property for any acts done in aid of the Confederate States in the prosecution of the war.

Taken as a whole the convention amounts to this, that the States of the Confederacy shall reënter the old Union upon the same footing on which they stood before seceding from it.

These States having, in their several conventions, solemnly asserted their sovereignty and right of self-government, and having established for themselves, and maintained through four years of bloody war a government of their own choosing, no loyal citizen can consent to its abandonment and destruction as long as there remains a reasonable hope of successful resistance to the arms of the United States.

The question, therefore, whether the terms of the military convention should be accepted will depend upon whether the Confederate States are in a condition further to prosecute the war with a reasonable hope of success, and this question will be answered by a brief review of our military situation.

The Army of Northern Virginia, for four years the pride and boast of the Confederacy, under the lead of the General-in-Chief, whose name we have been accustomed to associate with victory, after having been defeated and reduced to a mere remnant by straggling and desertion, has capitulated to the enemy. All who were not embraced in the capitulation have thrown away their arms and disbanded beyond any hope of reorganization.

Our only other army east of the Mississippi, the Army of Tennessee, contains now about thirteen thousand effective men, of infantry and artillery, and is daily melting away by desertion. It is confronted by one of the best armies of the United States, fifty thousand strong. Manifestly it can not fight, and if it retreats, the chances are more than equal that, like the Army of Northern Virginia, it will dissolve, and the remnant be forced to capitulate. If it should retreat successfully, and offer itself as a nucleus for reorganization, it can not be recruited. Volunteering is long since at an end, and conscription has exhausted all its force. East of the Mississippi, scattered through all the States, we have now about forty thousand organized troops. To oppose these the enemy have more than two hundred thousand. Persevering efforts for many months past have failed to overcome the obstacle to the removal of troops from the west to the east of the Mississippi. We can, therefore, look for no accession of strength from that quarter. If a returning sense of duty and patriotism should bring back the stragglers and deserters in sufficient numbers to form a respectable army, we have not the means of arming them. Our supply of arms is very nearly exhausted, our means of manufacturing substantially at an end, and the blockade of our ports prevents their introduction from abroad, except in small quantities, and at remote points. In view of these facts our two generals highest in command in the field have expressed in decided terms our inability longer to continue the struggle. Observation has satisfied me that the States of Virginia and North Carolina are finally lost to our cause. The people of the latter are utterly weary of the war, broken and despairing in spirit, and eager to accept terms far less liberal than the convention proposes. In the absence of a general arrangement they will certainly make terms for themselves. Abandoned by our armies, the people of Virginia will follow their example, and it will be impossible to arrest the process of disintegration thus begun.

This melancholy array of facts leaves open but one conclusion. I am unhesitatingly of the opinion that the convention ought to be ratified.

As to the proper mode of ratification, greater doubt may be reasonably entertained. The Confederate Government is but the agent of the States, and as its chief executive you can not, according to our governmental theory, bind the States to a government which they have not adopted for themselves. Nor can you rightfully, without their consent, dissolve the government which they have established. But there are circumstances so desperate as to override all constitutional theories, and such are those which are pressing upon us now. The Government of the Confederate States is no longer potent for good. Exhausted by war in all its resources to such a degree that it can no longer offer a respectable show of resistance to its enemies, it is already virtually destroyed. And the chief duty left for you to peform is to provide as far as possible for the speedy delivery of the people from the horrors of war and anarchy.

I therefore respectfully advise that upon the ratification of the convention by the Executive of the United States, you issue your proclamation, plainly setting forth the circumstances which have induced you to assent to the terms proposed, disbanding the armies of the Confederacy, resigning your office as chief magistrate, and recommending to the people of the States that they assemble in convention and carry into effect the terms agreed on.

GEORGE DAVIS.

Views of Mr. Breckinridge, Secretary of War:

CHARLOTTE, N. C., *April* 23, 1865.

To His Excellency the President.

SIR: In obedience to your request I have the honor to submit my advice as to the course you should take upon the memorandum or basis of agreement made on the 18th inst. by and between General J. E. Johnston, of the Confederate States Army, and Major-General W. T. Sherman, of the United States Army, provided that paper shall receive the approval of the Government of the United States.

The principal army of the Confederacy was recently lost in Virginia. Considerable bodies of troops not attached to that army have either disbanded or marched toward their homes, accompanied by many of their officers. Five days ago the effective force, in infantry and artillery, of General Johnston's army was but fourteen thousand seven hundred and seventy men, and it continues to diminish. That officer thinks it wholly impossible for him to make any head against the overwhelming forces of the enemy. Our ports are closed, and the sources of foreign supply lost to us. The enemy occupy all or the greater part of Missouri, Kentucky, Tennessee, Virginia, and North Carolina, and move almost at will through the other States to the east of the Mississippi.

They have recently taken Selma, Montgomery, Columbus, Macon, and other important towns, depriving us of large depots of supplies and of munitions of war. Of the small force still at command, many are unarmed, and the Ordnance Department can not furnish five thousand stand of small arms.

I do not think it would be possible to assemble, equip, and maintain an army of thirty thousand men at any point east of the Mississippi River.

The contest, if continued after this paper is rejected, will be likely to lose entirely the dignity of regular warfare, many of the States will make such terms as they may, in others separate and ineffective hostilities may be prosecuted, while the war, wherever waged, will probably degenerate into that irregular and secondary stage out of which greater evils will flow to the South than to the enemy.

For these and for other reasons which need not now be stated, I think we can no longer contend with a reasonable hope of success.

It seems to me that the time has arrived when, in a large and clear view of the situation, prompt steps should be taken to put an end to the war.

It may be said that the agreement of the 18th inst. contains certain stipulations which you can not perform.

This is true, and it was well understood by General Sherman that only a part could be executed by the Confederate authorities. In any view of the case grave responsibilities must be met and assumed. If the necessity for peace be conceded, corresponding action must be taken. The mode of negotiation which we deem regular and would prefer is impracticable.

The situation is anomalous and can not be solved upon principles of theoretical exactitude.

In my opinion you are the only person who can meet the present necessities.

I respectfully advise:

1. That you execute, so far as you can, the second article in the agreement of the 18th inst.

2. That you recommend to the several States the acceptance of those parts of the agreement upon which they alone can act.

3. Having maintained, with faithful and intrepid purpose, the cause of the Confederate States while the means of organized resistance remained, that you return to the States and the people the trust which you are no longer able to defend.

Whatever course you pursue opinions will be divided. Permit me to give mine. Should these or similar views accord with your own, I think the better judgment will be that you can have no higher title to the gratitude of your countrymen and the respect of mankind than will spring from the wisdom to see the path of duty at this time, and the courage to follow it, regardless alike of praise or blame.

Respectfully and truly your friend,

JOHN C. BRECKINRIDGE, *Secretary of War.*

General Sherman deserves thanks for bringing to light the above interesting and valuable historical papers.

CHAPTER XIX.

SNEERS AT THE STAFF—THE CONTROVERSY WITH THE WAR DEPARTMENT OVER THE CONTROL OF THE STAFF CORPS.

GENERAL SHERMAN, in his last chapter discusses at considerable length the same issues which he raised with the Secretary of War and the statute law, when he assumed the duties of general and promulgated an order assigning all officials in the War Department, except the Secretary himself, and possibly his chief clerk, to duty on his staff. In his treatment of this question he indulges in many undignified sneers at staff officers. For example:

"The subordinates of these staff-corps and departments are selected and chosen from the army itself, or fresh from West Point, and too commonly construe themselves into the *élite*, as made of better clay than the common soldier. Thus they separate themselves more and more from their comrades of the line, and in process of time realize the condition of that old officer of artillery, who thought the army would be a delightful place for a gentleman if it were not for the d——d soldier; or, better still, the conclusion of the young lord in 'Henry IV.,' who told Harry Percy (Hotspur) that 'but for these vile guns he would himself have been a soldier.' This is all wrong; utterly at variance with our democratic form of government and of universal experience; and now that the French, from whom we had copied the system, have utterly 'proscribed' it, I hope that our Congress will follow suit."

General Sherman's own military history, however, will show that it was not until he attained the rank of brigadier-general that his antipathy to staff duty began. But from that time forward it has been marked. Even the large body of staff officers in his own army, who, on the Atlanta campaign, had been continuously on duty and most of the time under fire from May till September, did not escape being made to feel this prejudice.

While the army was moving from Atlanta on Hood, who had passed to its rear, Lieutenant-Colonel Warner, inspector-general on the staff, was appointed by the Governor of Ohio to the command of one of the new regiments from that State. Whereupon General Sherman issued the following order:

[Special Field Orders No. 98.]

HEADQUARTERS MILITARY DIVISION OF THE MISSISSIPPI,
IN THE FIELD, SUMMERVILLE, GA., *October* 19, 1864.

1st. Lieutenant-Colonel Willard Warner, acting Inspector-General on the staff of this military division, having been appointed colonel of the One-Hundred and Eightieth Ohio, is hereby relieved from duty at these headquarters, and will proceed to Nashville and assume command of his new regiment.

2d. The General commanding thanks Colonel Warner for his most zealous and intelligent service during the past campaign, compliments him on his good sense in preferring service with troops to staff duty, and predicts for him the highest success in his professional career.

By order of *Major-General* W. T. SHERMAN.

Colonel Warner was an able and gallant officer. As lieutenant-colonel of an Ohio regiment, he was detailed for duty on the staff of General Sherman, and afterward, upon being appointed to a colonelcy, he naturally desired to assume command of his regiment. Certainly there were very few, if any, of the hundreds of staff officers serving with General Sherman who would not gladly have exchanged places with Colonel Warner. They were for the most part, men who had volunteered for the war without stopping to bargain for place or power, and accepted their staff positions and obeyed the orders detailing them for such duty as they would have obeyed any other military orders they might have received. It was a fact universally recognized that promotion came chiefly from the line, and none of them, with the same opportunity, would have failed to follow Colonel Warner's example.

In the nature of things it was impossible for many of them to receive such promotion in the line as would justify them in asking to be relieved from staff duty, and under the circumstances, General Sherman's order was to these officers both a cruel wrong and a gratuitous insult.

But if General Sherman in writing his final chapter had remembered the facts set forth in the opening of his book, he might have tempered his language in regard to staff service.

The Memoirs begin with the information that in the Spring of 1846 he was first-lieutenant in the Third Artillery, and present with his company at Fort Moultrie, South Carolina. In April of the same year he was detailed for recruiting service. In June he was ordered to California with Company F of his regiment, and assigned to staff duty as quartermaster and commissary. In March, 1847, he returned to company duty. The next month (April) he was assigned as aid-de-camp to General Kearney. In May General Kearney left California, and Lieutenant Sherman became acting assistant adjutant-general on the staff of Colonel R. B. Mason. In February, 1849, he was relieved from this service and assigned in the same capacity to the staff of General Persifer F. Smith. While thus acting his duties were changed to those of aid-de-camp on the same staff, in which capacity he continued to act until September, 1850, when he rejoined his company in St. Louis with the assurance that he would soon receive a regular staff appointment. This promise was soon after fulfilled, and on the 27th of the same month he was appointed captain and commissary of subsistence in the regular army. This position he held until his resignation some three years after, September 6th, 1853, having thus completed an almost unbroken record of seven years' service as an officer of the staff.

And when, after the hesitation about reëntering the army at the beginning of the war, which he details at length, he finally decided to take part in the struggle, he applied for staff duty again, as is plain from the close of the letter in which he tendered his services. "Should they be needed," he writes May 8, 1861, to the Secretary of War, "the records of the War Department will enable you to designate the station in which I can render the most service." As these records for seven preceding years of his former army duty pertained mainly to varied staff service, the intent of the application is manifest.

However, he was made colonel of the Thirteenth Infantry, and this was his "new regiment." But, instead of following Colonel Warner's example, who went from inspector on the staff to the command of a regiment, he reversed it, and with his colonel's commission in his pocket passed to duty as inspector on the staff of General Scott, and this duty continued until he was assigned to the command of a brigade some weeks later. From this time forward he "had the good sense to prefer service with troops to staff duty."

In this last chapter General Sherman argues that military correspondence with higher officials should pass through the hands of the intermediate generals, in order that they may never be ignorant of any thing that concerns their command. This has always been considered sound doctrine in the army, and yet General Sherman's records show that he constantly corresponded directly with General Halleck, on matters intimately affecting the whole army, without sending the letters through his own superiors. Now he writes: "I don't believe in a chief-of-staff at all." But up to the 18th of April, 1865, he sustained most intimate, cordial, and confidential relations with General Halleck as chief-of-staff, and on that date, as has been seen, wrote, asking him to influence the President, "if possible, not to vary the first terms made with Johnston at all." So close were these relations as to suggest the idea that his present non-belief in a chief-of-staff dates from a few days later, when, in addressing General Grant after his terms had been rejected, he wrote:

"It now becomes my duty to paint in justly severe characters the still more offensive and dangerous matter of General Halleck's dispatch of April 26th to the Secretary of War, embodied in his to General Dix of April 27th."

Out of the circumstances attending the rejection of the Johnston-Reagan terms, grew the controversy with the Secretary of War over the relative rights and powers of this officer and those of the General of the Army, which subject is discussed at some length in the Memoirs.

Ever since Secretary Stanton's fearless performance of duty in connection with the political features of Johnston's surrender, General Sherman has maintained that this officer was a mere clerk, and in his last chapter he contends that the General of the Army should have command of all the heads of staff-corps, and that the President and Secretary of War should command the army through the general. What he leaves to the Secretary of War is thus described: "Of course, the Secretary would, as now, distribute the funds according to the appropriation bills, and reserve to himself the absolute control and supervision of the larger arsenals and depots of supply."

And while he declares that the law or its judicial interpretation is against the right for which he contends, the removal of army headquarters to St. Louis resulted in great degree from the fact that when he became general he could not bring himself to conform to this law. The history of this controversy is pertinent to his present discussion of the organization and control of the staff-corps.

One of his first official acts, when made General of the Army, was to issue an order reducing the Secretary of War to the position which he had frequently before with great emphasis assigned him, namely, that of a mere clerk.

The preliminary order to effect this he obtained from the President. It was as follows:

[General Orders No. 11.]

HEADQUARTERS OF THE ARMY,
ADJUTANT-GENERAL'S OFFICE, WASHINGTON, *March* 8, 1869.

The following orders of the President of the United States are published for the information and government of all concerned:

WAR DEPARTMENT,
WASHINGTON CITY, *March* 5, 1869.

By direction of the President General William T. Sherman will assume command of the Army of the United States.

The Chiefs of Staff Corps, Departments, and Bureaus will report to and act under the immediate orders of the General commanding the Army.

All official business, which by law or regulations requires the action of the President or the Secretary of War, will be submitted by the General of the Army to the Secretary of War; and, in general, all orders from the President or Secretary of War to any portion of the army, line, or staff, will be transmitted through the General of the Army.

J. M. SCHOFIELD, *Secretary of War.*

By command of the General of the Army.

E. D. TOWNSEND, *Assistant Adjutant-General.*

General Schofield, who expected to retire in a few days, did not care to make issue upon it, and contented himself with pointing out that it violated or contravened some twenty-six express provisions of statute law, or regulations having the force of law. Based upon the above order General Sherman issued the following:

[General Orders No. 12.]

HEADQUARTERS OF THE ARMY,
ADJUTANT-GENERAL'S OFFICE, WASHINGTON, *March* 8, 1869.

By direction of the President of the United States, the undersigned hereby assumes command of the Army of the United States. His general staff will be:

Brevet Major-General E. D. Townsend, Adjutant-General.
Brevet Major-General R. B. Marcy, Inspector-General.
Brevet Major-General M. C. Meigs, Quartermaster-General.
Brevet Major-General A. B. Eaton, Commissary-General Subsistence.
Brevet Major-General J. K. Barnes, Surgeon-General.
Brevet Major-General B. W. Brice, Paymaster-General.
Brevet Major-General Joseph Holt, Judge Advocate-General.
Brevet Major-General A. A. Humphreys, Chief of Engineers.
Brevet Major-General A. B. Dyer, Chief of Ordnance.
Brevet Brigadier-General A. J. Myer, Chief Signal Officer.

His personal staff, Aids-de-Camp with the rank of Colonel from this date, will be:

Brevet Lieutenant-Colonel J. C. McCoy, Second Lieutenant, Second Infantry.
Brevet Lieutenant-Colonel L. M. Dayton, Captain, Seventh Cavalry.
Brevet Lieutenant-Colonel J. C. Audenried, Captain, Sixth Cavalry.
Brevet Brigadier-General C. B. Comstock, Major, Corps of Engineers.
Brevet Brigadier-General Horace Porter, Major, Ordnance Department.

Brevet Brigadier-General F. T. Dent, Lieutenant-Colonel, Thirty-third Infantry.

II. Generals commanding military departments, in addition to the duties heretofore required of them, will give their special atttention to the economical administration of all branches of the service within their command, whether of the line or staff, and to this end will exercise supervision and command of every part of the army within their limits not specially excepted.

III. The military academy, general depots of supply, arsenals of construction, permanent forts in process of construction or extensive repairs, general recruiting depots, and officers employed on duties not military, are excepted from the operation of the foregoing paragraph.

IV. All orders and general instructions to the troops, or to staff officers serving in military departments, must go from the headquarters of the army through the Adjutant-General's office, and through the Generals commanding the military divisions and departments in which the officers are serving; but ordinary correspondence relating to the details of execution may be carried on between the parties concerned and the heads of the staff department or corps charged with their execution. W. T. SHERMAN, *General.*

On the 13th of March General Rawlins assumed the duties of Secretary of War, and among his first acts he called the attention of the President to the various violations of law involved in Sherman's order. These were too plain to admit either of doubt or extended discussion, and the following order was issued by direction of the President, revoking those printed above:

[General Orders No. 28.]

HEADQUARTERS OF THE ARMY,
ADJUTANT-GENERAL'S OFFICE, WASHINGTON, *March* 27, 1869.

The following orders, received from the War Department, are published for the government of all concerned:

WAR DEPARTMENT,
WASHINGTON CITY, *March* 26, 1869.

By direction of the President, the order of the Secretary of War, dated War Department, March 5, 1869, and published in General Orders No. 11, Headquarters of the Army, Adjutant-General's office, dated March 8, 1869, except so much as directs General W. T. Sherman to "assume command of the Army of the United States," is hereby rescinded.

All official business which, by law or regulations, requires the action of the President or Secretary of War, will be submitted by the Chiefs of Staff Corps, Departments, and Bureaus, to the Secretary of War.

All orders and instructions relating to military operations, issued by the

President or Secretary of War, will be issued through the General of the Army. JOHN A. RAWLINS, *Secretary of War.*
By command of *General* SHERMAN.
E. D. TOWNSEND, *Assistant Adjutant General.*

The violations of law in General Sherman's Order No. 12, can be readily made to appear. The act of July 25, 1866, reviving the grade of General, authorized him, "under the direction and during the pleasure of the President, to command the armies of the United States." The same act authorized him to select "for service upon his staff such number of aids, not exceeding six, as he may judge proper," and the act of July 28, three days later, provided that "there shall be one General * * * * entitled to the same staff officers, in number and grade, as now provided by law." The law provided only six; Sherman's order assigned sixteen—an excess of ten; and more than this, each of the ten was, by law, directly under the Secretary of War.

But before following this branch of the subject to its conclusion, it will be well to present in brief some of the decisions upon the relations of the President as commander-in-chief under the Constitution, and those of the Secretary of War to the army:

"By the Constitution the President is made Commander-in-Chief of the Army and Navy of the United States. The departments of war and of the navy are the channels through which his orders proceed to them respectively, and the secretaries of these departments are the organs by which he makes his will known to them. The orders issued by those officers are, in the contemplation of the law, not their orders, but the orders of the President of the United States.—[1 Opinions, 380.

By the act of August 7, 1789, establishing the War Department, the duties of the Secretary of War are thus defined:

"There shall be an Executive Department, to be denominated the Department of War, and there shall be a principal officer therein to be called the Secretary for the Department of War, who shall perform and execute such duties as shall from time to time be enjoined on or intrusted to him by the President of the United States, agreeable to the Constitution relative to military commissions, or to the land or naval forces, ships or warlike stores of the

United States, or to such other matters respecting military or naval affairs as the President of the United States shall assign to the said department."

Subsequently, upon the establishment of a Navy Department, the supervision of naval affairs was withdrawn from the War Department.

"The Secretary of War is 'The regularly constituted organ of the President for the administration of the military establishment of the nation, and rules and orders publicly promulgated through him must be received as the acts of the Executive, and as such be binding upon all within the sphere of his legal and constitutional authority.'—[U. S. vs. Eliason, 16 Peters, 291.

"The War Department has a staff officer, the Adjutant-General, through whom the Secretary, in behalf of the President, that is, the President, speaks when he sees fit, in matters pertaining to the army."—[7 Opinions, 473.

And yet General Sherman, in the first line of his assignments, boldly invaded the official household of the President, his military superior, and ordered the chief staff officer there to report to him at the headquarters of the army. This did not differ, in any material respect, from what General Sheridan or any other general officer would be guilty of in issuing an order directing staff officers to report to him, who, by express provision of law, had been placed under the General of the Army.

The Quartermaster and Commissary Departments are placed by law directly under the Secretary of War, and yet General Sherman attached them both to his staff, and assumed that they were under his direction. The law regulating their duties reads as follows:

"In addition to their duties in the field, it shall be the duty of the Quartermaster-General, his deputies, and assistant deputies, when thereto directed by the Secretary of War, to purchase military stores, camp equipage, and other articles requisite for the troops, and generally to procure and provide means of transport for the army, its stores, artillery, and camp equipage.—[Act March 28, 1812.

"Supplies for the army, unless in particular and urgent cases the Secretary of War should otherwise direct, shall be purchased by contract, to be made by the Commissary-General * * * under such regulations as the Secretary of War may direct."—[April 14, 1818.

These officers are also severally directed by law to make their reports to the Secretary of War. And none of these acts were changed when the grade of General was revived.

By another section it is made the duty of the Quartermaster-General, "under the direction of the Secretary of War," to receive and distribute all clothing and camp and garrison equipage, and, "under the direction of the Secretary of War," to enforce a system of accountability for the same.

In the same manner the Surgeon-General by law performs his duties under the direction of the Secretary of War, and, in short, the whole general staff is, by law, governed by regulations which the Secretary of War is, by direct statute provision, obliged to make.

By the law creating it, the Bureau of Military Justice was "attached to and made a part of the War Department."

Paragraph 1,063 of Revised Army Regulations, which were enacted by Congress into law, reads as follows:

"The Signal Officer shall have charge, under the direction of the Secretary of War, of all signal duty, and of all books, papers, and apparatus connected therewith."

The following extracts from regulations, taken from many similar provisions, show clearly that Congress placed the general staff under the Secretary of War, and these regulations have been recognized by Congress since the office of General was established:

"Paragraph 1,010. The Chief of such Military Bureau in the War Department shall, under the direction of the Secretary of War, regulate, as far as practicable, the employment of hired persons required by the administrative service of his department.

"Paragraph 1,043. Chiefs of the Disbursing Department shall, under the direction of the Secretary of War, designate where principal contracts shall be made, etc."

Paragraph 1,197 makes the approval of the Secretary of War necessary to rules which the Surgeon-General may prescribe for supplying hospitals.

By various paragraphs of regulations the Paymaster-General is directed to report to the Adjutant-General, the legal staff officer of the Secretary of War.

"Paragraph 1,360. The Chief Engineer, with the approbation of the Secretary of War, will regulate and determine the number, quality, form, and dimensions of the necessary vehicles, pontoons, tools, etc."

By paragraphs 1,377, 1,378, 1,379, all the operations of the Ordnance Department are placed under the Secretary of War.

The officers of the Engineer Corps are placed under the sole direction of the President.

These various citations are quite sufficient to prove that the theory of Congress in all its legislation relating to army organization has been, that the President is Commander-in-Chief, while the Secretary of War is his representative at the head of the army, and his organ of communication with it; that the Adjutant-General is the staff officer of the Secretary of War, that is, of the President; and that the chiefs of the various staff corps form the general staff of the President, and are in consequence under the direction of the Secretary of War.

Thus it will be readily seen that Sherman's order contravened, or directly violated the laws and regulations which have the full force of law, for the government of the army. After that order was revoked, and his attention had been thus pointedly called to the law, every subsequent protest against it was unsoldierly, and in short, insubordination. The same conduct in any officer of less rank would not have been allowed to go unpunished. If the general of an army constantly frets over the restraints of the regulations, what attention can he rightfully expect to be paid them by the army at large?

Although at the time his order was revoked, he was made fully acquainted with the law, a few months later he was found not only violating it, but reporting and defending his disregard both of orders and the law. The facts upon which this statement is based will be found in his annual report for 1869.

General Rawlins died September 6, following the issuing of General Order, No. 28, given above. General Sherman was assigned temporarily to the desk of the Secretary of War. The following paragraph of the President's order, as given above, was still in force:

'By direction of the President, * * * * all official business which, by law or regulations, requires the action of the President or the Secretary of War, will be submitted by the Chiefs of Staff Corps, Departments, and Bureaus to the Secretary of War."

No order revoking this had been issued by the President. General Sherman was also aware that this order had been framed solely to control his official acts. It was not an order that he would for a moment forget. And yet, while speaking in his annual report of these same Chiefs of Staff Corps, Departments, and Bureaus, General Sherman said:

"The heads of these departments reside in Washington, and submit annually a written report of their operations for the past year. It so happened that I was Secretary of War during the month of October, when by law these reports were made in order to reach the Public Printer by the first of November, and I required all the annual reports to be addressed, like all other military reports, to the Adjutant-General for the perusal of the General of the Army, who could make use of such information as they contained, and then lay them before the Secretary of War. This is, in my judgment, the course that should always be pursued—though a different one has heretofore prevailed—for otherwise we would have the absurdity of a general commanding an army with his chief staff officer reporting to somebody else."

A little further on in the same paper he called attention to a report made by the Military Committee of the House, upon which, however, the House had taken no action, much less Congress, in which the Committee expressed the opinion that the staff corps should be as directly under the control of the general and the department commanders as the officers of the line. He then added: "I heartily concur in these views, and, so far as my authority goes, will carry them out." And this in a formal report, after he had been expressly ordered by the President not to carry out these identical views.

Throughout this controversy of General Sherman's own raising and pressing, there was no attempt by the War Department to assume unlawful authority over the General of the Army, nor had there been any other limitations placed upon his power than the law imposes. The case was simply this: The Secretary of War had been guided by the law as it exists. General Sherman had constantly protested against the law in the case, and, so far as he could, ignored it. The whole trouble on his side was this: He had not been regarded as Commander-in-Chief, and had not been allowed to command the army as such. Instead of exercising his authority under the law and in accordance with the terms of his commission—that is, "under the direction and during the pleasure of the President, to command the armies of the United States"—he insisted upon being allowed to exercise that authority as if both law and commission read, "under the direction and according to the pleasure of W. T. Sherman."

CHAPTER XX.

CONCLUSION—THE CASE AGAINST THE MEMOIRS SUMMED UP.

In closing this review, based throughout upon facts disclosed by the official files, the case against the author of the Memoirs may be summed up as follows:

Ten years after the close of the war, when the open, and all the secret official records, collected and arranged for ready reference, were at his service, he has published to the world a story of his campaigns, crowded with inaccuracies, and stained with injustice done associate commanders and coöperating armies.

The kindly years which, for most who followed the flag, have effaced whatever jealousies and misunderstandings arose in the field, leaving prominent in memory only the central and enduring fact of common service in a worthy cause, seem to have exerted no such influence upon him, but rather acted as mordants to fix all unpleasant things indelibly upon his pages. By following the statements of his book, and comparing them with the records of the same events, made at the time of their occurrence, and often by his own hand, many grave differences have been established.

Where the Memoirs give the credit of the move on Forts Henry and Donelson to Halleck, the records show that it belongs to Grant. Where General Sherman argues against the idea of a surprise at Shiloh, the records prove it to have been complete, and due mainly to his own blindness and neglect. Where he seeks to detract from the service rendered there by Buell and his army, the records set that service in

(272)

clear light. While he intimates that Rosecrans acted discreditably at Iuka and Corinth, and that Grant was deeply offended over some failure or blunder not clearly defined, the reports of the latter are found to commend Rosecrans strongly for these brilliant battles. Where he now visits severe censure, in connection with his failure at Chickasaw Bayou, his own report of the action, written at the time, commends the very officers, thus unjustly arraigned, for having done the heaviest fighting, and accomplished all that was possible. Where he assails General Sooy Smith for causing the partial failure of his Meridian expedition, his own orders, then issued, claimed complete success; and while he now declares he never had any intention of going to Mobile, the letters of General Grant (who ordered his movement) to Halleck and Thomas, informed these officers that in certain contingencies Sherman was to push for Mobile. He describes Rosecrans' flanking movement to capture Chattanooga as a march from that city to attack the enemy; and the battle which secured this stronghold, as a defeat before it, and its occupation after the battle as a retreat into it. He describes the terrible condition of affairs in Chattanooga, following the battle of Chickamauga, and seeks to create the impression that Rosecrans alone was in fault, when the records show that Burnside failed him on one flank and Sherman on the other—this too after the pressing necessities of the case had been repeatedly represented to them both—and that finally Burnside never came, and Sherman himself was seven weeks behind the time set for his arrival at Chattanooga, exhibiting no special activity in his advance until after Rosecrans was removed, when suddenly, under Grant's request to come on, the energy of his movement surpassed praise. While he states that Grant was afraid the Army of the Cumberland could not be drawn out of its trenches to attack Bragg, and wanted Sherman's men to come up and coax them into fighting by the power of their example, the records show that Grant had confidence enough in Thomas' army to order it—before Sherman was within supporting distance even—to do what the latter afterward failed to perform; and further, that when General Thomas insisted upon giving orders for an attack without waiting for Sherman, who was still delayed with the greater part of his troops, Grant assented, and Thomas actually accomplished that part of the battle assigned for the first day, before Sherman arrived; and lastly, that the Army of the Cumberland stormed and carried the whole line of Missionary Ridge hours before Sherman even received the news of the great success, he alone, of the three army commanders, having failed, though after splendid fighting, to carry the point assigned to him. While he contends that the failure to bring Johnston to battle at Resaca, was due to the timidity of General McPherson, the records show that this officer acted exactly in accordance with Sherman's own orders; and while the latter claims that from the outset of the movement, it was his intention merely to feign through Buzzard Roost on Dalton, and press the bulk of the army through Snake Creek Gap on Johnston's rear, the records show that for three days he "assaulted precipices" in front of Dalton, with Thomas' and Schofield's armies, before he allowed McPherson to make more than a diverson on Johnston's rear, so that the latter, being warned in time, withdrew safely. At Kenesaw he assaulted impregnable works to teach his veterans that flanking was not the only means of attacking an enemy, and failed at a cost of two thousand men, claiming now that Thomas, McPherson, and Schofield agreed with him that the assault was necessary, when the records clearly reveal Thomas' stern dissatisfaction, and a bold extension to the right by Schofield, which plainly indicates that the latter looked for success in the direction from which it finally came, through their old and sure method of flanking.

He describes the battle before Atlanta, where McPherson fell, in such a manner that no reader would dream of its being a great surprise, and well nigh serious disaster; but the records disclose an army, plunged by the flank against an enemy in position behind heavy works, on the supposition that Atlanta was evacuated, suddenly and unexpectedly attacked by the enemy upon its left and rear, before it had ceased to exult over the announcement from Sherman that the enemy had abandoned Atlanta, and his order for a vigorous pursuit. While he claims that he originated the March to the Sea, and had it in his "mind's eye" by the 21st of September, the records prove that Grant had planned the campaign through to Mobile in the previous January, notified Halleck of it on the 15th of that month, Thomas on the 19th, and that in February Thomas was arranging the details of the move as far as Atlanta. The records show further, that on the 10th of September Grant suggested a move from Atlanta on Augusta or Savannah, instead of Mobile, since the control of the latter had passed into the hands of the Union forces.

Concerning Savannah, the records reveal an escape of Hardee with ten thousand, from Sherman's sixty thousand, without disclosing even a plausible excuse. Here the Memoirs show Sherman looking back to Nashville, from whence alone, through defeat of Hood, could come a success that should vindicate his March to the Sea, and finding fault with Thomas, who, though crippled in all ways by Sherman, was through superhuman efforts there, saving him from the jeers of the Nation.

In treating of Savannah, he also attacks Mr. Stanton for carelessness in connection with the captured cotton, and transactions relating thereto, while the records show not only that he had absolutely no foundation for his charges, but that in most respects the exact opposite of what he wrote was true. After a magnificent and really wonderful march through the Carolinas, with every warning, as the Memoirs relate, that the enemy was rapidly concentrating in his front, the records show that he neglected all precautions, and marched the two wings of his army, neither moving in close order, so far apart that when the head of the left wing was attacked at 10 o'clock one forenoon, by the whole rebel army, estimated by himself to have been from thirty-seven to forty thousand, the advance of his right wing, marching to the sound of battle, to support the left, did not arrive till the next morning, while the bulk of this wing did not reach the field till the following afternoon; and then, when his whole force was in front of and on the flank of the enemy, the latter escaped. Such is the record history of Bentonville, the last battle of his army.

What shall be said of the political negotiations which followed? What need be said further than the records show, that, beginning with a proposition to receive the surrender of Johnston's forces upon the same terms Grant had extended to Lee, he ended by surrendering to Johnston upon terms drawn up by a member of the rebel Cabinet?

www.ingramcontent.com/pod-product-compliance
Lightning Source LLC
Chambersburg PA
CBHW032118230426
43672CB00009B/1776